Anglo-American Perspectives on the Ukrainian Question 1938-1951

A Documentary Collection

Anglo-American Perspectives on the Ukrainian Question 1938-1951

A Documentary Collection

Lubomyr Y. Luciuk
Bohdan S. Kordan

Foreword by
Hugh A. MacDonald

THE LIMESTONE PRESS
Kingston, Ontario — Vestal, New York
1987

This volume is the first in the series entitled
Studies in East European Nationalisms
Series Editor *Richard A. Pierce, Queen's University*

CANADIAN CATALOGUING IN PUBLICATION DATA

Main Entry under title:

Anglo-American perspectives on the Ukrainian
  question 1938-1951

(Studies in East European nationalisms; no. 1)
Bibliography: p.
ISBN 0-919642-26-8

1. Ukraine — Foreign opinion, British. 2. Ukraine —
Foreign opinion, American. 3. Ukraine — Foreign
opinion, Canadian. 4. Ukraine — Politics and
government — 1917-   — Sources. 5. Ukraine —
History — 1917-   — Sources. I. Luciuk, Lubomyr Y.,
1953-   . II. Kordan, Bohdan S. III. Series.

DK508.79.A54 1987   947'.71   C87-093492-9

61,561

This publication was made possible by a grant from the
Civil Liberties Commission, Ukrainian Canadian Committee.

THE LIMESTONE PRESS
Box 1604, Kingston, Ontario K7L 5C8
125 Southwood Drive, Vestal, New York 13850

Published simultaneously in the United
States of America and the United Kingdom.

Typesetting by *Multilingual on Whyte*
Printed in Canada by *Brown and Martin Ltd.*

For Our Fathers:
Danylo and Andrij

Preface

Drawn together in this volume, for the first time, are documents which indicate the pattern of the relationship between the Ukrainian independence movement and the leading powers of the western alliance just prior to, during and after the Second World War. These archival materials illustrate how these powers evaluated the impact Ukrainian statehood might have on their international relations, the strengths and weaknesses of the Ukrainian national movement (in particular its role as a political problem for a number of European states), and the question of whether Ukrainians in the emigration posed an internal security risk to their host societies.

Material culled from the national archives of Britain and the United States constitutes the bulk of this collection. Additional documents from Canadian government archives have also been included in keeping with the Anglo-American motif. While Canadian attitudes never completely reflected British and American perceptions of the Ukrainian Question, the peculiarities of the Canadian perspective nevertheless do not significantly detract from the central Anglo-American position. As these documents indicate, an admixture of 'high politics', indifference and opportunism underlaid, with few exceptions, the Anglo-American view of the Ukrainian nationalist movement, both in eastern Europe and elsewhere.

This collection has as its timeframe the years 1938-1951. This is not an arbitrary demarcation. These years marked a period of significant political activity and popular resistance by Ukrainians. It was also a time when the international balance of power became increasingly unstable and the prospect of Ukrainian independence again became a distinct possibility. During these years a paradox between the liberal democracies' proclaimed commitment to 'freedom and self-determination for peoples and nations' and the dictates of *realpolitik* emerged, resolved only in the sense that Ukrainian claims to national self-determination were neither recognized nor supported. At issue is *not* whether the Anglo-American powers were capable of action but the contradiction that arose from their failure to promote the claim of this nation to self-determination and those policies said to be based on support for such universal rights. The documents reprinted here suggest that, on one level, western statesmen were well-informed about the nature and extent of the Ukrainian national struggle while, on another, they were consistently cynical or indifferent to the idea of Ukrainian self-determination.

This collection of documents represents only a fraction of the large body of archives dealing with the Ukrainian Question in Anglo-American repositories. Several years of research in the national archives of Britain, the United States and Canada suggest that the reports, memoranda, minutes and despatches reproduced here basically, and fairly, reflect the official position of these governments toward the Ukrainian national movement between the years 1938-1951. The officials generating these materials were all senior diplomatic, military, and intelligence personnel whose assessments and reflections on the Ukrainian national movement could only have played an influential, and quite possibly decisive role, in shaping their respective governments' positions on this subject.

The volume contains fifty-four documents which, with one exception, have never been published before. Every effort has been made to preserve the integrity of these, although a few of the documents have been abridged to eliminate the redundancies, the obscure passages, or material irrelevant to the main themes being addressed in this collection. Passages which have been omitted are identified by elipses marks [........]. The occasional illegible word or signature has been indicated as follows [_____]. Different spellings of place-names and names of individuals have been retained for historical accuracy. Punctuation, however, has been changed for the sake of consistency. The language of the original documents in all cases was English.

The authors thank the staffs of the History Section of the Canadian Department of External Affairs, Public Archives of Canada, Public Record Office, and the United States National Archives. We are also grateful to Professors R.A. Pierce and P.G. Goheen, of Queen's University, and Dr. O. Romanyshyn for their critical comments on earlier drafts of this volume.

Hugh A. Macdonald expresses his thanks to Professor Anthony D. Smith, Department of Sociology, London School of Economics, for his helpful suggestions on recent literature in theories of nationalism.

Messrs. M. Bartkiw, J.B. Gregorovich, G.R.B. Panchuk, I. Rawluk, and Dr. M. Maleckyj mustered community support for the publication of this collection. Bill Rankin of the University of Alberta provided invaluable editorial advice. Hedy Later, of the University of Toronto's Department of Geography, prepared the maps which complement the manuscript; information for these maps was drawn in part from the recent publication *Ukraine: A Historical Atlas* (Toronto, 1985). Yarko Koshiw brought to our attention several documents referred to in our introduction. The authors also acknowledge, with thanks, the generous support of the Prometheus Foundation, the Shevchenko Foundation, and the Ucrainica Research Institute. Dr. Luciuk recognizes the Social Sciences and Humanities Research Council of Canada for the postdoctoral fellowship which helped make some of this research possible.

Finally, the authors are indebted to Professor Paul R. Magocsi of the Chair of Ukrainian Studies at the University of Toronto for his ongoing support of their research efforts.

Any errors, of commission or omission, are, of course, the responsibility of the authors and not of those whose generosity and encouragement made this volume possible.

LYL
BSK

Contents

Foreword

The Ukrainian National Question
in the Context of Great Power Conflict

This carefully compiled collection of documents highlights those developments and attitudes affecting Ukrainian nationalist groups during a period that takes the reader from the onset of the Second World War to the point at which effective armed resistance in Ukraine ceased. My task here is to sketch in the context for those interests and actions of Western governments – British, American and Canadian – under whose scrutiny and to some extent influence these organizations came, while providing a comparative framework in which the frustrated aspirations of Ukrainian nationalism can be placed. This objective will be met by examining the following questions: What do the documents in this collection show that is of general relevance to relations between governments and 'non-governmental actors' aspiring to statehood? What conditions determine the success or failure of national resistance movements, with particular reference to international politics today? and What are the prospects for Ukrainian nationalism in the light of these considerations?

Perhaps the most important factor of all revealed by this collection is the difference in approach to the Soviet Union's postwar security and frontiers which arose in Anglo-American wartime relations. Although in terms of military effort it was 1943-1944 before the contribution of the United States to the war in the west overtook that of Britain, already by 1940-1941 economic dependence upon American-manufactured war supplies meant that British Grand Strategy could not operate independently of Washington. And with the domestic economy strained to the limit

by war production, overseas trade cut to well under half its normal
level, reserves of gold and other investments overseas liquidated,
and a potential bill of nearly twenty billion dollars being ac-
cumulated for 'lend lease', the United States was not slow to exercise political and military leverage in London.[1] This comes through
with great clarity at two points in the documents: during the Eden-
Stalin negotiations over the Soviet Union's postwar frontiers in
December 1942 (Document 23), and at the time of the Yalta ac-
cords when not only frontiers but the status of displaced people
was of critical significance (Document 35).

President Roosevelt's policy was to postpone settlements as
far as possible until military victory had been attained. During the
early period of the Grand Alliance that was (broadly) British policy
too, however, the British were far more conscious of the changing
considerations of power, and were prepared to make settlements
(which in the main Stalin observed, as with non-intervention in
postwar Greece). This fundamental tension between London and
Washington carried major costs: leverage upon the Soviet Union
was foregone; and as *Soviet* military power grew, so did its
political influence over the terms of peace, especially in eastern
Europe.

This raises the question, what *was* American policy towards
European security issues, and eastern Europe in particular? The
answer is not evident from the documents presented here, and so it
is necessary to refer to other sources. Broadly, the United States
had no settled policy until after the end of the Second World War.
It wanted to abolish spheres of influence if possible; to break up
the British and other colonial Empires; and to work for
'democracy'. But none of these objectives could be achieved
without the exercise of direct power, and this the United States
was not prepared to do, until after the onset of the Cold War, by
which time the fate of eastern Europe was sealed.[2]

The Truman Doctrine, enunciated in March 1947, provided the
first American response to the collapse of co-operation with the
Soviet Union and showed the American Administration's recognition that there would need to be a continuing and perhaps permanent engagement in European affairs. But the Truman Doctrine
signalled the acceptance of a balance of power policy which took

---

[1] P. Kennedy, *The Realities Behind Diplomacy: Background Influences on British
     External Policy 1865-1980* (London, 1981), pp. 315-6.

[2] L.E. Davis, *The Cold War Begins: Soviet-American Conflict over Eastern Europe*
     (Princeton, 1974).

the postwar *status quo* for granted. It did not, despite ap-
pearances, signal the commencement of an ideological crusade to
reverse the new political and strategic facts created by Soviet
power.[3] Indeed, publication shortly afterwards of George Kennan's
famous 'X' article "The Sources of Soviet Conduct" in the influential journal *Foreign Affairs* provoked Walter Lippman to write
several major, critical, rebuttals of the logic of *Containment*. In
these he pointed out that *Containment* effectively meant the permanent division of Germany, the militarization of the continent,
and consequently the abandonment of any prospects of using
America's strength to negotiate a more acceptable *status quo*
within which change in eastern Europe would not be stifled in the
foreseeable future.[4]

The direct consequence of *Containment* was, therefore, that
nationalist resistance in eastern Europe, and above all in Ukraine,
never received more than contingent assistance from the Western
powers (Document 44). Even such *sub rosa* intervention as did occur was more or less abandoned when the Korean War generated
new military and political demands, although it is also clear
(Documents 47, 53, 54) that it was periodically reviewed as an 'indirect strategy'.

In the main, however, nationalist resistance in eastern Europe
was regarded as a futile, fanatical struggle which could not lead to
the defeat of Soviet power without war, assisted directly by the
West (Document 49). That would have meant atomic war, carrying
risks and consequences which these powers were not prepared to
contemplate, even while the United States enjoyed a monopoly of
nuclear weapons. Hence, despite many differences over how to
operationalize *Containment;* the creation of a permanent conservative caucus in the West which has never accepted Yalta; and
much rhetoric about 'Rollback', 'Liberation', and 'Human Rights',
there has never been a time when any British or American government has been willing to sacrifice the bones of its Grenadiers to
retrieve national societies dominated by Soviet power.

However, we are entitled to ask, would things have been much
different even if a more 'political' strategy had been pursued during
the war, or in the peacemaking process? Here again the documents
provide interesting direct and indirect evidence. Both Britain and

---

[3] J.L. Gaddis, *Strategies of Containment: A Critical Appraisal of Postwar American National Security Policy* (New York, 1982), p. 66.

[4] R. Steel (ed.), *The Cold War: A Study in US Foreign Policy by Walter Lippman with an Essay by George Kennan* (New York, 1972).

the United States assumed the continuing existence of the Soviet Union in frontiers beyond those of 1939; and both placed more stress upon preserving the interests of Poland than on creating new arrangements of territory (Documents 10, 11, 13). The British used Ukrainian nationalist organizations as a tool in the struggle against Germany and considered them a possible political and military factor had the Soviet Union collapsed (Documents 1, 2, 12). But neither Britain, nor later America and Canada, was much interested in the real claims of Ukrainian nationalist groups, although all three were interested in harnessing their economic and social influence (Documents 14-22). There is no sign in all of this of any alternative external policy, and there is every indication that it is silly to distinguish between more and less 'political' strategies; the West acted politically, and it is largely through hindsight that it can be said it might have acted more astutely.

What accounts for this? The documents suggest several reasons. Firstly, even when it was understood with considerable sophistication and in its full economic and strategic context, Ukrainian nationalism was not regarded as politically strong (Document 49).

Secondly, at least for Britain, by 1938 the discerned enemy was Hitler's Germany, and the search was on for allies: no other aim was allowed to confuse the central one, and allies and enemies were identified according to that dominant criterion. While the documents show that it is a travesty of the truth to believe that Ukrainian nationalist organizations, in Ukraine or abroad, were dominated by Germany (Documents 17, 21, 22, 28), it is beyond doubt that the appeal of a New Order divided the movement and caused it to be treated with suspicion by the Western powers.

Thirdly, the documents show, indirectly at least, how little effective power Britain – or even the United States – possessed in eastern European affairs. Although as we have already seen, this was a situation that arose to some extent out of political choice, it would be foolish to overlook the fact that it was also a systematic feature of geopolitical and military technological circumstances which had operated for over a century. With the special exception of the general re-alignment of frontiers after the First World War, the last occasion on which Britain intervened directly against Russia was the Crimean War. Nor indeed was this lack of operational power confined to relations with the Soviet Union, for even though the Polish government in exile was patronized and pushed by the allies, it was able to stubbornly resist their blandishments for changes in its policies, both towards Ukrainian nationalism and the re-alignment of its own territorial frontiers (Documents 9, 10, 13). Hence, it is a category error to identify influence and interest with power (Document 36).

Lastly, the documents show up three extremely interesting points about Ukrainian nationalist organizations operating in the United States and Canada. Their real power lay in numbers and economic significance, while their greatest effectiveness lay in united action and their gravest weakness in factionalism. They were also inevitably presented with the dilemma of how to reconcile relative freedom of organization in the democracies with lack of power in eastern Europe, particularly since the main thrust of the West's postwar strategy was not to challenge the Soviet Union.

In general, then, the experiecnce of Ukrainian nationalists in the West during this period was bitter and deeply frustrating. Not only did their numbers, organization, economic significance and constant efforts to find the key to political recognition of their aspirations lead to little; in Ukraine itself the outcome of the war presented Stalin with an opportunity to appease those whom he had previously dreadfully oppressed. This was done through the creation of a Ukrainian SSR which now encompassed much of historic Ukraine, and was given the *facade* of sovereign government (Documents 38, 40, 41). All in all, the lessons of this period point to the painful paradox that if the aim is to create a new state, then there is no substitute for being able to use the power of a state to realize that aim. It is this which leads us to examine more generally the dynamics of nationalism in the experience of creating, or failing to create, new states.[5]

Most of the sovereign states of today were created after 1945 as a direct or indirect consequence of the collapse in the ability of the European colonial powers to go on controlling the vast territorial estates which they had built up across the globe, in the face of the new conditions which prevailed after the end of the Second World War.

The Second World War brought the deaths of well over forty million people, most of them in Europe, and thereby an enormous need to rebuild societies, which had suffered much spiritual as well as material damage. The development of the Cold War ensured that as their power was rebuilt, the West Europeans would need to

---

[5] An essay of fundamental theoretical importance is A.W. Orridge, 'Separatist and Autonomist Nationalisms: the Structure of Regional Loyalties in the Modern State', in C.H. Williams (ed.), *National Separatism* (Cardiff, Wales, 1982).

focus most of it within the region. During the previous half-
century at least, the more powerful and progressive colonial
powers had allowed nationalist aspirations to be cultivated. The
war itself showed hundreds of millions of people beyond Europe for
the first time that the European master races could be defeated,
and gave them military experience. Hence, even in the best of circumstances, after 1945, nationalism in the developing world would
have been a pervasive and difficult force to manage.

But the anti-colonial tradition of the United States supported
the abandonment of formal empires and their replacement by new,
open, global institutions; and thereby found cause to hasten the
departure of the Europeans from such areas as the Middle East
and South East Asia, on the twin (and often confused) arguments
that this was the best way of containing the communist threat,
while promoting the national interests of the United States. In the
series of costly and sometimes humiliating struggles which saw
the Europeans driven out from the Indian sub-continent, Palestine, Indo-china, Iran, Egypt and elsewhere, the United States consistently *opposed* the policies of the colonial powers in these
regional and local areas, even as it was building a mighty alliance
with them to contain communism in Europe. The great defeats of
French arms at Diem Bien Phu in 1954 and of British and French
strategy during the Suez crisis of 1956 therefore mark a psychological watershed, after which the Europeans – with the partial
exception of the British, and the near total exception of the Por-
tuguese, whose economic dependence on colonies in Africa was increased by the economic strategy of the Dictatorships in Lisbon –
retreated to fortress Europe, leaving the United States unpre-
cedented scope to act as arbiter of the global *status quo,* committed by its own self-image to promoting a world in which, somehow,
political independence and economic interdependence would be
reconciled.

Strangely, therefore, despite their fundamental antagonism,
both superpowers have acted as agents of political revolution outside Europe. Ideas of a free-world, of national self-determination,
of socialist revolution, and of sovereign economic development
have interacted heavily; by the early 1970s there were more than
twice as many members of the United Nations as in 1945. But in
all of this it must be emphasized that the pace of change could not
have been so hectic, nor the results so universal, without the agency of American support for nationalism. Compared with that, the
impact of Soviet communism in creating political transformations
outside Europe has been small, though of course the effort con-

tinues and the resources available have grown.

Many of the world's newly independent states were, and are, weak: they lack a tradition of professional, bureaucratic management; they are also without an adequate physical infrastructure to sustain an integrated domestic economy, let alone one which could hope to compete for development through international trade; and they frequently lack the trained human capital to be truly independent, the ideas of tolerance and pluralism to make democracy effective, and even the scientific and social facts necessary to make institutions work successfully in the face of underlying myths, fears and social enmities. Nigeria is perhaps the classic case of a type found throughout Africa, and in other continents; a great, well-endowed land which through a combination of internal shortcomings and over-dependence upon external actors has not governed itself well.

And the world of putative nationalities turned into nationally independent states has shown other weaknesses. Even where the pre-conditions for sovereign independent development did exist in sufficient measure, external conditions might intervene to wreck everything, as happened during the 1960s and 70s to Vietnam and Cambodia, and more recently to Lebanon. Other states have been scarcely more fortunate, condemned by some combination of strategic location, internal division, or external intervention to a constant struggle to keep themselves in being: Cuba, Angola, Sudan, Nicaragua, Afghanistan, Iran; these are just some important examples from a lengthy list.

However, the central point in all of this is how exceptional the combination of circumstances was which induced this rash of new state building for about three decades after 1945. Already by the beginning of the 1970s such permissive conditions were exhausting themselves, as the United States slowly learned the craft of being a *status quo* power and global policeman; as new regional powers developed, such as India or Iran, prone to act severely against nationalist movements in their vicinity, like the Sikhs, Tamils, or Kurds; and as the Soviet Union and China began to temper their support for wars of national liberation. In many ways the creation of Bangladesh in 1971 was the exception which proved that conservative conditions had re-asserted themselves.

In Europe after 1945 such conditions never prevailed. Indeed, European history bears out the generalization that a cumulation of exceptional conditions are required for an established state to be extinguished and one or more new states established in its place. Let me briefly examine the historical record in modern times, from the development of industrialization and 'nation states' in their familiar, contemporary form. From this I shall draw out an account of some of the main forces which have frustrated Ukrainian nationalism.

The partitions of Poland in the later eighteenth century meant its disappearance for some time as a sovereign entity, but it then reappeared after the First World War. Meanwhile, the restructuring of Germany under the impact of the French Revolution reduced almost three hundred self-governing polities into a comparatively small number of 'regional states', most of which had previously existed as significant forces in European politics. The nineteenth century creation of the German Empire was based on their consolidation under a single centre of authority. But although the shift of economic and military power from south to northern Germany made Prussia the determining actor in that process, the political structure of the German Empire continued to express its distinctive regional identities. In the Italian peninsula, unification also derived its most important successes from the pre-existence of 'regional' and 'historic' entities, most importantly Piedmont-Sardinia, which managed to take advantage of the new forms of technological development and the rivalries of the Great Powers to create a viable army and a respectable cause.

These last two factors were less important in the establishment of self-determining national states in southern Europe and the Balkans, as Ottoman power slowly declined. That Empire was by its nature centrifugal, since it lacked any theoretical justification for absorbing into Islam distinctive subjugated religious minorities (a striking contrast with the dynamics of pan-Slavism and Great Russian nationalism in the Romanov Empire); and it also lacked (until the Kemalist revolution) the technological, commercial and administrative forms of logic which in other modern states tended to help create a dominant 'nationalist' centre. Moreover, some of the Ottoman sub-nationalities could claim 'historic' descent transmitted by effective aristocracies or neo-commercial bureaucracies — Greece, Romania, and Albania; or acquired powerful popular appeal — Serbia, and Bulgaria.[6] In any case, at least from the middle of the nineteenth century, the factor of Great Power rivalry, inducing continuous competitive interventions and compromises, was another agency of erosion and of sponsorship of politically aspirant nationalisms.

---

[6] P.F. Sugar, 'External and Domestic Roots of Eastern European Nationalism' in P.F. Sugar & I.J. Lederer (eds.), *Nationalism in Eastern Europe* (Seattle, 1971).

That factor stands in striking contrast to the Habsburg Empire, where German protection created a decisively different context in which the Austrian and Hungarian 'dominant minorities' could fend off the challenges presented by other groups. Furthermore, the Habsburg nationalities could work within a constitutional and cultural framework that recognized ethnic diversity, and, by the later nineteenth century, had learned to make political accommodations with them. This helps to explain why Polish, Czech, and Hungarian nationalities were so well adapted to arguing their respective causes as 'historic' rather than 'political' nations when it came to reconstructing the international order of Europe after the First World War. Indeed, the comparative freedom of thought and action in Habsburg lands encouraged the Ukrainian intelligentsia's strongest growth in Galicia, though this was not unconnected with rivalry between St. Petersburg and Vienna over the Slav peoples.

By contrast, however, with the exception of the Finns, whose cultural distinctiveness was respected until the outbreak of the 1905 revolts, the nationalities of the Romanov lands were suppressed and absorbed throughout the nineteenth and early twentieth centuries – and indeed earlier – mainly as a consequence of the repressive nature of Tsardom,[7] though also out of a growing sense of Russian national domination. And whereas in Austria-Hungary the minority of Germans needed to respect Hungarian (and other) nationalities in order to gain their co-operation, the near majority position of the Russians, and the fact that the two most important minorities, Ukrainians and Belorussians, were also Slav nations made 'Russification' a far more attractive instrument.

The collapse of the Russian and Habsburg Empires during the First World War ushered in a chapter of new national-state building in central and eastern Europe. But the successor states were strongly shaped by the considerations of the Great Powers, concerned as much with containing Bolshevism and German revanchism as with the purity of the principles enunciated by President Woodrow Wilson, embodied in the Charter of the League of Nations. And while the nationalities policy of the Bolsheviks in the revolutionary phase promised much, through civil war, external intervention, and the renewed growth of *raison d'etat*, it delivered little.

It was this combination of circumstances that conspired

---

[7] R. Pearson, *National Minorities in Eastern Europe* (London, 1984), pp. 68-70.

against the short-lived Ukrainian *Rada*. Moreover, this combination of factors, set against the background of the dreadful collectivization and induced famine of the early 1930s, led many Ukrainians in the home territories and abroad to place their hopes in the
New Order heralded by Hitler. But what was not recognized widely enough or soon enough was that Hitler sought to destroy
modern international political relations, not to develop them: indeed, he sought a new Imperial Europe. Through this miscalcula-
tion, tragedy was redoubled. As one eminent historian has written,
"The ex-Soviet nationalities were treated worst of all and were consequently alienated most ... by 1944, two thirds of the *Ostarbeiter*
in Germany were Ukrainians".[8] Not surprisingly, the nationalist
intelligentsia which came under Nazi control was liquidated.[9]

In this period, then, Ukrainian nationalists were forced into a
three-way choice, and every choice was wrong: Hitler was never
prepared to offer even limited autonomy, and when presented with
the evident disutility of the policies of enslavement, reaffirmed
them; after the war there was no hope that the West would once
again seek to pick its way through the impossible contradictions of
the claims of competing east European nationalisms; and, finally,
despite Stalin's temporary appeasement of 'Ukrainian nationalism'
for its tremendous struggle in defence of the Soviet Union, the
false independence of the Ukrainian SSR could never satisfy the
dreams of those who refused to accept Soviet socialism.

The 'lessons' history provides for the creation of new states
are, therefore, paradoxical and even contradictory. In the first
place, to become a new state it is important in some sense to be, or
appear to be, a 'historic' state. This is not the same thing as having
a 'populist' national identity: for example, Polish and Hungarian
nationalisms were by no means 'populist' before 1945; while in
Yugoslavia there is no binding tradition worth speaking of, despite
the breadth of Serbian populism. But when the accidents of history
happen, it is important to possess strongly developed,
documented, culturally entrenched, 'historic' claims to a social,
political, and territorial arena. Unfortunately, however, this
'lesson' carries with it the corollary that it is by no means sufficient

---

[8]   A. Dallin, *German Rule in Russia 1941-5: A Study of Occupation Policies* (London,
      1957), pp. 166-7.

[9]   On the important social role of the intelligentsia in nationalism — and against
      other theories which tend to discount this in favour of a close link between na-
      tionalism and 'economic development', see A.D. Smith, 'Nationalism, Ethnic
      Separatism and the Intelligentsia' in C.H. Williams (ed.), *National Separatism* (Car-
      diff, Wales, 1982).

in the light of historical experience to identify a prospective nation-state with its ethnographic dimensions; if nation states are political outcomes of a process of social strife, then nationality is also, in effect and at least somewhat in definition, a political construct.

Thus, to be a 'political' nationality seems in practical terms even more important: political revolutions and the aftermath of great wars provide those occasions of the most fundamental redrawing of territorial arrangements. However, the record of revolutionary activity leading successfully to the creation of a new state is not good. Irish nationalism has lived in continuous frustration for well over two centuries, despite the subsistence of its revolutionary identity. The Basque people have little or no prospect of translating their autonomy within Spain into an independent state that would unite all Basques. Although Yugoslavia is a troubled and only provisionally stable state, Croatians, Albanians and others aspiring to separate political existence must struggle against the forces which make for the continuity of the Yugoslav state. Ukrainian nationalism has lived and suffered through several major revolutions, and during the Second World War existed at the very epicentre of the biggest and most destructive battles of history; yet it has been smothered, divided, and driven to distraction by the working through of those very same dynamics of change which in other places have led secessionist movements to success in creating new states.

So can one generalize about the randomness of history? It seems that the interplay between aspiring nationhood and the major fissures which from time to time crack the surface of international politics demands that revolutionary organizations put the preservation of themselves and their traditions, through possibly very long periods of time, ahead of any priority to create such fissures by their own independent efforts. No movement, however enormous its potential, can act against the currently prevailing pattern of international political action.

However, there is much more to it than this. Whatever theory we adopt to explain the spread of nationalism and its corresponding political forms, there can be little doubt that it provides the single most important key to the growth, distribution, and management of political power in today's world. So crucial is this nexus that, once it is reached in an attainable form, nationalities seldom die out, though some, like Scottish nationalism, may be effectively de-politicized. This means, or it may mean, that while the nationalities which 'succeed' in realizing the form of states never voluntarily diminish their power, there is everything to be gained by unrealized nationalities probing continuously for a share in that power; that indeed the history of nationalism is less the history of transcendence than of the ultimate plasticity of our self-made social universe.[10] It may not be going too far to suggest that the underlying political power of nationalism is precisely this: a reflection of the maturation of society in which social morality ceases gradually to be eschatalogical, and becomes transactional.

But whether that be accepted or not, it is today difficult to gainsay the underlying strength of nationalism in eastern Europe and the Soviet Union, and increasingly problematical to sustain the argument that the socialist regimes can maintain their power without increasing accommodations to it. In the light of recent international political history, that is a remarkable phenomenon.

The documents in this collection demonstrate that Ukrainian nationalist organizations never acquired the political power or cohesion to influence the strategic priorities of the Western powers during the crucial war and postwar years; and that, despite Cold War mistrust, the Soviet Union's legitimacy as a territorial state within its 1941 frontiers, and its geostrategic presence in eastern Europe, were accepted as beyond effective dispute. If my account of the difficulties which international politics usually place in the way of nationalities becoming state-nations is accepted, then several additional factors serving in a systematic way to frustrate Ukrainian nationalism also need to be considered. So does this nationalism have much of a future outside its Western emigré and Soviet dominated formations?

The answer I have tried to suggest is that despite the unique accumulation of tragedy, accident and error which depicts the history of Ukrainian nationalism to date, the broader history and theory of nationalism suggests that the past does not predetermine the future. So while the past may provide useful, indeed absolutely necessary, bedrock for building the politics of national aspirations, it is the nature of the aspirations themselves that should count for most.

Hugh A. Macdonald
London School of Economics

---

[10] Ernest Gellner is perhaps the most logically rigorous proponent of the theory that nationalism is reducible to empirical and functional aspects of social structure, and specifically state-centric development. The difficulty with his theoretical approach is that it makes nationalism so instrumental that its quite specific command of sentiment and loyalty is lost sight of. See, for instance, E. Gellner, 'Ethnicity between Culture, Class and Power', in P.F. Sugar (ed.), *Ethnic Diversity and Conflict in Eastern Europe*, (Santa Barbara, Calif., 1980).

Introduction
The Anglo-American Powers
and the Ukrainian National Question

The failure of Ukrainian nationalism to establish a permanent state in the twentieth century has been at times ascribed to the underdeveloped character of a Ukrainian national consciousness. Such a perspective, however, represents an oversimplification of the complex economic, social, and historical realities which confronted the Ukrainian population in eastern Europe. It is also incomplete in that it ignores both the importance which established states historically assign to the maintenance of the international balance of power and the logic of the modern state system which favours fixed borders and known relationships over the uncertainties attendant on change. Recognizing the relevance of this bias is, therefore, critical to any study of the prospects of success for national liberation movements, since rarely, in modern political history, have these proved successful without either external recognition and support, or, minimally, non-interference from abroad.

The inability of the Ukrainian *Rada* to gain widespread legal and political recognition during the turbulent years 1917-1921, for example, was a decisive factor in the collapse of the Ukrainian Republic.[1] The period 1938-1951, also years of political flux,

---

[1] On Ukraine during the World War I see J.S. Reshetar, *The Ukrainian Revolution, 1917-1920: A Study in Nationalism* (Princeton, NJ, 1952); T. Hunchak, (ed.) *The Ukraine, 1917-1921: A Study in Revolution* (Cambridge, Mass., 1977); and J. Borys, *The Sovietization of Ukraine 1917-1923: The Communist Doctrine and Practice of National Self-Determination* (Edmonton, 1980).

marked another time when the Ukrainian national movement was
unable to garner the type of support that would have lent itself to
the formation of an independent polity. Arguably, in the latter
case, Anglo-American unwillingness to accord legitimacy to the
struggle for Ukrainian independence had as much to do with the
defeat of the aspirations of the Ukrainian nationalists as did the
political-territorial ambitions of Soviet Russia and Nazi Germany.
Why this occurred, and the degree to which Anglo-American re-
ticence played a role in the failure of the Ukrainians to establish a
lasting state has yet to be explored.

In the unsettled political conditions prevailing in Europe during the late 1920s and 30s, complex international relationships
were forged which aimed at containing or promoting changes to
the existing geopolitical balance. Ukrainian nationalism, as a force
which favoured a restructuring of the political geography of
Europe, was generally considered a destabilizing factor by the
policy-making elites of those states which sought to maintain the
European *status quo*. To reduce the political effectiveness of
Ukrainian separatism, decision-makers − whether in London's
Whitehall or Warsaw's Ministry of External Affairs − often put
forward arguments intended to counter Ukrainian claims to national self-determination. These included arguments that ques-
tioned the historical legitimacy of Ukrainian claims; challenged the
idea of a distinct Ukrainian nation in ethnological terms; or simply
gave precedence to geopolitical considerations, suggesting that
further territorial fragmentation in eastern Europe would promote
regional instability. Since some of these policy-makers believed
there had never been a Ukrainian nation-state, they argued there
was no need to create one now. Indeed, Ukrainian demands for a
state of their own were increasingly perceived to be nothing more
than an 'Austro-German invention'. On this premise, it was asserted that Ukrainian aspirations were illegitimate and, as such, could
be ignored. This was a view often repeated, especially when it
became evident that German ambitions in the east once again
threatened the peace of Europe.

Undeniably, some of the leading proponents of Ukrainian
statehood would look to and did receive political support from Germany, although never to the extent nor the kind most had hoped
for. But in seeking external recognition and aid, as they did in
1918, Ukrainian leaders differed little from their Czech or Polish
counterparts. Nor did they restrict themselves in their political options having sought diplomatic recognition from every possible
quarter both during and after the war. Ukrainian delegates to the

postwar peace negotiations at Versailles, for example, tried to extract guarantees of the political and legal right of the Ukrainian people to national self-determination. Yet being associated with the defeated Central Powers, they were rebuked and, in the case of Western Ukrainians, given only minimal constitutional guarantees of minority rights within a restructured Polish state.

The 1920s and the period of *NEP* were initially hopeful years for those Ukrainians who found themselves under Soviet rule (*vide* Map 1). A programme of Ukrainianization, whose origins were in the national renaissance of 1917-1921, was implemented during the short-lived period of national communism. It suggested a partial realization of Ukrainian expectations. These, however, were left unfulfilled with the consolidation of Stalinism in Soviet Ukraine; Ukrainian social and political elites were suppressed as were the Ukrainian language, culture and various national institutions. Stalinism would culminate in the Great Famine of 1932-1933 during which the Ukrainian nation would suffer a demographic loss of several millions.[2]

The policy of denationalization in Soviet Ukraine paralleled to a lesser degree developments in Polish East Galicia or Western Ukraine (*vide* Map 2). Social, legal and economic rights were denied the Ukrainian minority while the Polish government's "pacification" of the Ukrainian population in the early 1930s reminded them of their tenuous position in the newly formed state. Under these circumstances certain sections of the Ukrainian populace became increasingly alienated. Among the more militant element of the Ukrainian nationalist leadership, the notion was reinforced that there could be no political accommodation with those states which ruled over Ukrainians.

Although the diplomatic and intelligence sources of the Western powers provided sufficient information for their respective governments to comprehend the magnitude of the distress being experienced by the population of Soviet Ukraine, little was done to protest or ameliorate the situation. When, for example, Sir Waldon Smithers and Lord Charnwood raised questions in the British Parliament during the summer of 1934 about famine in Ukraine, the Foreign Office's reply was evasive.[3] Nor were British

---

[2] See J.E. Mace, *Communism and the Dilemmas of National Liberation: National Communism in Soviet Ukraine 1918-1933* (Cambridge, Mass., 1983); R. Conquest, *The Harvest of Sorrow: Soviet Collectivization and the Terror-Famine* (New York, 1986); and R. Serbyn and B. Krawchenko (eds.), *Famine in Ukraine 1932-1933* (Edmonton, 1986).

[3] The relevant British Foreign Office (FO) file is FO 371/18321, dated 2 July 1934. In considering Sir Waldron's question, L. Collier disclosed:

officials very critical of the Polish government's treatment of non-Polish nationalities living within its state borders, especially the Ukrainians. This unwillingness to protest anti-Ukrainian actions, at least on the part of Britain, was rooted in fears about a resurgent Germany's political and territorial designs as well as Britain's self-interest in preserving the balance of power in which it enjoyed a favourable position. Since Poland played a crucial regional role in eastern Europe, this meant Britain would not risk complicating relations with this important ally over the Ukrainian Question. The British also preferred a strong and united Soviet Union acting as a potential deterrent to German ambitions.

Aware of some of these complicating factors, the Ukrainian nationalist leadership nevertheless sought Britain's support for the movement since it was understood that British recognition would considerably strengthen the case for Ukrainian independence within international forums. In June 1935, Colonel Evhen Konovalets, leader of the Organization of the Ukrainian Nationalists (OUN),[4] addressed a letter to the British Foreign Office in which he enumerated the beneficial effects which the creation of a sovereign Ukrainian state in eastern Europe would have for European democracy. He concluded his appeal by noting:

> During the last years affection and reverence for English culture, and for the tolerant foreign policy of the British Empire, have increasingly penetrated the minds of the Ukrainian people and widely so. The Ukrainians are grateful for the expressions of sympathy which have been manifested by the English nation during the last years. We are hoping that in the future it will be possible to coil the interests of Great Britain with the interests of Ukraine in such a way that both countries shall derive benefits therefrom.[5]

> The truth of the matter is, of course, that we have a certain amount of information about famine conditions in the south of Russia [sic] similar to what has appeared in the press, and that there is no obligation on us not to make it public. We do not want to make it public, however, because the Soviet Government would resent it and our relations with them would be prejudiced... We cannot give this explanation in public.

A particularly detailed account of how famine conditions were developing in Ukraine was prepared for the Foreign Office by A. Cairns (FO 371/16329, 12 August 1932). In a report, FO 371/17253, 30 September 1933, W. Strang noted that *New York Times* correspondent, Walter Duranty, "thinks it quite possible that as many as 10 million people may have died directly or indirectly from lack of food in the Soviet Union during the past year."

[4] See J.A. Armstrong, *Ukrainian Nationalism,* 2nd rev. ed. (New York, 1963). The OUN split into two competing factions in 1940, known popularly as the *Banderivtsi* (OUNb) and the *Melnykivtsi* (OUNm) after their leaders, Stepan Bandera and Andrii Melnyk.

[5] A translation of Colonel Konovalets' letter is found in FO 371/19455, 15 June 1935.

Similar arguments, consonant with the liberal-democratic views expressed in British foreign policy statements, were advanced by other Ukrainian nationalist representatives. Their attempts to establish a rapport with Britain's foreign policy-making circles, however, failed. The Ukrainian nationalist movement was, as a result, restricted in whom it could seek political support from. Only the revisionist powers of the European Right seemed willing to promote the kinds of political and territorial changes that might increase the likelihood of Ukrainian independence.

British unwillingness to accord legitimacy to the concept of Ukrainian statehood had its origins in at least several other preconceptions about the nature and intentions of the nationalist movement. There was, for example, concern over the growing use of violence by Ukrainian nationalists against Polish state institutions and representatives. Equally important was the British view that Ukrainian irredentism might somehow be exploited by Germany. The latter's diplomats had sporadically raised the Ukrainian Question in the councils of Europe and, reportedly, enjoyed a measure of influence over parts of the Ukrainian nationalist movement. Since it was felt that Ukrainian nationalism could become a potential political force, British officials decided that it would bear more careful scrutiny. Just before the outbreak of the Second World War, they would inform their American counterparts of their point of view. The latter would, essentially, adopt it. The Canadian authorities, on the other hand, were already monitoring their Ukrainian minority in an attempt to forestall any security problems which the factionalism evident in this population might engender.

The concern over whether a connection existed between the Ukrainian nationalist underground in Europe and the Ukrainian emigration in countries as far flung as Cuba, Canada, Argentina, the United States and Ecuador would come to be shared by the Anglo-American powers — Britain, the United States, and Canada. Recognizing that widespread sympathy existed in the Ukrainian emigration for the creation of an independent Ukrainian state, each of these governments initiated policies of surveillance aimed at controlling their respective Ukrainian communities. With the prospect of a European war, they were particularly concerned about containing any threat which the ostensibly foreign political sympathies of Ukrainians in their societies might generate to their war efforts. These internal security measures would often have deleterious effects on these communities.[6]

The Ukrainian nationalists by the late 1930s were left with little alternative but to deepen their existing contacts with the revisionist powers. These ties were mainly with the military and intelligence services of the Tripartite Alliance, reflecting the belief of
many Ukrainians that an independent Ukraine would emerge only
after war had altered the prevailing political order in eastern
Europe. There were Ukrainians, including leading members of the
nationalist movement, who, while rejecting Nazi ideology as im-
perialist and anti-Christian, were drawn to the corporatist and conservative aspects of the programme of the European Right. In
some measure, this orientation reflected the perception that the
failed Ukrainian attempt at state-building during the period of the
Rada was also the failure of the social-democratic leadership in
Ukraine. The programme of the OUN would place much emphasis
on discipline, obedience to the leadership of the movement, and the
notion of subordinating social conflict to the principle of national
unity, all with the aim of attaining Ukrainian statehood.[7]

The Ukrainian movement was nurtured by those within Germany who recognized that the Ukrainian Question could be used to
the discomfort not only of Poland and other east European states
but also the Soviet Union and Britain. Such sympathy within certain official German circles, however, left the Nazi worldview largely unaffected. The Nazis continued to regard Ukrainians as a
"racially inferior" people and scheduled Ukrainian territory for
depopulation and German colonial settlement. Thus, despite the
relatively sympathetic attitude to Ukrainian independence by party ideologist, Alfred Rosenberg, the ruling Nazi elite, from Hitler
to his *Reichskommissar* for Ukraine, Erich Koch, remained
vehemently opposed to Ukrainian nationalism and refused to
entertain the idea of an independent Ukraine. For most Nazis, co-
operation with the Ukrainian national movement was deemed

---

[6] For documentation on policies of control and internal security directed against
Ukrainians in the emigration see, for example, Documents 28, 31, 33, and 37 in B.S.
Kordan and L. Y. Luciuk, *A Delicate and Difficult Question: Documents in the
History of Ukrainians in Canada 1899-1962* (Kingston, Ont., 1986).

[7] The Ukrainian nationalists were inordinately interested in manifestations of national activism everywhere. Their leading ideological journal, *Rozbudova Natsii*
contained articles on revolutionary nationalist movements such as Pilsudski's anti-
Russian underground, *Zemlia i Volia*, the Irish Sinn Fein, and similar groups in
Korea, Finland, Lithuania, Afghanistan and the United States. On the question of
the relationship between Ukrainian nationalism and fascism, see A.J. Motyl, *The
Turn To The Right: The Ideological Origins and Development of Ukrainian Nationalism, 1919-1929* (Boulder Co., 1980).

ideologically objectionable and unnecessary, a position reinforced after the spectacular German military advances against Soviet forces in 1941-1942.[8] This attitude toward Ukrainians, and the policies it informed, would later be modified, only insofar as the exigencies of wartime dictated and, at that, only fitfully. The Nazis had come to Ukraine to exploit and rule, not to liberate.

The dismemberment of the Polish state by Nazi Germany and the Soviet Union, in September 1939, temporarily altered Anglo-American perspectives on the Ukrainian Question. The Soviet Union was now perceived by western analysts as an opportunistic and imperialistic power, one closely tied to Britain's chief rival, Nazi Germany. Within the British Foreign Office the option of negotiating a *rapprochement* between the Poles and Ukrainians was considered; other strategists even pondered the feasibility of instigating a Ukrainian revolt in eastern Galicia in order 'to bring down' the Nazis and their Soviet ally. This did not mean that Polish sensitivities on the question of Poland's prewar eastern boundaries were forgotten, but it was understood that such considerations would be jettisoned if British interests required it.

While such options were considered by the statesmen of Britain's Foreign Office, Soviet security forces in eastern Galicia began to eliminate systematically the sources of potential resistance to Soviet rule. Selected categories of individuals – embracing ethnic Poles, Jews, Belorussians, and Ukrainians – were deported to Kazakhstan and Yakutsk in Central Asia as well as to the Kolyma region of northeastern Siberia.[9] For some time

---

[8] See I. Kamenetsky, *Hitler's Occupation of Ukraine, 1941-1944: A Case Study of Totalitarian Imperialism* (Milwaukee, 1956); *Secret Nazi Plans for Eastern Europe: A Study of Lebensraum Policies* (New York, 1961); and G. Reitlinger's *The House Built on Sand: The Conflicts of German Policy in Russia, 1939-1945* (New York, 1960).

[9] A detailed account of Soviet deportations of the population from eastern Galicia was provided by British Intelligence in a report dated December 1943. Of the approximately 2 million individuals registered for deportation, approximately 1 million were taken; reportedly 52% of them were Poles, 30% Jews, 20% Belorussians and 18% Ukrainians. Of these, 115,000 survived in the ranks of the Polish Anders Army, or as civilians attached to this force, while another 272,000 were later accounted for. A copy of the report, entitled *Soviet Deportation of the Inhabitants of Eastern Poland in 1939-41* can be found in the archives of the Department of External Affairs (Canada), File: 266-40-C. The report includes a cover letter which states:

> The aim of the present report is not to contribute to any further dispute in the camps of the United Nations.... Nevertheless, it seems advisable that a few persons, especially selected for this purpose, be confidentially informed of the fate of Polish citizens under Soviet rule, and thus to avoid any misunderstanding which may arise and to refute certain false statements emanating from specific sources.

American Intelligence also produced a report which documented these population losses. See *Wartime Population Changes in Areas Incorporated into the Soviet*

thereafter what information the British could obtain about conditions in Western Ukraine was contradictory, often spurious, and
sparse.

British plans for a Ukrainian revolt in Western Ukraine were
pre-empted by the June 1941 German invasion of Soviet-controlled
territories. The invasion forced the Soviet Union to align itself
with Britain and its allies. In these changed international circumstances it was in Britain's interest to preserve the territorial
and political integrity of the Soviet Union as a much needed ally in
the war against Germany. British analysts had long since concluded that the loss of Ukrainian territories to the Soviet Union would
likely result in economic dislocation and the political collapse of
the USSR. Thus no action would henceforth be sanctioned which
might appear to demonstrate British support for any Ukrainian
nationalist group. American and Canadian authorities came to
share this perspective, although they were more circumspect in
voicing it, mainly because of their serious and ongoing concerns
about provoking anti-Allied sentiment among the large Ukrainian
communities working in the key industries of North America.
Surveillance against Ukrainian emigrés was increased and detailed
information on a number of Ukrainian groups was regularly ex-
changed between the various internal security services of Britain,
the United States and Canada. Simultaneously, an attempt was
also made to monitor developments in Ukraine, although during
the war and in the immediate postwar years this proved to be a difficult process.

In the wake of the German invasion of the Soviet Union,
Ukrainian nationalists proclaimed the renewal of an independent
and sovereign Ukrainian state.[10] The Nazi leadership immediately
demonstrated its hostility toward Ukrainian aspirations by suppressing the OUN. Indeed, a large number of the organization's
leading cadres were executed or incarcerated in the concentration
camps of the Third Reich.[11] The OUN network went underground to
regroup and continue its organizational and political work. Those

---

tion losses. See *Wartime Population Changes in Areas Incorporated into the Soviet
Union in 1939-1940* produced by the Research and Analysis Branch of the Office of
Strategic Services. *OSS, RAND A Report No. 2325*, US National Archives, Microfilm
Publication, M 1221, Intelligence Reports: 1941-1961.

[10] On the initiative of the OUNb faction the renewal of an independent Ukrainian state,
headed by Yaroslav Stetsko, was proclaimed in Lviv, on 30 June 1941. The OUNm
faction established a Ukrainian National Council in Kiev, on 5 October 1941, headed by Prof. M. Velychivsky.

[11] On the OUN's losses under Nazi occupation see J.A. Armstrong, *Ukrainian Nationalism*, 2nd rev. ed. (New York, 1963), pp. 104-117.

nationalist cadres despatched to proselytize and consolidate popular opinion on the national question and who escaped the initial arrests by German police were able to achieve some success in the various parts of eastern and southern Ukraine to which they were sent.[12]

The repressive policies of the Nazis in the *Generalgouvernement* and in the *Reichkommissariat Ukraine* prompted the underground leadership to organize the growing armed resistance which had developed spontaneously among the civilian population against German rule. In the autumn of 1942 the nucleus of the Ukrainian Insurgent Army (UPA) formally came into being, and by 1944, foreign intelligence circles estimated UPA forces numbered as many as 100,000 combatants.[13] Reportedly, the influence of UPA and the civilian OUN network supporting it, especially in Western Ukraine, was so extensive that German forces retained effective control only in the larger urban centres. By late 1944, the Ukrainian partisan war against the Nazis and their occupation policies was suspended as the Germans retreated; Ukrainian resistance was redirected against Soviet administration as Soviet armed forces once again reoccupied all of Ukraine. The insurgency continued into the 1950s although the scale of resistance had been much reduced by 1948, when Soviet security forces, in collaboration with Polish and Czechoslovak units, eliminated UPA's base of support through the deportation of Ukrainians from insurgent-dominated areas. With this, the last vestiges of an extensively organized armed resistance to Soviet rule in eastern Europe disappeared.

During this decade of armed conflict (1941-1951) a transformation took place in the worldview of the Ukrainian underground. Although the primary objective of creating an independent Ukrainian national state was still emphasized, the movement's programme evolved to include not only a critique of partocracy, and

---

[12] On the success of the OUN expeditionary force in the Donbas region of Ukraine, see B. Krawchenko, *Social Change and National Consciousness in Twentieth-Century Ukraine* (London, 1985), p. 168.

[13] An organized Ukrainian resistance coalesced around various village and regional self-defence units, the most effective of which seems to have been the group headed by Bulba-Borovets, which operated in Volhynia. It was later incorporated by the OUNb into the UPA. Estimates about the size of UPA vary although a figure of 40,000 partisans is generally accepted. The figure cited probably includes the OUN civilian network, which co-operated closely with UPA. On the UPA, see Y. Tys-Krokhmaliuk, *UPA Warfare in Ukraine: Strategical, Tactical and Organizational Problems of Ukrainian Resistance in World War II* (New York, 1972). The *Litopys UPA* series (Toronto, 1978-1987) reproduces documentary materials and personal reminiscences about UPA.

specifically Bolshevism, but also promulgated a position that was anti-imperialist, anti-capitalist and anti-colonial in nature. This reformulation of Ukrainian nationalist ideology had its origins in a number of factors: the need to develop a critical analysis of both Nazi Germany and the Soviet Union as warring imperialisms, the political isolation of the insurgency, and the programmatic changes which had taken place as a result of incorporating the specific social and economic concerns of those Ukrainians who had experienced nearly a generation of Soviet rule.[14]

The appeal of the resistance, the location of the front, and the high incidence of desertion within the Soviet army, all combined to attract other national minorities to the ranks of UPA. These were organized within UPA as non-Ukrainian units after a special conference of national representatives was convened in November 1943 which called for a united and co-ordinated front against German and Soviet military and civil administrations. During this same period, a new political body, the Supreme Ukrainian Liberation Council (UHVR), also emerged. Although dominated by members of the OUN, the Council included representation from a range of political tendencies in Ukraine. The formation of UHVR represented in part the idea of historical continuity in the struggle of the Ukrainian people for self-determination.

In the immediate postwar period the isolation of the Ukrainian

---

[14] Outlining a possible future social and economic order in an independent Ukrainian state, the nationalist ideologue P. Poltava wrote:

> The concept of an independent Ukraine is also the concept of a future social order in the Ukrainian state that will be free of any exploitation of one person by another. This social order will be based upon state and co-operative ownership of industry, banking and trade, and upon state ownership of land with individual or collective managements, depending upon the will of the population.
>
> This concept of the social and economic order of the future Ukrainian state is in accord with the actual situation in Ukraine at the present time. At present there is no private ownership of industry, trade or banking and no private land ownership in Ukraine. The present economic exploitation of the Ukrainian people is due to the colonial status, both political and economic, of Ukraine within the Bolshevik USSR. The Ukrainian labouring masses are enslaved by a class of Bolshevik overlords who enjoy both political and economic privileges. These two facts alone – Ukraine's colonial status within the Bolshevik Soviet system and the social enslavement of the Ukrainian toiling masses by the Bolshevik overlords – are the main reasons for the present economic misery of the Ukrainian people. When the Ukrainian people attain their full political independence and establish a just and democratic internal political and social order, these conditions will no longer apply. Then and only then will it be possible to put the principle of public ownership fully at the service of the Ukrainian people – the peasants, workers and intellectuals.

See P.J. Potichnyj and E. Shtendera, (eds.), *Political Thought of the Ukrainian Underground 1943-1951* (Edmonton, 1986), p. 177. On the official OUN position with respect to social-economic policy, see Document 9 "Programmatic and Political Resolutions of the Organization of Ukrainian Nationalists. Third Congress – 1943" in Y. Boshyk (ed.), *Ukraine During World War II: History and Its Aftermath* (Edmonton, 1986), p. 186-188.

insurgency led to a re-evaluation within the underground of the role of Britain and America. The political situation of the Ukrainian nation came to be seen as much a consequence of policies formulated in Washington and London as Berlin and Moscow.[15] For them, the moral and political bankruptcy of the Western powers was further evidenced by the Alliance's forcible repatriation of displaced persons to Soviet-dominated territories under the terms of the Yalta Agreement[16]. And although a global war involving the USSR and the United States seemed imminent, the prospect of an Anglo-American intervention in the Soviet Union was viewed with much uncertainty. Some even argued that, for economic and political reasons, the structure of the Soviet Union would be preserved by the West should the former be defeated in the expected war. Commenting on the Ukrainian position with respect to this scenario, the nationalist ideologist P. Poltava wrote:

> It may be true that the Anglo-American bloc has no aggressive intentions toward the Soviet Union or, more specifically, toward Ukraine. But if it supports forces that take a hostile attitude toward the liberation of Ukraine and strive to maintain, in one way or another, Russia's colonial rule over non-Russian territories and peoples, then its policy towards the peoples of the USSR and, above all, the forty-million-strong Ukrainian people, automatically takes on an anti-liberation character. If the Ukrainian people and the other peoples of the USSR cannot expect that during the next war the Anglo-American bloc will take a sympathetic view of their struggle for independence, if they can expect only that the Anglo-American bloc will abet their renewed subjugation by a new breed of Russian great-power imperialists, then they can only assume that the stance of the Western bloc in the coming war is to be anti-liberation in character.
>
> In such an event, the Ukrainian people and all the other subject peoples of the USSR will not welcome this war as a war of

---

[15] An example of the alienation of the insurgency from the West is evident in the reported statements of 'Zalizniak' the Chief of Staff, UPA-*Zakerzonia*, who declared that should a war break out between the Anglo-American bloc and the Soviet Union, and if an amnesty were granted, he would personally lead a number of Soviet divisions on Washington. The latter had, he believed, abandoned the Ukrainian nation and was ultimately responsible for the situation Ukrainians found themselves in. Interviews with 'Kozak' [pseudonym], The Canadian Institute of Ukrainian Studies, *Oral History Project*, Eastern Region, October, 1983.

[16] On the forcible repatriation of Ukrainians and others to the USSR during the latter part of World War II and the immediate postwar period, see N. Tolstoy, *Victims of Yalta* (Toronto, 1977), his *Stalin's Secret War* (New York, 1982); and M.R. Elliott, *Pawns of Yalta: Soviet Refugees and America's Role in Their Repatriation* (Urbana, Ill., 1982).

> *liberation; they will not regard the opponents of the USSR as their
> true friends.*
>
> *In such an event, the Ukrainian people, and, we expect, all
> the other non-Russian subject peoples of the USSR, will regard
> this war as another war of world imperialism, a war in which the
> national and social aspirations of the peoples subjugated by the
> Soviet Union will be attained only to the extent that they
> themselves might bring these things about.*[17]

While ignoring the evolving political character of the Ukrainian national movement, the Western states which developed policies aimed at containing the Soviet Union did review what future potential a Ukrainian insurgency might have as a strictly anti-Soviet military force. They also made limited use of a number of Ukrainian political refugees for intelligence-gathering missions inside the USSR, and considered how Ukrainian emigré groups might be exploited as a destabilizing element in eastern Europe in the event of war. In the end, however, it became clear to Western statesmen that an accommodation would have to be reached with the Soviet Union. The Ukrainian Question — even as a military-strategic question — faded into obscurity, thereafter being discussed only from the viewpoint of what advantages might accrue from establishing diplomatic 'listening posts' in Ukraine. Any kind of brinkmanship involving the Ukrainian Question was overruled in the uneasy atmosphere of coexistence which came to characterize postwar relations between the Anglo-American powers and the Soviet Union.

The dictates of 'high politics' underpinned Anglo-American unwillingness to recognize and support Ukrainian claims to national self-determination. In later years similar considerations would lead to equally vacillating policies with respect to the struggle of various peoples for self-determination in eastern Europe and the developing world. Preserving the international *status quo*, and distancing themselves from any political movements challenging it, became and remained cornerstones of Western geopolitical thinking. In this context it becomes clear that the Anglo-American powers never wanted, nor felt they needed a free Ukraine.

Bohdan S. Kordan   Lubomyr Y. Luciuk
Department of Political Science   *Department of Geography*
Arizona State University   *University of Toronto*

---

[17] See P. Poltava, "Preparatory Steps Toward the Third World War and the Tasks of the Ukrainian People," in P.J. Potichnyj and E. Shtendera (eds.), *Political Thought of the Ukrainian Underground 1943-1951* (Edmonton, 1986), pp. 275-276.

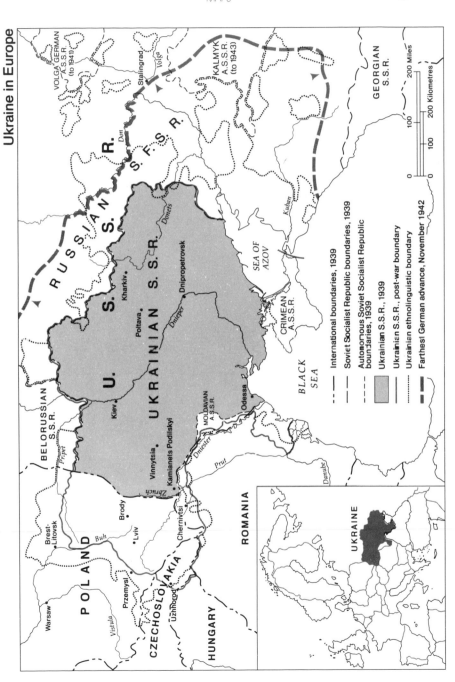

Ukraine in Europe

International boundaries, 1939
Soviet Socialist Republic boundaries, 1939
Autonomous Soviet Socialist Republic boundaries, 1939
Ukrainian S.S.R., 1939
Ukrainian S.S.R., post-war boundary
Ukrainian ethnolinguistic boundary
Farthest German advance, November 1942

RUSSIAN S.F.S.R.

U.S.S.R.

UKRAINIAN S.S.R.

VOLGA GERMAN A.S.S.R. (to 1941)

KALMYK A.S.S.R. (to 1943)

GEORGIAN S.S.R.

Stalingrad

Volga

Don

Donets

Kharkiv

Poltava

Dnipropetrovsk

Dnieper

Kuban

SEA OF AZOV

CRIMEAN A.S.S.R.

BLACK SEA

Kiev

MOLDAVIAN A.S.S.R.

Odessa

Vinnytsia

Kamianets Podilskyi

Dniester

Prut

Danube

BELORUSSIAN S.S.R.

Pripet

Zbruch

Brody

Lviv

Chernivtsi

Uzhhorod

POLAND

Buh

Brest-Litovsk

Przemysl

Warsaw

Vistula

CZECHOSLOVAKIA

HUNGARY

ROMANIA

UKRAINE

200 Miles
200 Kilometres
0   100   200
0   100   200

Western Ukraine

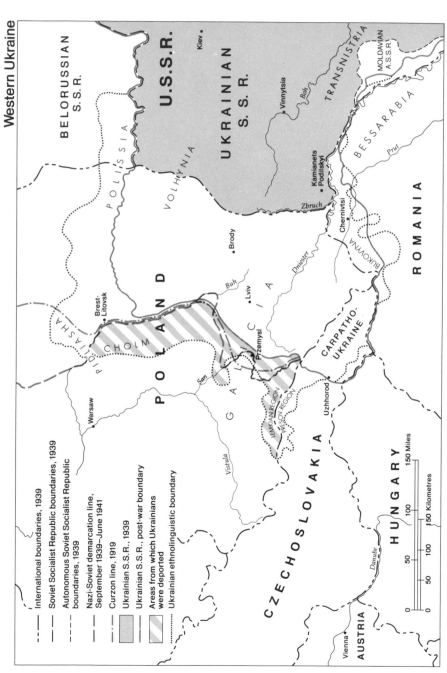

International boundaries, 1939

Soviet Socialist Republic boundaries, 1939

Autonomous Soviet Socialist Republic boundaries, 1939

Nazi-Soviet demarcation line, September 1939–June 1941

Curzon line, 1919

Ukrainian S.S.R., 1939

Ukrainian S.S.R., post-war boundary

Areas from which Ukrainians were deported

Ukrainian ethnolinguistic boundary

BELORUSSIAN S.S.R.

U.S.S.R.

UKRAINIAN S.S.R.

Kiev

Vinnytsia

Buh

TRANSNISTRIA

MOLDAVIAN A.S.S.R.

BESSARABIA

Prut

Kamianets Podilskyi

POLISSIA

VOLHYNIA

Zbruch

Chernivtsi

BUKOVYNA

Brody

Dniester

POLAND

PIDLIASHIA

CHOLM

Brest-Litovsk

Buh

Lviv

GALICIA

Przemysl

San

CARPATHO-UKRAINE

LEMKIAN REGION

PRESOV REGION

Uzhhorod

Warsaw

Vistula

ROMANIA

CZECHOSLOVAKIA

HUNGARY

Danube

Vienna

AUSTRIA

150 Miles

100

50

0

150 Kilometres

100

50

0

Documents

1

Despatch from British Embassy, Moscow, 17 October 1938, to the British Foreign Secretary, Commenting on the Inability of the Ukrainian Communist Party to Attract Recruits to its Ranks.

BRITISH EMBASSY

No. 440

Moscow
17TH OCTOBER, 1938

My Lord,

In my despatch No. 293 of June 27th last, I had the honour to acquaint Your Lordship with the publication of certain figures relating to the membership of the Ukrainian Communist Party and to point out how low the percentage of Party members was in comparison with the total population of the Ukraine.

2. The Ukrainian newspaper, the Kiev *Communist*, published on September 19th some interesting supplementary figures in this connexion, which were made available at a recent meeting of the Central Committee of the Ukrainian Communist Party. It appears that from November 1st, 1936, when the ban placed on further admissions to the Party was removed, up to August 1st, 1938, 20,740 persons were admitted to the grade of candidate members, while during the same period 13,891 persons were admitted to full membership of the Party. Of this total of 34,631 candidates and full members, 7,450 were admitted between November 1st, 1936, and January 1st, 1938, and 27,181 during the first seven months of this year.

3. After referring to the improvement as regards admissions to the Party which had taken place in 1938, the article in the *Communist* declared that nevertheless certain Party organizations were very behindhand. For instance, from November 1st, 1936 to August 1st, 1938, not a single new member had been admitted to the Party in 469 Party organizations in the Kharkov area, in 217 organizations in the Nikolayev area and in 209 organizations in the

Vinnitsa area. The Central Committee of the Ukrainian Communist Party had accordingly addressed a sharp warning to Party Secretaries in those areas. It appears, however, that, at the same meeting, the Central Committee passed a resolution stating that politically suspect and hostile elements had found their way into a number of local Party organizations and laying down that in future only those persons who came from the ranks of the workers and who had proved themselves in the campaign against internal foes should be admitted to Party membership.

4. It seems likely that, so long as the intensive drive to increase membership of the Party is accompanied by warnings with regard to the admission of suspect and hostile elements, the growth of membership will be slow, and that the marked reluctance of Ukrainians, owing to their nationalist proclivities, to join an organization which is wholly under the control of Moscow, will only be deepened.

I have the honour to be,
with the highest respect, My Lord,
Your Lordship's most obedient,
humble servant,

[sgd.] CHILSTON

SOURCE: FO 371/22295
Public Record Office

2

Despatch by Sir H. Kennard, British Embassy, Warsaw, 14 December 1938, Regarding International Aspects of the Ukrainian Question and the Possible Appearance of Autonomous Ukraine. Minutes by R.L. Speaight.

BRITISH EMBASSY

WARSAW
14TH DECEMBER, 1938

My Lord,

In my immediately preceding despatch I have endeavoured to throw some further light on the present situation in the Ukrainian provinces of Poland. In the present despatch I propose to deal with the international aspects of the Ukrainian problem. Necessarily any remarks on this subject must be very tentative indeed. There is much loose talk and even more loose thinking about it, and no one so far as I know has any concrete knowledge of what exactly is in the mind of Monsieur Beck. It is, however, certain that the Polish Government are giving the matter serious consideration.

2. The whole Ukrainian question is intimately bound up with Poland's security against Russia. If by some means the open rolling land south of the Prypet marshes could be neutralized politically, Poland would have better chances of holding the Russians at bay among the forests and marshes to the north of them.

3. Moreover, the Russian Ukraine has close affinities with Poland. Most of it formed part of the Polish-Lithuanian Empire of the sixteenth and seventeenth centuries. The west bank of the Dnieper was only lost to Poland in the First Partition. There are also ethnographical considerations, for Ukrainians and Poles have suffered together from the denationalizing policy of Imperial Russia. Great numbers of Poles come from near Kiev. It is commonly estimated that there were four million Poles in the Russian Ukraine at the end of the last war, and there are still said to be a great many there. It is even now less than twenty years since a Polish army captured Kiev.

4. Pilsudski favoured the setting up of an autonomous Ukrainian state which would have acted as a buffer against Russian aggression in the south and which (in the nadir of Germany's misfortunes) would have had to look for political and military support to Poland. To ensure the friendship of such a Ukrainian state, Pilsudski would apparently have been prepared even to cede a certain amount of present Polish territory.

5. The times were not propitious. Poland had failed in 1919 to free the Ukraine by force. The policy of good neighbourly relations with Russia was adopted instead. But the idea of an autonomous and pro-Polish Ukraine has never been entirely forgotten. A senior member of the Eastern section of the Ministry of Foreign Affairs, in one of his more fantastic moments, touched on it playfully in conversation with a member of my staff a year ago. The serious decline of Russia in the last year and the possibility of chaos if and when Stalin dies or is eliminated, have revived the idea. An article in a periodical called *Polityka*, which used to have some relations with the Ministry of Foreign Affairs, caused a minor sensation in October by adumbrating the so-called "Promethian policy" of creating buffer states under Polish protection in White Russia and the Ukraine. More recently it has become clear that the Polish General Staff are thinking about this problem. Colonel Sword, Military Attaché to this Embassy, recently had a conversation on the subject of Russia's internal situation and of Poland's attitude towards the possible appearance of an autonomous Russian Ukraine, with a member of the Deuxième Bureau. I enclose, in two parts, a record of this conversation, which it is interesting to compare with that between Colonel Mason MacFarlane and the Polish Military Attaché in Berlin, recorded in Sir G. Ogilvie-Forbes's despatch No. 1260 of November 23rd. It will be seen that both the Polish Military Attaché in Berlin and Major Slosarczyk were preoccupied by the danger to Poland of German expansion to the Russian Ukraine, but although Major Slosarczyk was the more cautious of the two, both showed an interest in the possible emergence of an autonomous Ukraine under Polish patronage.

6. I do not think that Monsieur Beck is contemplating any adventures in the Ukraine at present. He is an opportunist and the opportunity is not there. Moreover, there are now other dangers. The Polish Ukraine is being unsettled by the existence of an autonomous Ukrainian province of Ruthenia, or Carpatho-Ukraine as the German press delights in calling it. How much more would it be unsettled were it the only part of the Ukraine not to enjoy autonomy. For the Poles do not intend to grant autonomy to their

Ukrainian population. It is impossible to agree with Major Slosarczyk's words about "a scattered proportion" of Ukrainians in
Poland, but the intention behind the words is obvious, namely that
the South Eastern provinces are to remain an integral part of
Poland. There is here a fundamental difficulty in Poland's cham-
pioning a Ukrainian autonomist movement in Russia. In Ruthenia
her policy is the direct opposite.

7. Then there is the German aspect. It seems clear from Sir
George Ogilvie-Forbes's despatches that no decision as to German
policy has yet been reached in Berlin, and I think that is probably
also the impression of the Polish Government. But Germany's attitude cannot be of indifference to Poland. I cannot conceive of any
greater danger for Poland, short of direct partition, than the
emergence of an autonomous Russian Ukraine encouraged by Germany to look for the union of all Ukrainians in Russia, Poland,
Roumania and Ruthenia, more especially as about one-third of
Poland is claimed to be Ukrainian. The Polish Military Attaché in
Berlin suggested that an autonomous Russian Ukraine might be
anti-German. With the spectacle of Slovakia and Ruthenia before
their eyes, I cannot believe that the Polish Government will allow
themselves to be misled by any such delusion, at any rate so long
as they have any hope at all that the Western Powers have not
abandoned them utterly to their fate. Indeed the recent public reaffirmation of the non-aggression pact between Poland and Russia is
in itself direct *prima facie* evidence that Polish thoughts are not
moving in the direction of any adventures in the east.

8. I have ventured, in a despatch which is largely speculative,
to indicate the way some minds are moving here and the direction
in which Polish interests seem to lie. I would emphasize again that
I do not think that the creation of an autonomous state in the Russian Ukraine is at present the policy of the Polish Government.
They are obviously worried at the possibility of Germany showing
an unhealthy interest in the Ukraine, and the fear of such a
development is largely what underlies Monsieur Beck's continued
insistence on the idea of Hungary's absorption of Ruthenia. It
seems incredible that Poland could ever lend herself to any German plans in the Russian Ukraine, and the only circumstances in
which this would appear possible would be in the event of Monsieur Beck becoming convinced that the Western Powers had finally decided to yield Eastern Europe into Germany's hand and that
no other course offered any chance of salvation.

[........]

I have the honour to be, with the highest respect,
My Lord,
Your Lordship's most obedient, humble Servant,

[sgd.] Sir H. KENNARD

The Right Honourable
The Viscount Halifax, K.G., G.C.S.I.

* * *

Minutes

[........]   14TH DECEMBER, 1938

The only definite conclusion reached in this despatch is that the Poles
are most unlikely to co-operate in any German designs on the Soviet
Ukraine. If this attitude is maintained, it is difficult to see how an armed
conflict between Germany and Poland can be avoided; for even if the
former were concentrating primarily on the Soviet Ukraine for the present
(and our information from other sources points rather to the contrary), she
could not establish any effective contact with the province except across
Polish territory. The whole situation, however, is still very confused.

[sgd.] R.L. SPEAIGHT

*

Poland under Pilsudski was anxious to set up an autonomous Ukrainian state which would have formed a barrier against Soviet Russia.
Pilsudski was apparently even ready to cede a certain amount of present
Polish territory to form part of the Ukrainian state. The essence of the idea
was, however, that the Ukraine should be friendly towards Poland and
under her influence. The Poles today — at any rate the Polish General Staff
— are under no illusions and realize that an autonomous Ukraine would be
under German control. Nor would they today be prepared to cede any ap-
preciable amount of Polish territory even to form a pro-Polish Ukraine. Sir
H. Kennard therefore concluded that Poland will be unable to lend herself
to any German plans in the Russian Ukraine unless, perhaps, Mr. Beck
were to become convinced that the western Powers had washed their hands

of eastern Europe. In that event the Poles might feel obliged to run the risk of an alliance with the Germans, which might involve the loss of the western provinces and the Corridor, in the hope of getting compensation elsewhere. Against this would be many Poles who would [wonder] whether compensation would be forthcoming and many who would fight rather than abandon the present framework of the Polish state (with Posen and access to the sea) which expresses the recovery of Poland from the partitions. In either event the outlook for Poland is a dark one though the Poles themselves argue that Germany is unlikely to risk a war, with a country in which the roads are so bad and the targets for effective bombing so scanty, which would cost her half a million men and still leave her face to face with Russia. Many Poles conclude, therefore, that if the Germans advance anywhere they will advance through Rumania.

[sgd. _____]

SOURCE: FO 371/21810
Public Record Office

3

Report by A.J. Drexel Biddle, Jr., Embassy of the United States of America, Warsaw, 15 December 1938, to President Roosevelt and the US Secretary of State, Relating Views on Suspected German Plans for a "Greater Ukraine."

EMBASSY OF THE
UNITED STATES OF AMERICA

No. 848

WARSAW
DECEMBER 15, 1938

STRICTLY CONFIDENTIAL
FOR THE PRESIDENT AND THE SECRETARY

Sir:

I have the honour to supplement my despatch No. 844 of December 10, 1938, and to report the following observations on the currently widespread press "play-up" of Berlin's reportedly envisaged establishment of a "Greater Ukraine" under German auspices.

When Czechoslovakia had been eliminated as a potential fortress against German eastward infiltration, a wave of rumored projects emanated from Berlin, subsequently *Post Munich Nazi-inspired rumors aimed at spreading confusion in all European quarters.* traceable to the inspiration of Nazi "extremist" circles in Berlin and obviously aimed at inciting confusion in all quarters of Europe. It may be recalled that almost before the ink of the signatures to the Munich pact became dry, Munich-dateline forecasts were published in the foreign press, pointing to the Corridor, Danzig and Memel as next in line as objects of Berlin's "attention." Then came stories of a projected *putsch* in Hungary, later followed by a succession of rumors that colonies would next engage Berlin's consideration, and that perhaps even Holland might soon become the focal point of Berlin's roving eye in view of its strategic position vis-à-vis Britain and its colonial possessions.

During the period leading up to the Munich Conference and the early phase of the post-Munich period, the question of an independent Ukrainian state was very much in the background and engaged merely a certain amount of vague speculation in sensationalist press quarters.

[........]

Now, however, as Berlin's reportedly envisaged "Greater Ukraine" looms into the foreground and increasingly engages the attention of political observers and correspondents of the press of European states other than Germany the following aspects call for consideration.

"Play-up" of Greater Ukraine in foreign press.

Examination reveals that while the press outside of Germany is rendering the project a steadily increasing "play-up" and is devoting more and more columns to the various aspects thereof, the press of Germany itself is silent on the subject. It is obvious, therefore, that the foreign correspondents in Berlin are eagerly grabbing for the bait handed them by the various Nazi press bureaus and have succeeded in focusing public interest to an important degree on the subject. Accordingly, in my opinion, the Nazi propagandists have put the foreign correspondents to work for them, and I look for the German press to stand aloof until such time as (a) the Nazi Propaganda Bureau will have had time to appraise world reaction to current publicity and (b) operations in Ruthenia might have shown signs of definite progress. My belief on this score is borne out by disclosures of an informed Nazi, who recently visited Warsaw, in reply to my discreet inquiries.

Significant silence of German press.

Further examination, moreover, points to the "Greater Ukraine play-up's" having been deliberately inspired by Berlin as a tactical maneuver aimed: (1) as a diversion activity to cover up other contemplated intermediate moves; and (2) as a simultaneous campaign to propagandize and "start the ball rolling" and stimulate interest in Berlin's envisaged eventual Ukrainian project.

Press campaign a tactical play.

In connection with (a) above, my interest was engaged by the following remarks of an informed Nazi (connected with the Nazi Party Propaganda Bureau in Berlin) to a Polish official, who subsequently imparted them to me. He said that the Nazis counted upon their exploitation of the "right of self-determination" to play an important rôle in their formula for eastward infiltration. They looked for it to spread confusion, not only in states standing in the path of projected infiltration, but also in the western democratic states. In connection with latter, the Nazis looked for impor-

Nazi opinion that exploitation of "right of self-determination" will help their eastward drive.

tant elements in the democracies to play into Nazi hands, by rallying to the support of Berlin-inspired and Berlin-supported
demands of the various minorities for autonomy. (Subsequently
the aforementioned Nazi spoke to me somewhat along the same
lines.)

In connection with (b) above, my observations lead me to
believe that Hitler might hardly be expected to risk a war with the
Soviet over the Ukraine (in the event his formula of subversive
machinations failed to shake the Ukraine loose from the Moscow
orbit) until Hitler might have assured himself either of the alignment of, or domination over, states lying in the area between
Berlin and his objective. However, I look for Hitler to lose no time

Unlikelihood
of Hitler's risk-
ing a conflict
with Soviet until
assured of align-
ment of inter-
vening states.

in setting the scene in Ruthenia for immediate
and future anti-Soviet, anti-Polish, and anti-
Rumanian activities. In connection with the
foregoing, it is pertinent to recall the
substance of my reported conversation with
an observer, enjoying close contacts with in-
ner Nazi circles [........]. This observer remarked that Germany was not building
a ramshackle road, such as that which Na-

poleon built. The road which present-day Germany was construct-
ing would not tumble. While Napoleon was a great General, he had
lacked the opportunity to learn many things present-day Germany
had learned, and which only the modern world understood – such
as, economics and the regularized expansion of population. I interpret this to mean that an almost "power-drunk" and super-
confident Germany intends to have no unsympathetic or un-
digested portions along the way towards its eastward goal.

Moreover, Soviet Embassy circles here inform me that
Moscow is of the definite opinion that Hitler is not yet prepared to

Hitler still un-
prepared to risk
major conflict.

risk a major conflict. Moreover, I am aware
these same circles concur in my impression
that Hitler has a number of "axes to grind"
of minor character before "sticking out his
chin" too far vis-à-vis his Ukrainian objective.

In line with this thought, Berlin pressure is steadily increasing
against Warsaw at various points: (a) agitation of the Ukrainian
minority; (b) anti-Polish activity in Ruthenia, obviously identified
with Berlin; (c) Berlin-inspired radio broadcasts in the Ukrainian
language from Prague, Vienna and Leipzig; (d) Danzig Nazis'
reported establishment of a political course for Ukrainians – with

*Increasing
Berlin pressure
vis-à-vis Warsaw
at various points.*

sixty-five Ukrainians already enrolled, some from Poland, others from Ruthenia and Rumania; (e) evidences of Czechoslovakia's reportedly Berlin-inspired rôle in the campaign to set up a Ukrainian state in [the] form of an illuminated map of the projected state displayed on Czech territory close to the Polish border near Morawska Ostrawa; (f) Prague's continued publication of articles favoring the establishment of a "Greater Ukraine" and support of the Polish Ukrainian minority's desire for autonomy. (In fact, it is discernible that Prague is increasingly becoming a center for anti-Polish propaganda – placing an added burden on already strained Polish-Czech relations); and (g) Berlin's recent fresh approach towards bringing the Danzig and Corridor questions to issue in the form of a Goering-inspired article in his *National Zeitung,* suggesting a permanent German right of way through the Corridor, to provide for construction of a combined auto and rail *bahn* [........].

Of pertinent bearing, my attention has recently been drawn to reports from usually reliable sources that Hitler's plans now envisage bringing Rumania to terms: (a) through "sicking" Hungary on to Transylvania; and (b) using Ruthenia as a base for operations to shake Bukovina loose from Rumania and attaching it to Ruthenia as an increased nucleus for a projected "Greater Ukraine." (Accomplishment of the latter, according to the opinion

*Various aspects
of Hitler's re-
ported plan vis-
à-vis Rumania.*

expressed by [a] Nazi informant, would probably signal the first signs of Berlin's identifying itself directly with a movement envisaging the "liberation" of the Ukrainians.) My informant added that in the event Bukovina joined up with Ruthenia and Berlin's envisaged project developed a more positive course, the extremist clement in Berlin might conceivably press Hitler to move troops into the Ruthenian area with the aim of accelerating the Ukrainian movement. These extremists had in mind the German elements inhabiting the Soviet, as well as their scheme to push the Ukrainian project – indeed the position of Germans across the border in an area of potential disorder might become endangered and require protection, thus serving as a pretext for forceful action should circumstances prove favorable.

In addition to the foregoing, however, the following aspects also call for consideration: (a) reported internal weakness in the

*Severe decline
in Soviet's eco-
nomic trend; in
morale and
efficiency of
military.*

Soviet in terms of a measurable decline in industrial production and a set-back in the efficiency of the agricultural and industrial
cooperatives, also a reportedly marked decline
in the standard of the military structure in
general – and the commissioned personnel in
particular; (b) Moscow's reportedly drastic
measures against all detected signs of Ukrainian nationalism and foreign agents.

In connection with (a) my information from British and
Japanese diplomatic circles here tallies and corresponds in effect
with that imparted to me confidentially by Polish Intelligence Service circles to effect that in general the standard of efficiency
throughout the economic structure of the Soviet has suffered an
important decline during the past year. Particularly the standard
of industrial production in the Leningrad district had fallen off.
Among other features included in these reports, as representing in-

*Economic
decline impor-
tantly at-
tributable to
scarcity of
engineers and
technicians.*

dications of distinct weakness, were the following: marked loss of efficiency in the system
of petroleum and fuel storage; signs of growing weakness in the agricultural cooperatives,
presaging a complete breakdown in event of a
potential crisis; a notable lowering of efficiency in the operation both of industrial and farm
machinery. In this connection there was now a
distinct lack of trained technicians and
engineers capable not only of operating the machinery but also of
understanding the system of repairs and replacement.

Moreover, the British Military Attaché of the British Embassy in Moscow reported that in his opinion about 70% of the officers of the Soviet Army had been "purged," thus reducing the
morale and efficiency of the military establishment. He added that
due to a lack of engineers and technically trained personnel the
aviation authorities were having a difficult time keeping their air
fleet up to date.

[........]

The Japanese Ambassador here imparted that Moscow had
recently come down so hard on any kind of a nationalistic tendency
among the Ukrainians and on anyone suspected of being a foreign
agent that information from the Ukraine was becoming steadily
more scarce. He added that several weeks ago over fifty officers of
Ukrainian origin, serving in the Soviet Army of the Far East, were
accused of Ukrainian nationalistic tendencies. They were

transported to Kiev, where they were tried and "purged" as a demonstration of Moscow's drastic attitude toward nationalistic

Japanese Am-
bassador's report
of Moscow's
strong hand.

activities amongst the Ukrainians. The Japanese Ambassador, moreover, remarked that these and other signs presaged Moscow's adoption henceforth of an increasingly strong hand in dealing with matters concerning the Ukraine territory.

If Moscow's efforts to isolate the Ukraine from outside communication proved effective, Hitler, if he continued in his deter-

Japanese
opinion Hitler
would have to be
prepared to fight
if he failed to
shake Ukraine
loose.

mination to accomplish his Ukraine objective, would have to be prepared to measure his military strength with that of the Soviet as an alternative to shaking loose the Ukraine from Moscow's orbit, through "boring from within" and other machinations characteristic of Berlin's formula of infiltration.

The foregoing reports on Russia's weakened internal condition are important in the light of their potential bearing upon the attitude both (a) of the power-drunk Nazi extremist element in Berlin who reportedly envisage increasing the pace of their machinations vis-à-vis the Ukraine with the anticipated decline in the Soviet; and (b) upon those elements in London and Paris official circles who are inclined to look upon Moscow with distrust and hopelessness as a potential European balance and who advocate Moscow's isolation from the British and French Government's forward-looking considerations in terms of European appeasement and pacification.

Of pertinent bearing, the Rumanian Ambassador informed me for the second time that informed observers of Rumanian Government circles are inclined to look for Berlin to accelerate the pace of her campaign toward the envisaged establishment of a Ukrainian state. In the opinion of my informant and his associates, the tendency of upper Nazi circles would be to take advantage of the period of the Soviet's internal weakness rather than risk the possibility of the passage of time's playing in Moscow's favor. The Ambassador, in conclusion, emphasized his opinion that Berlin was rapidly setting the scene for carrying out its long-envisaged "mission" of Ukrainian "liberation."

Of connected bearing, I am aware that Sub-Carpathian Ruthenia is now openly and facetiously referred to by agents of the Nazi extremists as *Carpatautostrada.* Signs of Germany's increasing interest are indicated by reports that Berlin has established a

Consulate in Chust, a town of about 30,000 inhabitants and now
the new capital of Ruthenia. Recent reports, moreover, indicate increased movements of German military observers in Ruthenia,
who headquarter at the German Consulate in Chust.

[........]

In considering the foregoing aspects of Hitler's envisaged
Ukrainian project in an effort to appraise his next move, I am personally disinclined at the moment to look for him to accelerate the
pace of his campaign towards this objective to the maximum
degree or to risk coming to military grips with the Soviet until he
might have fully established his ascendency over the intervening,
middle and eastern Danubian area. Indeed, an informed Nazi
secret agent recently imparted to me that for such an operation as
an invasion of the Ukraine across a hostile Poland or a Poland
whose neutrality was suspect would, according to high German
military authorities, involve an army of no less than one hundred
divisions. When the Germans and the Austrians had occupied the
Ukraine in 1918 they had in all forty odd divisions. These had
merely sufficed to police the large cities and the main railways but
not to occupy and subdue the rest of the country where the population, an armed one, remained free and indulged in considerable
sabotage. In line with these remarks it is conceivable that,
although the present British Government and certain elements of
the present French Government appear to be trying to divert the
German "cyclone" eastward, an actual German thrust vis-à-vis the
Soviet might spell an eventual trap for Germany. With the majority of her divisions engaged in conflict of questionable outcome in a
territory which has already spelled disaster to the invaders, Germany would naturally weaken her potential resistance against a
possible attack on her western front. Moreover, by that time, opinion in London and Paris might conceivably have altered in
respect to a desire to divert Germany's aggressive attention
Ukraine-wards. Even now British agents are reportedly busy in
the Caucasus region with a view to establishing a foothold therein
should it eventually become necessary to establish therein a bas-
tion for the protection of British oil interests and against potential
growth in Germany's appetite to infiltrate India in the event Germany succeeded in marching into the Ukraine. Indeed, the British
Intelligence Service is not blind to the reported ambitions of the
Nazi extremists to reach out eventually for the Caucasus and
neighboring oil fields. Moreover, my aforementioned Nazi informant imparted that the more experienced officers of the German
high military command did not fail to take the foregoing aspects

into consideration.

On the other hand, my talks with Soviet diplomatic circles here disclose that Moscow would never come to terms on any sort of a deal with Germany on the Ukraine. Indeed, Moscow would resist with all the forces at its command. I am therefore inclined to feel that, while Berlin will lose no time in setting up the mechanics in Ruthenia as a center for campaign for the annexation of Bukovina, possibly Bessarabia and the Polish Ukraine, Berlin may not be expected to risk coming to grips with the Soviet until Hitler will have become assured of his ascendency over the intervening area.

Respectfully yours,

[sgd.] J. DREXEL BIDDLE, Jr.

SOURCE: M1286 Reel 3
US National Archives

4

*Letter from G. Vereker, British Embassy, Moscow,
24 December 1938, to British Foreign Office,
Describing Conversation with M. Litvinov on the
Ukrainian Question.*

BRITISH EMBASSY

Moscow
December 24th, 1938

My Dear Collier,

At the conclusion of my talk the other day with Litvinov about the Grover case, about which I am reporting separately, I asked him whether he had anything of interest to tell me. To this he replied in effect that the Soviet Government, conscious of their strength, were not going to allow themselves to be unduly alarmed by the latest German bogey — an independent Ukraine. He asked me if I seriously believed that the frontiers of the Soviet Union were likely to crumble at the horn blowings of a handful of Ukrainian emigrés. To this I said that I had always understood that it was something more than a mere blowing of horns, and that, in fact, it was nothing less than an earthquake that had caused the collapse of the walls of Jericho.

However much Litvinov may profess calm over the Ukrainian question there is, I think, little doubt that the Soviet Government are, naturally enough, seriously perturbed as to possible developments in this connexion. For the present, as reported in my telegram No. 198 of December 15th, there is no reason to believe that there is any exceptional trouble in the Soviet Ukraine or that the population there has any inkling that the Ukrainian question has been raised elsewhere. But if there were to be any kind of armed intervention or threat of armed intervention with the intention of bringing about the inclusion of the Soviet Ukraine in a Greater Ukraine State, the Soviet Government would be faced with a war, as they would undoubtedly, I think, fight to oppose any cession of territory. A war anywhere on their own frontiers, of course, is, as we have always said, the one development which might endanger the régime and which it cannot envisage with equanimity, especially in the still disorganized condition of the Soviet higher command and of the officer cadres.

Yours

[sgd.] GORDON VEREKER

* * *

Minutes

JANUARY 5TH, 1939

I agree with Mr. Vereker that the Soviet gov't must be perturbed. They cannot renounce the Ukraine — yet the prospect of fighting Germany for it in present circumstances is pretty grim! Possibly they hope that Hitler will get involved in war difficulties when he deals with Poland (as he must do before he can deal with them); but there seems no reason why he should if he plays his cards only reasonably well and if Poland remains isolated.
[........]

[sgd.] L. C[OLLIER]

Source: FO 371/23677
Public Record Office

5

G. Vereker, British Embassy, Moscow, 10 January 1939, to the Rt. Hon. Viscount Halifax, British Foreign Secretary, Reporting German Agitation on the Ukrainian Question and Soviet Reaction. Minutes by R. L. Speaight, L. Collier, W. Strang and Sir A. Cadogan.

BRITISH EMBASSY

Moscow

No. 14 JANUARY 10TH, 1939

My Lord,

As reported in my telegram No. 50 (Saving) of December 28th last, the first direct reference in the Soviet press to the Ukrainian question was made on December 27th in a leading article which bore the stamp of an official pronouncement since it appeared in the *Journal de Moscou* which is generally supposed to reflect closely the views of the People's Commissar for Foreign Affairs. This article took the line that the recent agitation by the German and German-inspired press in other countries on the subject of the Ukrainian question, could not be taken seriously as a threat to the Soviet Ukraine but was probably intended to distract the attention of the Western European Powers from the real aims of German policy. The article declared that the Soviet Ukraine was indissolubly attached to the rest of the Soviet Union and that any attempt to interfere with it would mean war.

2. I must confess that there seems to be considerable force in the arguments set out in this article, the full text of which was transmitted to Your Lordship under cover of my despatch No. 527 of December 28th last. As I see it, the so-called "Ukrainian question" resolves itself into whether there is going to be an attempt by Germany with or without the support of Poland or Rumania to bring about the incorporation of the Soviet Ukraine in some Greater Ukrainian State. Such incorporation, it seems to me, could

only come about as a result of:

    (a) An internal independence movement in the Soviet Ukraine to which the Soviet Government would not be able to oppose effective resistance;

    (b) An external attack on the Soviet Ukraine or a combination of both (a) and (b).

The first of these alternatives, in my opinion, is most unlikely. Although the Ukrainians are historically an independence-loving people, and, although the idea of an independent Ukrainian State incorporating the Ukrainian minorities in Poland, Rumania and Czechoslovakia might, in theory, have much attraction for the Ukrainian population of the Soviet Union, there seems to be no likelihood of an independence movement gaining any ground under the present Soviet régime with its widespread and active police system and its close control over all activities within the State. It also seems impossible to believe that any propaganda from abroad in favour of an independence movement could make any headway at the present time in the Soviet Ukraine, in view of the Soviet Government's complete control of all printed and wireless matter, the possibility which it has of blocking the transmission of foreign wireless emissions and of preventing the entry into the Soviet Union of all foreign nationals. Moreover, it must also be taken into consideration that the younger generation, brought up under the Soviet system, is not likely to be as susceptible to the attraction of an independence movement as the older generation might be. As I pointed out in my telegram No. 198 of December 15th last, the vast majority of the population in the Soviet Ukraine has probably no inkling at all that the idea of an independent Ukrainian State has been raised outside this country. Were, however, the Soviet Ukraine to be invaded, it is possible that some enthusiasm might be engendered for an independence movement though this would be likely to take some time owing to the fact that the Ukrainian population has, in company with the population of the rest of the Soviet Union, lived in a vacuum for so long a period and has been without any contact with either the rest of the world or with the Ukrainian minorities elsewhere.

3. If, therefore, we discard the possibility in present circumstances of an independence movement in the Soviet Ukraine against the Soviet Government with or without the support of foreign propaganda, the only possible way in which the Soviet Ukraine could be detached from the Soviet Union and incorporated in some Greater Ukrainian State would be by way of conquest.

Such an operation seems to me to present the greatest difficulties but I assume that if it is seriously contemplated in Germany it is because the German Government feel that an attack on the Soviet Ukraine might bring about in a comparatively short space of time the downfall of the present Soviet régime and that in such circumstances no strong régime capable of taking its place and continuing the war could be set up.

4. In the first place, however, it seems clear that for geographical reasons any invasion of the Soviet Ukraine can only take place either with Polish or Rumanian approval or in opposition to Polish and Rumanian wishes. The arguments set out in Sir H. Kennard's despatch No. 414 of the 14th December, a copy of which he was good enough to send me direct, seem to demonstrate that Poland is not likely to cooperate voluntarily with Germany in an invasion of the Soviet Ukraine. While, as pointed out by Sir H. Kennard, Poland may have some sympathy with the idea of a buffer State between her and the Soviet Union and might therefore in certain circumstances welcome an independent Ukraine and White Russia [Byelorussia], she would almost certainly now be compelled, if she supported an independence movement in the Soviet Ukraine, to contemplate the grant of wide autonomous powers to her own Ukrainian minority. This, according to Sir H. Kennard, she has no intention of doing. In the event of the exploitation of the Soviet Ukraine by Germany, Poland might expect to be compensated for her assistance possibly by the annexation of White Russia [Byelorussia] or the formation of White Russia [Byelorussia] into a buffer State under Polish control, but such compensation could only be obtained for Poland if the Soviet régime were to collapse and would in any case sow the seeds of much future trouble for Poland. Furthermore, strategically, it would seem that Poland could not tolerate a Soviet Ukraine under German influence since Poland would then be open to German pressure on three fronts.

5. Assuming, therefore, that Poland is not willing to cooperate with Germany in the invasion of the Soviet Ukraine and that she could only remain neutral if the invasion took place through Rumanian territory (which would avoid in the first stage a direct attack on Poland and has certain strategic advantages in that the attack could be directed against the flank of the Soviet forces), it would seem that Poland would be forced into active support of the Soviet Union in resisting such an invasion. In this connection the recent reaffirmation by the Polish and Soviet Governments of the Polish-Soviet Non-Aggression Pacts seems definitely to show which way

the wind is blowing. Furthermore, if the invasion were to take place through Polish territory and led to Germany being involved in a war with Poland and the Soviet Union, it seems not unlikely that France, despite the hesitation which she now feels with regard to the fulfilment of her commitments towards Poland and the Soviet Union, might come to the assistance of both those countries in accordance with her treaty obligations.

6. It is possible that Germany may contemplate, by conducting the invasion through Rumania, the neutrality of Poland and of the Western Powers but it can, I think, definitely be assumed that the Soviet Government would resist with all the forces at their disposal, any attack on the Soviet Ukraine from whatever quarter, since they could not possibly contemplate the cession of that territory without resistance. The Soviet Ukraine is, from the point of view of population, with the exception of the RSFSR, the largest republic of the Soviet Union and is of immense importance on account of its agricultural and mineral wealth, not to speak of its strategical value at the head of the Black Sea, one of the few ice-free seas to which the Soviet Union has access, and of its neighbourhood to the *terra irredenta* of Bessarabia. It is not, I think, an exaggeration to state that the Soviet Ukraine is the life-blood of European Russia.

7. The Soviet army would be fighting a war on its own territory with internal lines of communication and even though it may have been seriously weakened as an offensive force by the recent purges in the ranks of the officers it would, I feel convinced, by sheer weight of numbers present a serious obstacle to any aggressor. Russia has, moreover, in her past history displayed remarkable resilience to purges from which she seems to recover with greater rapidity than other countries would and although this Embassy would be the last to underestimate the effects of the purges on the morale and military value of the Red Army, I would certainly not agree with the view expressed on December 6th to the Military Attaché in Paris by the head of the Deuxième Bureau of the French Army, in a conversation, the record of which was transmitted to me under cover of Your Lordship's despatch No. 765 of December 13th last, to the effect that the Soviet Union was

> *militarily entirely impotent and that she would find it very difficult to offer any effective resistance to a movement for independence in the Soviet Ukraine if such a movement were actually supported by Germany.*

This Embassy has always confined itself to expressing the view that the Soviet Union would be very reluctant to take part in any war outside its frontiers and that if by any chance it became involved in one the Red Army would be unlikely to distinguish itself greatly. On the other hand, it has always been the view of this Embassy that any Power which tried to invade the Soviet Union would not have at all an easy task. It must be remembered that the Red Army commands the entire resources of the Soviet Union, both material and human, which are by no means inconsiderable and that as a defence force it still possesses considerable value. It may well have lost a large percentage of its value even for defence purposes during the last two years and its transport system may be weak, but an army which can put no less than one hundred infantry divisions into the field within three months, even if it is badly handled, is still a formidable obstacle to an attacker. To these obstacles of men and material must be added the not inconsiderable factors of climate and the lack of East-West communications in the frontier districts which would hinder an attacking force.

8. It would thus seem that unless an invasion led within a very short space of time to the collapse of the Soviet régime, Germany would have to contemplate, in order to ensure the realization of the limited objective of separating the Ukraine from the rest of the Soviet Union, the defeat of the whole Soviet army, not to mention the possible allies of the Soviet Union operating from the region of the Black Sea. As regards the probability of the collapse of the Soviet régime it is difficult to make any prophecies but I do not feel that this could be brought about by the mere threat by Germany of the invasion of the Soviet Ukraine. It might well come about as the result of a war, but it seems evident that for some time at any rate there would be much popular enthusiasm in the Soviet Union for a war against a fascist aggressor. This enthusiasm is likely to be shared, at any rate at the commencement of hostilities, by the Ukrainian population which cannot retain pleasant recollections of the German occupation in 1918-1919 nor of Pilsudski's advance in May 1920 and more precipitate retreat, the memory of which has been sedulously kept alive by the Soviet Government.

9. In view of the foregoing considerations I am inclined, though it is dangerous to prophesy in these matters, to agree with the article in the *Journal de Moscou* that the so-called "Ukrainian question", if by that is meant the separation of the Soviet Ukraine from the rest of the Soviet Union, is being exaggerated. The question is no doubt seriously exercising the minds of the Soviet

Government, but there seem to be so many difficulties in the way of Germany achieving the objective with which she is credited, unless she is prepared to contemplate a general as opposed to a localized conflict, that I cannot believe that any action can be contemplated by Germany, at least until there are far clearer signs of a collapse of the existing Soviet régime than are evident at present. Another situation might, of course, arise if such a collapse did eventually occur and if a state approaching chaos then prevailed in this country.

10. I am sending a copy of this despatch to His Majesty's Representatives at Warsaw, Berlin, Prague, and Bucharest.

> I have the honour to be, with the highest respect,
> My Lord,
> Your Lordship's most obedient, humble servant,

> [sgd.] G. VEREKER

The Right Honourable
Viscount Halifax, K.G.

✦ ✦ ✦

Minutes

10TH JANUARY, 1939

Mr. Vereker's views on the possibility of a German attack on the Soviet Ukraine are quite interesting although they might have been expressed more clearly. (I have ventured to make his despatch rather more readable by re-paragraphing it).

Mr. Vereker discounts from the outset the possibility of an internal revolt in the Soviet Ukraine, and I think his arguments on this point are irrefutable. An independence movement in the Ukraine might, and probably would, follow upon the downfall of the Central Soviet régime, but it is difficult to see how it could possibly precede it.

In the event of a German attack upon the Soviet Ukraine, Mr. Vereker agrees with Sir H. Kennard in thinking that Polish co-operation with Germany would be unlikely. He thinks indeed that Poland would inevitably find herself fighting on the side of the Soviet Union, although he admits she might remain neutral if the attack were first made through Rumanian territory. This view too seems logical enough, but I still find it difficult to envisage any circumstances in which the Poles would be prepared to fight side by side with the Red Army. One has to reckon with the intense hatred of the governing classes in Poland for both the Russian race and the Communist idea: and it must be remembered that the Germans will all the time be doing their utmost to exploit this hatred and will be in a position to submit the Poles to the severest political and economic pressure. I am still more doubtful as to the likelihood of France going to the aid of Poland or the Soviet Union, as suggested by Mr. Vereker in paragraph 5.

When speaking in paragraphs 6 and 7 of the determined resistance with which any German attack on the Soviet Ukraine would be met and of the probable effectiveness of this resistance, Mr. Vereker is on firmer ground. It has always seemed to me dangerous to assume that, because a number of Generals have been executed, the Red Army, regarded a few years ago as probably the most formidable in Europe, should suddenly have become completely impotent. If Herr Hitler, persuaded by his "yesmen" to the view that the Soviet Union is ripe for disintegration at the first touch, and its Army incapable of resisting the armed might of Germany, should attempt a direct attack on the Soviet Ukraine, it seems most unlikely that he will obtain the quick success on which he counts.

At the same time one must bear in mind that everything that is written about the Soviet Ukraine is based almost entirely on speculation. Neither we nor, I imagine, the Moscow Embassy, have any concrete evidence whatsoever about what is happening there or about the present temper of the large majority of the Ukrainian population living East of the Soviet frontier.

Copy War Office   *[sgd.]* R. L. Speaight

*

We have a certain amount of evidence about what is happening in the Soviet Ukraine and the state of feeling there; but it is not from very reliable sources. Such as it is, however, it confirms Mr. Vereker's view that there is no general feeling of Ukrainian nationalism and that the whole country is so well controlled by the Soviet Government and so "atomized" by the precautions taken to prevent anything like a concerted political movement or the propagation of any political views other than their own, that there is no chance of any anti-Soviet movement developing there unless and until the country is first conquered by a foreign army. There is undoubtedly widespread discontent among the peasantry, who have been forced into the collective farms with even greater ruthlessness than elsewhere in the Soviet Union; but it is the unorganized discontent of individuals and is economic rather than political; and though there is some evidence that Ukrainian nationalism has affected the upper ranks of the town population, and even Soviet officials of Ukrainian race, this, too, does not seem to have produced any organized nationalist movement, the accusations of "bourgeois nationalism" levelled against the victims of the recent "purges" being usually the excuse rather than the true reason for the proceedings against them. If an independent Ukrainian State could be established in the Polish Ukraine and determined attempts made to smuggle a large number of propagandists and subversive literature from that State over the Soviet border, it is perhaps just conceivable that a Ukrainian nationalist movement of serious dimensions might be started by this means in the Soviet Ukraine; but even then it would have no chance of creating an armed rising without military assistance from abroad, and, as Sir H. Kennard has pointed out, it is difficult to imagine the Poles voluntarily committing suicide by agreeing to the establishment of such a State.

As regards the Soviet army, it is difficult to say how much its defensive power has been weakened by the recent "purges"; but I agree with Mr. Speaight that it cannot safely be assumed that the Germans have only to win one battle against it for its resistance to collapse. It seems clear, therefore:

(1) that the Soviet Ukraine cannot be detached from the Soviet Union without a larger [_____] invasion from abroad;

(2) that the Poles will fight the Germans rather than permit a German army to launch such an invasion from their territory, both since that must in the long run involve the loss of the Polish Ukraine and since in any case they would never allow German troops into their country; but

(3) that they might, if subjected to sufficient pressure, be forced to remain neutral while the Germans launched their attack on the Soviet Ukraine through Rumania, and even perhaps, if sufficient inducements were combined with the pressure, to join in the attack themselves in the hope of securing some of the spoils; though

(4) the ultimate consequences to Poland are so obvious that it would require the very strongest pressure, coupled with the conviction that they could get no support from France, to make them amenable to any scheme of this sort.

[sgd.] L. COLLIER

*

I agree with Mr. Collier's analysis.

[sgd.] W. STRANG

This seems to me to make sense. And that might point to the conclusion that Hitler, if he feels he must explode, will explode towards the West first.

[sgd.] Sir A. CADOGAN

*

Yes, if there is any inference to be drawn from all this, it is the one drawn by Sir A. Cadogan. Such an amazing amount of facile nonsense has been talked about the Ukrainian project, that it is well to have the almost insuperable difficulties plainly put.

[_____]

*

There are no ripe plums in the Ukraine.

[_____]

SOURCE: FO 371/22461
Public Record Office

6

*Exchange of Telegrams, British Chancery,
Washington, and the British Foreign Office, January
1939, Commenting on the Weakening of the Central
Authority in Moscow and Implications for
Ukrainian Independence. Includes Foreign Office
Minutes by Mr. Jebb.*

DECYPHER. MR. MALLET
(WASHINGTON)

JANUARY 6TH, 1939

No. 11

Acting Secretary of State told me today that the Polish Ambassador had recently informed him that reports from Russia indicated serious weakening of the central authority and that a break up involving independence of the Ukraine might be expected in the next nine months. Reports received by State Department were scanty but there were certain indications confirming the above.

Acting Secretary of State asked whether you had any recent information on this subject.

I should be grateful if you could furnish me with material for reply.

*

CYPHER TELEGRAM
TO MR. MALLET
(WASHINGTON)

JANUARY 13TH, 1939

No. 20

Your telegram No. 11 [of January 6th: Situation in Soviet Ukraine].

I have no confirmation of these reports, though "purges" which

are still continuing throughout Soviet Union must have reduced efficiency of the administration in Ukraine as elsewhere, and Ukrainian nationalist sentiment is undoubtedly a *potential* source of
trouble.

[........]

* * *

Minutes

*Please see in this connexion Moscow tel No. 198 of December 15th, in
which W. Vereker says that he has no reason to believe that the situation
in the Soviet Ukraine is more strained than anywhere else in the Soviet
Union.*

*It must be remembered that the Moscow Embassy is not well placed to
gain early information of troubles in the Ukraine; but our own information
from "other sources" on this subject tends to confirm what he says. Violent
purges continue, there as elsewhere in the Soviet Union, and steps are apparently being taken to evacuate more and more Ukrainians not only from
the frontier zone, but also from many districts West of the Dniepr. But all
this is probably prophylactic in the main, and we have nothing more
positive to indicate a "serious weakening of the central authority." The
Germans, from whom the rumours to this effect probably emanate, are undoubtedly working to convert their hopes into reality, but so far as we
know they have not yet achieved anything positive.*

[........]

[sgd.] MR. JEBB

SOURCE: FO 371/23677
Public Record Office

7

Report Compiled for British Foreign Office by Department of Overseas Trade, 2 February 1939, Describing Economic Assets of Ukraine and Probable Effects of an Independent Ukrainian State on Economies of USSR and Germany.

DEPARTMENT OF OVERSEAS TRADE (I.I.C.)

ICF/1153   2ND FEBRUARY, 1939

[........]

UKRAINE

Boundary and Population

Were its boundaries fixed on an ethnological basis, an independent Ukrainian State should include not only the greater part of the administrative district of Soviet Russia known as the Ukrainian SSR but also certain border areas of Poland, Czecho-Slovakia and Rumania. On the other hand, a true ethnological boundary would exclude some areas now within Soviet Ukraine. In practice, it is impossible to delimit accurately the territory inhabited by persons of Ukrainian origin* without a detailed population census. Thereafter, the subsequent fixing of a frontier, even by an impartial Boundary Commission, would inevitably exclude Ukrainians from the new State and include a number of persons of other nationalities.

It is assumed for the purpose of this paper, however, that the underlying drive of the present Ukrainian independence movement is less concerned with satisfying national aspirations than with

Note: * Some authorities assert that Ukrainians are of artificial origin without any real claim to race distinction and are in fact a collection of magnificent crossbred scallywags. There seems at least a case that their origin and development has been more due to political than ethnological causes.

cutting off from the USSR valuable economic assets and making them available to Germany. From this point of view, territory inhabited by Ukrainians but now lying outside the USSR is relatively unimportant, the real economic assets being found within Soviet Ukraine. This is not to suggest that potential Ukrainian territory outside the USSR is without importance, but that the effect of its inclusion in an independent *Ukrainia* would lie rather in the political and strategic than in the economic field.

Insofar as Soviet Ukraine is concerned — if the underlying purpose of the independence movement be as described — there is little doubt that the plan must imply the inclusion in *Ukrainia* of the independent Soviet republic of Moldavia on the borders of Bessarabia and of the autonomous Soviet republic of the Crimea, neither of which could, for geographical and economic reasons, exist as separate entities, were Soviet Ukraine independent.

The total area thus envisaged lying within the USSR is about 470,000 square kilometres in extent, or somewhat larger than Poland, with a population of about 36 millions, i.e. nearly 20% of the population of the USSR. It stretches from the frontier of Poland to the Black Sea, half of whose northern shores would come within its boundaries, and takes in practically the whole western shore of the Sea of Azov. The entrance to the latter would be commanded by the port of Kerch in the Crimean Republic, where lie also the ports of Sevastopol and Feodosia, the former having the only ice-free natural harbour on the Black Sea.

RESOURCES OF THE UKRAINIAN SSR

The administrative district of the Ukrainian SSR is the richest economic unit of the Union of Soviet Socialist Republics. [........]

Ukraine includes the greater part of the "Black Soil Belt," probably the most fertile district of Europe. In addition to grain, vegetables and oil-bearing seeds, cotton, hemp and tobacco are cultivated, while the rich grazing lands support large numbers of horses and cattle. There is very little timber.

Though lacking in large deposits of non-ferrous metals or petroleum, the area is rich in the highest quality coal in the Donetz basin; iron ore of high metallic content in the Krivoi Rog district; limestone, manganese, near Nikopol, and salt.

Central Ukraine was the seat of the iron and steel, heavy engineering and chemical industries of Imperial Russia which have been further expanded and developed under the Soviets. Among major industrial units erected and enlarged in the last ten years, is the well-known Dniepropetrovsk hydro-electric power station, with its dependent industrial area; the Krammatorsk machine construction works, which is the largest in the USSR; the Makeevka iron and steel works; the Nikopol steel tube works; the Kharkov tractor and railway works; the Lugansk locomotive works; the Slaviansk chemical works and many others. Here, too, are found Russia's principal coal-tar recovery, distillation and allied plants. The armament sections of all these factories, producing armament stores, aircraft, AFV's, explosives, war chemicals and other war stores, form a very important part of the armament industry of the USSR. The only important shipbuilding yards on the Black Sea, including the naval yard at Nikolaev and the naval base at Sevastopol, are on the Ukrainian coast. Notwithstanding recent developments of the metallurgical industry in other parts of the Soviet Union, Ukraine is still responsible for the production of well over half the pig iron and nearly half the raw steel output of the whole of the USSR.

SOME EFFECTS ON THE USSR OF THE LOSS OF THE UKRAINIAN SSR

The figures [........] for the agricultural production of Soviet Ukraine are misleading if compared statistically with the percentage of the population of the USSR living in the district. In point of fact, there is an average annual surplus of over 5 million tons of grain alone, which represents the main source for the supply of Central and Northern Russia, who also rely on Soviet Ukraine to make good their deficiency in vegetables and meat. Since three-quarters of the sugar production of the USSR is derived from Ukraine, the loss thereof would be irremediable insofar as that important commodity is concerned.

Whereas it might be argued that the loss of Ukraine would not necessarily spell absolute, immediate disaster to the USSR from the point of view of agricultural products alone, there is no doubt that, from the point of view of iron and steel production it would be fatal to the economy of the Union. Not only would the USSR lose well over half its supply of coal, coke, iron ore and pig iron, but also half, or nearly half, of its manganese, steel and salt. Moreover, coal mined in excess of local requirements feeds the important industrial districts of Central and Northwestern Russia, as well as the lower Volga, the Kuban and Northern Caucasus. In fact, the output of coal, coke, steel, iron, and of a number of important manufactures as well, forms an integral part of the industry of the Union, lacking which many works in other parts of the USSR would cease to function. To give but one example, the loss of the Ukrainian output of casing tubes for petroleum wells would, failing import from abroad, put a stop to all drilling and well repairs in the Caucasian oilfields and bring about an early and heavy fall in production.

In the event of the loss of Ukrainian territory, the USSR would suffer a further grave blow in the disorganization of Soviet communications, both internal and external. The major north-south railway trunk lines, including those leading to the Caucasus, pass through this area. The severance of these lines and the loss of all important ports on the Black Sea except Novorossisk, Poti and Batoum, as well as of the waterways leading inland from the Black Sea and the Sea Azov, would seriously affect transportation between Russia and the Caucasus and greatly reduce the flow of Caucasian products, including liquid fuels, from the Caucasus to the industrial districts of the USSR.

Some Effects on German Economy from the Gain of Ukrainian Surplus Products

The gain to Germany of free access to Ukraine produce can only be assessed on very broad lines, unless the surrounding circumstances are known or postulated. Assuming, however, that by some means Germany could, without hindrance, import and render counter-value for any surplus Ukraine output [that is] of immediate value to her, she could obtain from this source sufficient bread grains, vegetables and dairy produce, to make good all German deficiencies in peace and war. The surplus vegetable oils, cotton, hemp and tobacco would be of great value to Germany, but even if she took the whole Ukrainian output of these commodities, it would still leave a margin of deficiency relatively large in certain cases.

Germany might be able in emergency to dispense with imports of iron ore from Sweden, were she able to obtain the whole Ukrainian production of pig iron and steel, while Ukrainian manganese would more than meet German needs. On the other hand, the German non-ferrous metal and liquid fuel situation would not be directly improved, though the nearer approach of German influence to the Caucasian oil wells might eventually alter the situation.

Several Ukrainian surplus products, for example, coal, coke and salt, are already exported by Germany, and would therefore not be required by her for her own use. Conditions whereby Germany directly controlled all Ukrainian products as by right of ownership and could, therefore, export to her own account an absolute surplus to other countries have not been considered, but it may be borne in mind that the present output figures for Soviet Ukraine do not represent the true potential of the area in the matter either of agricultural or of industrial produce. With German organizing ability and scientific methods and with the full range of necessary equipment available from German industry, Ukrainian output might be materially increased in a comparatively short time and the variety of agricultural produce adapted to coincide more closely with the requirements of the Reich.

Conclusions

Though this survey is necessarily superficial, certain conclusions are indicated.

The loss to the USSR resulting from an independent Ukraine, re-oriented as far as possible in a German direction, would be far greater than would the economic gain to Germany. It might greatly improve Germany's position in peace or war but would not solve all her economic problems. On the other hand, since the existence of the Soviet Union depends primarily on the maintenance of an interlocked Union wide economic balance, the destruction of this balance would presumably entail the collapse of the Soviet régime and therefore a general disintegration of the USSR. It seems more likely, however, that, in view of the vital importance of these areas to the latter, the loss of the Ukraine and the greater part of the Black Sea coast could only result from a decisive military defeat. Hence, the surrender of the Ukraine to exploitation by Germany should follow and not precede the collapse of the Soviet Union.

These conclusions, however, depend primarily on the correctness of the assumption in paragraph 1, namely that the real object to be achieved through an independent Ukraine would be cutting-off supplies from the USSR and making them available to Germany. Were a *Ukrainia* to be created truly independent not only of Moscow but also of Berlin without entailing the collapse and disruption of the Soviet Union (though it is hard to imagine how this could be brought about) so that she could trade freely in any market, the Soviet Union having the means of rendering acceptable counter-value to the Ukraine for her exports would presumably make great efforts to satisfy Ukrainian needs and is at present in some respects better placed to do so than is Germany.

* * *

Minutes

2ND FEBRUARY, 1939

This is useful.

As regards the passage marked "A" in paragraph 1, the Ukrainians themselves certainly regard the independence movement as being concerned solely with the satisfaction of their nationalist aspirations: but the motive of the Germans, without whose aid the movement has little chance of ever coming to anything, is, of course, largely economic.

[R.L. SPEAIGHT]

SOURCE: FO 371/23056
Public Record Office

8

Report of Tour in Non-Soviet Ukraine, June-July 1939, by J. H. Watson, Intelligence Officer, British Foreign Office.

REPORT OF TOUR OF THE NON-SOVIET UKRAINE
MADE IN JUNE AND JULY 1939

Ukrainians today tend to regard their country as portioned unevenly between the Soviet Union, Poland, Roumania and Hungary. Sub-Carpathia is, however, such a special case that in spite of the events of the last few months it is really legitimate to consider the Ukraine *divisa in partes tres.*

Detailed statistics are hard to obtain. The Ukrainians officially claim some 34½ millions in the USSR, 5.87 millions in Poland, 1.12 millions in Roumania and ½ million in Hungary. They usually aim at the erection of a state to include 564,000 square kilometres in the Soviet Union, 122,000 square kilometres in Poland, 18,000 square kilometres in Roumania and 15,000 square kilometres in Hungary and Slovakia, making 719,000 square kilometres in all. The population is some 48 millions, not all of which would be Ukrainians and in which not all Ukrainians would be automatically included. The statistics furnished by the governments affected are of course, considerably smaller.

Much confusion has resulted from the use of the term "Ruthenian," which used to denote those Ukrainians formerly under Austria. The older people in Galicia still regard themselves *ruski*, whereas the younger people tend to call themselves Ukrainians. (There is little doubt that these two terms are interchangeable, but a complication is introduced in Poland by the fact that many people in the former Russian territories consider themselves *russki*, and that when confronted with the option of declaring themselves in a census to be *ruski* or *russki*, the peasants are confused, and the picture effectively blurred).

All Ukrainians seem to agree that the capital of their country is Kiev. And indeed so much of the territory, wealth and population which would fall to any greater Ukrainian state is now in the Soviet Union; that unless and until Russia consents, or is com-

pelled, to withdraw from the Soviet Ukraine, the predominant concern of the Ukrainians in Poland and Roumania must be their position inside those countries. Little contact, if any, seems now to be
maintained between Polish and Roumanian Ukrainian organizations, and of course contact with people inside the Soviet Union is
more or less impossible. Most Ukrainians, naturally, dream of a
united state, and are prepared to take action should the moment
arrive. But they realize that such a moment can only arrive as a
result of circumstances beyond their control.

The Ukrainian issue therefore, tends to resolve itself into two
separate lines of speculation: the position of the Polish and Roumanian minorities, and the international combinations necessary to
permit the establishment of an independent Ukraine. Guessing the
latter has now degenerated into a drawing-room pastime, and a
source of revenue for literary hacks; and the subject is in any case
beyond the scope of this enquiry, which can only deal with the position of the Ukrainian minorities outside the Soviet Union.

The principal political organization in the Polish Ukraine is the
UNDO, the Ukrainian national democratic organization, whose present leader, Mudrij, is a vice-marshal of the Polish *Sejm*. It springs
from the Ukrainian national democrat party of before the war in
Galicia, and has always been more or less the only organization
which counted for anything in the ex-Habsburg areas. Members of
the party as such are only enrolled in the towns; but there is in each
Ukrainian village apparently one active member of the party, one
of the *intelligenz*, and the peasants are supposed to take their cue
from him. Most of the soberer ones apparently still do. The party
claims to be democratic, anti-communist and anti-fascist, national
but not nationalist, [and a] champion of peasant rights.

The UNDO has inherited from prewar days the tradition of
preparedness to co-operate on the whole with the State, while
attempting to secure such privileges as may be possible. But Warsaw, far more than Vienna, is fascinated by the mirage of a national state, – *un pays, un peuple, une langue, une capitale,* – and
even the most moderate members of the party, whose counsels
have hitherto carried the day as far as the policy of the organization is concerned, are being ruefully forced to admit that the attainment of the sort of position which the French enjoy in Canada
is out of the question. Mudrij himself was most pessimistic about
the future policy of his party. He said he was unable to suggest
any line of action, that he saw no possibility of the Poles meeting
him half way on any visible tomorrow, and that the only thing to
do was to hold the organization together and hope that somehow

or other something would turn up. The hopelessness of co-operation as Ukrainians with the Polish régime seems gradually to be driving the moderate leaders, by a natural process of thought, to look for a solution in some sort of more formal autonomy. They now demand an internal administration of their own linked federally to Poland by comparatively loose ties; but they do not even say that they think this solution will in fact ever be adopted.

While the moderate leaders are reluctant in themselves to look to Germany, the hopelessness of their position, the restlessness of the younger generation and of much of the peasantry, and the visible success of more radical groups has created a longing for a *deus ex machina;* and the melting-pot of war tends more and more to suggest itself. Mudrij disclaims any wish for war. But he admits that he considers the peasants and the *intelligenz* are sick of the present disorder, the lack of organization and legality, and the claustrophobia caused by the blocking of every peaceful settlement; and that they feel the position after a war could hardly be worse. He points out cautiously, that in 1919 the Ukrainians were able to set up a national state for awhile, and with better management next time it might be permanent. There would, he feels, after all be no fundamental objection by England, France and America, if victorious, to an independent Ukraine, supposing Russia collapsed and Poland had been too badly mauled to resist. However, the second in command of the party is apparently hopeful of the outcome of a war; and certainly the editors of *Novii Chas* and *Dilo*, the two UNDO newspapers openly consider a war desirable.

In 1933 the leader of the more radical wing of the UNDO, Paliev, (who was also a member of the OUN) split off from the party and founded the FJN, the Front of National Unity. He was sentenced to a considerable term of imprisonment on account of his activities in the Pacification of 1930, I understand, and though pardoned in a year he grew more radical in prison and more convinced of the final futility of Mudrij's policy (which Mudrij himself now more or less admits). When he came out of gaol he declared that in his absence the more opportunist and time-serving wing of the organization had prevailed, and that a more radical affirmation of the unbreakable national spirit of the Ukraine was the only answer to Polish chauvinism and irresponsibility. The FJN has never taken part in elections because, according to the Polish electoral law the appointment of candidates depends ultimately on the Government; but Paliev claims an organization of 10,000 members, and that if a democratic election were held he would get a majority of Ukrainian votes, (a safe boast). Unlike all other organizations in Poland, apparently, the members make regular contributions to the party funds, and meetings, lectures and talks are held in the villages. Special attention is paid to Volhynia, where the Ukrainians are proportionally more numerous than anywhere else, but where the UNDO organization is weak, as it is outside Galicia. Paliev swears he has no connection with the Germans; and indeed the Jewish editor of *Hvila*, vouches for the fact that Paliev has no use whatever for the Germans, and that in fact the OUN, now generally regarded as under German influence, hates his party more than the UNDO, partly no doubt because both organizations tend to appeal to the same people, but also on account of personal feuds dating from the time when Paliev left the UNDO. Though the FJN is by no means negligible, and its recent rapid growth is symptomatic of present trends, the importance of the movement should not be overestimated.

The other organizations, such as the Clerical Party, the Peasant Labour Party, − strongest in Ternopil and Stanislaviv, − and who have since 1930 had an electoral pact with the UNDO, − the two Socialist Parties, one of which cooperates with the Polish Socialist Party, and the Women's Organization, are of little importance. The OUN, the organization of the Ukrainian Nationalists, is a terrorist organization about which information is not easy to obtain. It is generally asserted to be in German pay, and is very firmly dealt with by the authorities. While it has lost much of its former importance, only Poles claim that it is virtually disbanded. Mudrij admits its romantic fascination, and says many of the young men toy with the idea of joining the organization "if anything happens." Its policy in wartime would be assassination and sabotage of every kind. It aims, of course, at the breaking of every connexion with Poland, however constituted.

An example of the waning influence of the UNDO was afforded by the recent election to the committee of *Prosvita*, a very powerful cultural organization founded by the UNDO and usually regarded as their monopoly. The committee should consist of fifteen members; early in June an election was held in which Bryk, the UNDO president was defeated, and an independent Greek Catholic priest elected in his stead, the others being all either Clericals, Palievists, or mysterious people said to flirt with the OUN. This total defeat was a blow for the UNDO, but the authorities declared the election null and void on the ground that though the list contained fifteen names, only fourteen had been elected (I am unable to discover what this means). Another election has no doubt been held by now; in any case the result this time will be quite different, because the UNDO will prepare the ground, and because Archbishop

Szepticky is not in favour of a breach with the UNDO.

Archbishop Szepticky explained to me that in this as in other internal Ukrainian matters he is in favour of a compromise, both because of the necessity for a common front and because he does not want the Uniate clergy to be disliked. His church must be a unifying not a disrupting influence. This means, I gather, that for various reasons Szepticky has no wish to see the UNDO seriously weakened, and that he realizes that although the UNDO have felt bound to choose unpopular paths in the past and yet have nothing to show for it, nevertheless any other course might lead to more positive disaster. His Excellency gives one the impression of being a cautious man, closefisted, well aware of the advantage of the status quo, untroubled by generous and romantic visions; – whereas Mudrij is the Girondin, the *vrai modéré, (celui qui s'oppose aux extrêmes, mais qui s'y oppose modérément)*. The Archbishop says he considers the establishment of a Great Ukraine under Polish or German aegis, with or without Galicia, to be now a very remote possibility. He disclaimed any ideas of looking on the Catholic Orthodox Church as a Ukrainian National Church, and said he had no hope of converting the Ukrainians still under Russia to the Uniate faith should religion become tolerated there again, – let alone the Ukrainians in the Volhynia and Roumania. He said he advocates loyalty to the Polish state, in the sense of obeying the law and fulfilling all the legal duties of a citizen. Ukrainians could not be expected to feel as Poles, nor to fight ardently for Poland unless they were given some *solde*, or at any rate their right to exist. He said that too many Ukrainians looked towards Germany, and that he himself doubted whether she would ever be in any position to set up an independent Ukraine under her control, or whether it would be much pleasanter than life in Poland if she did. He admitted the force of the remark of the Carinthian Nazis: *In der Systemzeit ist uns Unrecht geschehen; jetzt geschieht uns recht,* – a remark in accord with his outlook. On the other hand, he complained with all the usual bitterness that the Ukrainians were handicapped at every turn simply because they were Ukrainians, however ready they might be to accept the Polish state. His complaints about the Uniate Churches which have been handed over to the Roman Catholic authorities emphasized the stupidity of these acts; but he did not agree that the religious issue could or should be divorced from the national and political one.

In Roumania the Ukrainians are much less organized and on the whole represent a much less serious problem than in Poland; but one of the same nature. Unlike other minorities, they have no

part in the Front of National Renaissance. While the Ukrainians in
Poland have in bygone days been promised and are till clamouring
for a Ukrainian university in Lwów, in Roumania Ukrainian is not
even taught in the schools, in purely Ukrainian country districts;
with the result that the children benefit very little from education
at all. The fact that the Ukrainians in Roumania belong to the
State Church means that, unlike the Uniate and Orthodox churches in Poland, the ecclesiastical hierarchy is in the hands of the
Staatsvolk, not the minority. On the other hand, the *intelligenz*
seems to be much less numerous in Roumania than in Poland; and
the relatively easy-going administration of Roumania, – where
nothing is eaten as hot as it is cooked, – enables her peasants to
manage better in many cases than those across the border.

The recent re-grouping of the Roumanian Departments into
(often somewhat fantastic) federal provinces, each with a royal
resident who apparently exercises a considerable amount of influence in practice, may well tend to benefit the Ukrainians, in
spite of their very natural disappointment at not being given any
official minority status in the new state. The northern province of
Suceava, with Czernowitz as its capital, includes the Bukovina and
Northern Bessarabia, or in practice, the bulk of the Ukrainian area.
In place of the petty administrators from the old kingdom, often of
gypsy origin, the royal resident is now George Flondor, the head of
an aristocratic Bukovinian family known and respected in the
neighbourhood, and imbued in spite of his traditional Roumanian
sympathies with an understanding of the administrative methods
which made prewar Austria so regretted in all that part of the
world. The leader of the Ukrainian minority is Dr. Vladimir
Zalosiecki, a relation of Flondor's with whom he was brought up.
Dr. Zalosiecki professes to be very conscious of the advantages
which the Ukrainians enjoy by being in Roumania. He sees little
prospect of the erection of any state in which they would fare much
better, and his hope is that the Roumanian Government will make
it possible for Ukrainians to become loyal citizens of Roumania
and serve the State. He has hopes that Flondor will be able to con-
vince the King and the more far-sighted of the Roumanian officials
of the wisdom of such a policy; that gradually Ukrainian will be
unobtrusively taught in the schools, (one hour a week at first), and
used in certain churches; and, of course, especially that selected
loyal Ukrainians will be given small Government jobs of various
kinds. Flondor himself, I understand, realizes that the vast majority of the Ukrainian population could be conciliated simply by dis-
regarding politics and ethnography in the Suceava Province and

just governing in the best interests of the area, showing as much national tolerance as possible and making use of such loyal talent as was available. He is, however, most worried that his policy is not likely to be understood in the old kingdom, where, of course, quite other ideals and theories of government prevail. Nor must it be forgotten that the Iron Guard, so many of whose policies the King has adroitly taken over, was bitterly anti-Ukrainian; the organization was particularly strong among Roumanians in the Bukovina, and the new administration is therefore on slippery ground. The Orthodox Church too, tends on the whole to make a policy of conciliation more difficult; and indeed, Father Vascá, the Rector of the local theological seminary has several times made public anti-Ukrainian utterances of an inflammatory nature.

Such *intelligenz* as there is — editors of the newspaper *Chas*, an occasional lawyer and so on — talk in much the same strain as their opposite numbers in Poland. They deny German activity more, however, and produce no atrocity stories, though of course their complaints about the lack of educational facilities and such matters are more serious than those in Poland.

In essentials, then, the problem in Poland is the same as that in Roumania. One cannot help being impressed by the absolute hopelessness which fills most Ukrainians above the level of peasants on account of the apparent impossibility of becoming loyal citizens of the country in question unless they sacrifice every distinctive trace of nationality, and in all probability not even then. The *intelligenz*, see every avenue virtually closed to them in the civil and military services; they are reminded on every hand that they come from a subject people governed by and in the interests of the *Staatsvolk*, whose ultimate idea is to stamp out all that they hold so pathologically dear, (and which the *Staatsvolk* in the time of its own subjection held just as dear), and so it is inevitable that they should gradually abandon all hope of leading a self-respecting existence in a uniate state, and find themselves driven to see their salvation if not in detachment, at least in some sort of autonomy, where they would have their own civil, military and religious services, and where their national culture and traditions would be preserved. From this, of course, it is a short step to the demand for absolute independence and fusion in a Greater Ukraine, a hope which was so nearly realized at the end of the Great War and which recent events have seemed to bring almost within their grasp again.

The peasantry on the whole are naturally not so concerned as

the white collar classes with these aspirations. A majority of them
would probably be content, both in Poland and in Roumania, with
any administration which guaranteed them their land, provided
them with reasonable economic conditions free from ethnological
discrimination, and which did not interfere over much with their
local village life. It is true, of course, that many of the peasants are
already imbued with nationalistic ideas and that the incitement of
the peasantry by the *intelligenz* is a potentiality which the administration must always take into account. How much easier is it,
however, for the *intelligenz* to inflame the peasantry when, for instance, they can point to Monsieur Witos' demands on behalf of
the Polish peasantry – that, as there is no room in Poland for the
½ million increase in the population each year, the Polish peasantry should gradually colonize the Ukraine and that the Ukrainians
rather than the Poles should emigrate to Canada and the Argen-
tine. Up to date not a very great deal of settlement of Poles or
Roumanians in Ukrainian areas has taken place. But sufficient has
undoubtedly been done to give just cause for alarm; and apparently neither the Polish nor the Roumanian Government dares give a
guarantee that the process will not be continued further. There are
also various cases of Uniate churches in the Polish Ukraine being
handed over to the Roman Catholic authorities – and of a slow but
steady Polonization of various schools in doubtful areas. In
Roumania, of course, the whole education and ecclesiastical ap-
paratus in the Suceava Province is in non-Ukrainian hands,
whereas other minorities receive many privileges which are denied
to Ukrainians.

This all forms part of a general tendency on the part of both
Poland and Roumania to create a national state with one language
and one capital and to abandon the more or less non-national
technique of administration evolved by Austria. It appears quite
natural to the Poles and Roumanians that if anyone is to emigrate
from their country it should be the minorities rather than
themselves. So long as all the governmental white-collar posts in a
country, and even such jobs as that of village postman, can be
filled by members of the *Staatsvolk*, the administrative classes
both in the civil and military services can hardly be expected not to
employ their own nationals in preference to members of the
minorities, about whose loyalty they are bound to feel a certain
doubt. This attitude is, of course, a vicious circle, as the members
of the minority *intelligenz*, seeing so many avenues closed to them
simply on account of their nationality, gradually abandon all hope
of co-operating loyally within the framework of the State and turn

instead more and more to the solution of autonomy. The more this attitude prevails generally, the more difficult it becomes for the Central Government to make the concessions that are asked for, all of which inevitably have autonomist and thus eventually a secessionist flavour.

The essential tragedy of so many minority groups in the east of Europe is that young states, desirous of making all the area which fortune has given them an integral part of their own *Volksraum*, can conceive of only one sort of minority, namely the alien unassimilated group which must be attenuated as far as possible as its ambitions are directed at least to autonomy if not to secession. And indeed, in cases where this really represents the facts, such as that of the virtually irreconcilable Hungarian minority in Roumania, it is hard to recommend seriously any other attitude but that at present adopted. On the other hand, I am not convinced that even now the Ukrainians in Poland and Roumania belong to this category. The surest way of counteracting the propaganda of Germany and her conscious and unconscious helpers, is to treat the Ukrainians as far as possible without discrimination against them on the score of their nationality. The root of all the trouble is the sense of frustration which Polish and Roumanian Governments have succeeded in giving to these people and the peasantry at any rate would, in the opinion of competent neutral observers, in most cases be quite reconciled to being citizens of the states concerned, and willing to give up playing Ukrainian politics, provided that they felt themselves, their lands and their economic organizations to be secure. Many of the Ukrainian *intelligenz* too, would be only too thankful to serve Poland loyally on condition that their spiritual integrity was left to them, (just as, for instance, Count Goluchowski, whose statue has a place of honour in Lwów, became Foreign Minister of the Austria-Hungarian Empire, while remaining a patriotic Pole).

This process of absorption could, of course, only be done very gradually at present; and its counterpart should be a firm refusal on the part of the State to discuss any projects of autonomy with the Ukrainians as such. For such concessions can never hope to satisfy Ukrainian aspirations, which will only become more vocal as each new concession is made, and make the recipients more hopelessly conscious of their own nationality. The more far-seeing Poles and Roumanians are prepared to admit that the only way to destroy the case for autonomy is to make no distinction between their own people and the Ukrainians, and to repress impartially, both consciously Ukrainian national movements and the corresponding Polish and Roumanian demands for preferential treatment. They see the fundamental contradiction between refusing to regard Ukrainians as partners with themselves in the State, and then chastising them for not being so. They admit that it would not be possible for England to maintain the loyalty of Wales if the Central Government adopted a policy of colonizing Wales with English settlers, letting the Welsh emigrate; if every obstacle were placed in the way of accepting Welshmen for Government employment; and if the resultant disaffection were met on the one hand by ferocious "pacifications" and on the other by abortive discussions on the subject of autonomy with people who were being driven to dream of a great Gaelic Empire.

The Poles also sometimes realize that the "Promethean policy" of setting up a Ukrainian State under Polish protection would have much more chance of successful realization if Poland could count on the loyalty of her own Ukrainian minority and if the talent which is now wasting itself in hopeless opposition could be trained into an efficient civil and military *cadre*, loyal to Poland and capable of filling key positions in the Russian Ukraine.

However, most Poles and Roumanians are convinced that these things are only possible in an atmosphere of confidence and territorial integrity which no longer exists. The Ukrainians, they declare, are too disloyal to be trusted; and whatever might have been possible at the beginning, the only course now is to give positions only to their own people. The difficulty of this policy is that it is not being pursued with the atrocious thoroughness which is really necessary. The Poles and the Roumanians know that Prussia and Hungary were unable to destroy the Polish and Roumanian character of Posen and Transylvania. They realize that spasmodic brutalities exacerbate Ukrainians rather than cow them. They often reluctantly admit what almost every Ukrainian will assure a foreigner, that even if the able-bodied men were not left in the Ukraine to rebel in time of war and even if they can be put to work where sabotage is hardly possible, nevertheless the countryside in the present circumstances will certainly welcome a German army on the whole, while it will do what it can to damage the war efficiency of its oppressors.

I came to the personal conclusion that not enough responsible Poles saw sufficiently clearly the tragedy of what was happening — that too few of them were anxious enough, in their own interests, to break the vicious circle. In Roumania, where other minority problems overshadow the Ukrainian one, there is as much or more complacency. But there the blithe acceptance of waste and risks that one meets in Poland is rather replaced by indifference or resignation; which may stifle the efforts of anyone who sees the bogs into which the will o' the wisp of exclusive nationalism can lead, and who tries to stand on firmer ground.

The problems of sub-Carpathia seem to me separate from those of the Polish and Roumanian Ukraine. For one thing the area is ethnologically very mixed; there are at least three main dialects shading from fairly pure Ukrainian to something very like Russian and to a unique dialect perhaps resembling Slovak. The country consists of a series of mountain valleys not really connected very much with one another but all moving down to the valley of the Tisza and to the Hungarian towns at the foothills. The peasantry are all comparatively poor; and much more than elsewhere, they openly admit that their chief anxiety is to gain a livelihood. "We starved under the old government, we are starving now; we hate all governments." There is very little Ukrainian *intelligenz* so far as I could see, though a certain amount had grown up in Czech times and has now disappeared. Most of the peasantry which regarded itself rather as *ruski* than Ukrainian was somewhat bewildered by the events of the last few months. Much of the "Sich" was made up of Garibaldi-like individuals from over the borders and in any case most of it has been shot or has fled into Slovakia. (At the frontier just outside Ungvár, for instance, the Slovak guards told me that some twenty Ukrainians and Germans came over the border each day). Even Father Voloshin recognized the peculiar nature of the territory by evolving a "Ruthenian language" which differed in some respects from orthodox Ukrainian. Large numbers of the inhabitants seem to have regarded Hungary as their natural market and their inevitable destiny; and there was a very widespread belief that if only the country could be linked to Hungary the peasants would be able to sell their wood (their principal product) which had proved somewhat difficult in Czech times, and that all would be well.

As even informed opinion in Budapest is willing to admit, however, most of this goodwill was forfeited in the first weeks of the occupation by the blunders of the "redeemers" and their apparent helplessness to alleviate the economic distress. The territory was occupied, first of all by the military authorities and then later by civilians who were often given jobs for nepotic and other reasons which they were quite incapable of filling. However, these mistakes are gradually being remedied and not only are satisfactory arrangements at last being made for the taking of sub-Carpathian wood, but the whole mountain area is rapidly filling with Hungarian tourists who are eager to visit mountains once again and who are bound to bring a certain amount of wealth into the country. The people are conscious of a stable equilibrium, of a solution in accordance with the laws of gravity, which for years they had not known.

It is perhaps worth mentioning that only with the greatest difficulty was it possible to cross the frontier into Hungarian sub-Carpathia at Uzsok or to leave it again either at Sobranc (into Slovakia) or Körösmező (formerly Jasiňa), although I had a Hungarian laisser passer and though the only road was closed, while the railway was stated to be theoretically open. The petty military officers in charge refused to do anything about the tryptique of the car. It always proved possible to proceed in the end, however, on the principle that however afraid you are of the tiger in the jungle, he is even more afraid of you. The Slovaks and the Poles never made any difficulties of any sort. The frontier hotel at Uzsok was so full of half-drunk Hungarian tourists that it was literally physically impossible to enter; all along the Tisza valley from Huszt up to the frontier at Körösmező there were small groups of tourists bathing in the river or picnicking along the banks, driving cars with Budapest number plates or pitching tents for the night. The restaurants are a mass of Hungarian flags. It is reasonable to suppose that in these days of lack of devisen Hungary, which suffered from a total lack of such scenery, will be able to make more of the area as a tourist centre than Czechoslovakia, which had a plethora of it, was ever able to do; just as Hungary ultimately offers a much better market for sub-Carpathian timber than Czechoslovakia could. Ungrár and Munkacz too, offer a much less deserted appearance than towns like Kassa and Losonc where the Vienna frontier still runs some two kilometers from the last house, and which, cut off from their mountain hinterland and emptied of their Slav populations, are mere shells of their former serves, and a problem to their new administrators.

At a shooting Fest at Kliemec, on the common frontier, where Polish and Hungarian sportsmen met one Sunday in June to celebrate their becoming neighbours, and which representatives of President Mos[c]icki and Admiral Horthy attended, the Archduke Franz Josef, after parades of troops and hoisting of flags, made a speech in Hungarian followed by one in shocking Ukrainian in which he said he was speaking only to the Ruthenians who had now returned to Mother Hungary, and who enjoyed full cultural autonomy. The Poles might have been expected to take this speech, made in mid-Ukraine, somewhat amiss, but their reaction seems to have been "oh their autonomy is all a farce, just like their army." The autonomy which the Slav population enjoys is said to be "cultural but not administrative." Certainly if one asks any inhabitant of the territory what cultural autonomy means he says he doesn't know. In pointed contrast to Poland and Roumania, the villages all have their Magyar and Slav names written up (the two are very often totally different), but the latter in prewar Russian characters, not Ukrainian ones. The Huszt newspaper too is written in these characters, and the language used seems to differ from normal Ukrainian as well as from *Voloshinese*. A certain amount of this language is taught in schools, though it is clear that in a country almost devoid of an Aryan middle class there will be little demand for any higher instruction in anything but Magyar; in any case, the level of schooling is expected to fall off from the level of Czech days.

On the whole it seems as if sub-Carpathia will settle down — unless another convulsion upsets everything — as a sort of Hungarian Wales, with such slender ranks of the *intelligenz* as may exist gradually becoming more and more Magyarized, and so more and more accepted by the State as loyal citizens. The anti-semitic tendency of modern Hungary will produce ever greater gaps in the present virtual Jewish monopoly of trade and such activities; and so any Ukrainian intelligenz which may grow up will be fairly easily accommodated. Dissatisfied people are rapidly getting out; and even if a Greater Ukraine were ever erected, the Carpathians might well form its frontier, the enthusiasts moving over the mountains.

[sgd.] J.H. WATSON

SOURCE: FO 371/23056
Public Record Office

9

Note to Mr. Makins, Foreign Office, from
Mr. Leeper, Political Intelligence Department,
20 October 1939, Suggesting no Official Contacts be
Maintained with Ukrainian Representatives.
Advocates Federal Solution to the Polish-Ukrainian
Problem. Minutes by F. Roberts and L. Collier.

COPY   OCTOBER 20, 1939

Mr. Makins.

I have looked through this Ukrainian file and I should like to make a few comments on the Ukrainian question, as I am dealing myself with Poland in the Political Intelligence Department. May I first state my qualifications such as they are? I dealt with this Ukrainian question from the outbreak of the Russian Revolution in 1917 and through the whole of the Petliura period. After the Treaty of Riga between Poland and Russia in 1921 the Russians suppressed the Ukrainian movement within their own territory, but the Ukrainian question remained a very live issue in Poland, especially in Eastern Galicia. When I was in Poland in 1923-4 and again from 1927-9 I visited the whole Ukrainian area in Poland including Volhynia as well as Eastern Galicia, and again and again I discussed it with Poles from Pilsudski downwards and with Ukrainians. I have, therefore, a certain amount of background, though I admit that I am not up to date in the sense of knowing the names and the value of the different Ukrainian politicians who may now appear on the scene.

After this introduction may I make a few general observations? The British and French Governments in 1917 played with the Ukrainian question and burnt their fingers, as the Ukrainian leaders were men of no real standing in their own country and Petliura himself was little better than a brigand. The Bolsheviks suppressed the movement without any difficulty. I do not imply that there is nothing in Ukrainian national sentiment, but there is no organization and nothing to build on. From that point of view the movement is still in a very backward stage and I do not believe that various Ukrainian politicians who address us on the subject of an independent Ukraine count for anything at all outside a small area. The only area where the movement is actively organized is in Eastern Galicia where it came into being through direct encouragement given by the Austrian Government before the war with the object of keeping the Poles in check.

The Poles after the war had an opportunity of coming to terms with the Ukrainians which they missed. There were many Poles who were far-sighted enough to realize the importance of an agreement and who worked for it sincerely. They were thwarted by the intransigence of the Poles in Lwow who in many ways resembled the Ulsterman of Belfast. As a result no real progress was made, although far more liberty was given to develop the movement than was the case in Russian Ukraine. It was, however, one of the real weaknesses of Polish policy.

Recent events may have taught the Poles a lesson. I gather that the new Polish Government realize that the only way of recovering their territories now occupied by Russia is to come to a federal arrangement with the Ukrainians. They are already contemplating this new State as a federal Polish-Ukrainian State. We should, I submit, encourage this mood in every way we can. Just as the new Czecho-Slovak State should be federal and not the old Benes State, so too should the new Polish State be federal. Could some such indication be given to Sir Howard Kennard? Mr. Savery knows this question well.

I am all in favour of embarrassing the Russians over this Ukrainian question, but not through direct action by us, only indirectly through the Poles. They will know how to play their cards in this part of the world much better than we can, but we should make them do so. If Poles and Ukrainians come together they should be able together not only to embarrass Russia, but create as much trouble as possible between Russia and Germany where the two frontiers meet.

I suggest, therefore, that we should not treat direct with the Ukrainians or give any publicity to their pronouncements, but should handle this question entirely through the Poles.

[sgd.] R. A. LEEPER

* * *

Minutes

20TH OCTOBER, 1939

We have told Dr. Kissilevski who represents the UNDO in this country that he can occasionally bring to the Foreign Office any Polish Ukrainian leaders who may come to England. We have, moreover, asked Paris to acknowledge the letter of M. Prokopovitch, President of the Paris organization. This in itself does not commit us to very much. [........]

As to the future it is agreed that the Ukrainian movement is one to be encouraged. It is merely a question of the best method by which to encourage it — directly or through the Poles?

It might be worthwhile to send a copy of this memorandum to Sir H. Kennard, asking for his observations and suggesting that if he has no objection, he should broach the subject to M. Zaleski. The Poles have not as yet taken any open steps to make clear that the future state which they have in mind is a Polish-Ukrainian federation.

Northern Dept.

[_____]

*

I am afraid I am not competent to express any opinion about the actual merits of the Ukrainian question, but on the question of machinery, I agree with Mr. Leeper that we should not ourselves enter into negotiations with the Ukrainians or give them any publicity. I do not, however, see any objection, to our continuing to receive quite informally individual Ukrainians, as we did in the case of Doctors Kissilevski and Solowij. I assume that the last paragraph of Mr. Leeper's minute is not intended to rule out such private conversations.

We should, I think, first get the advice of Sir H. Kennard and Mr. Savery on Mr. Leeper's minute [........] I think it would be better to await Sir H. Kennard's observations beforing instructing him to discuss the matter with M. Zaleski.

[sgd.] F. ROBERTS

*

I see no objection to trying to work through the Poles in the first instance; but if — as I fear is quite likely — the Poles will not play properly, and if the attitude of the Soviet Government makes it desirable for us to raise up Ukrainian trouble for them, I trust that we shall not be deterred by undue regard for Polish susceptibilities from dealing directly with any Ukrainian leaders one can get hold of.

I would also venture to suggest that, while Mr. Savery has an unrivalled knowledge of the facts of the Ukrainian question, he may not be a good advisor on policy. My experience of him has been that he thinks, in these matters, more as a Pole than as an Englishman. That caveat, however, is for the future and does not affect the action now proposed, with which I agree, subject to what I have said above.

[sgd.] L. Collier

Source: FO 371/23138
Public Record Office

10

*Letter from F. Savery to W. Strang, 6 November
1939, Commenting on Leeper's Note. Advocates
British Participation in Bringing about Federal
Solution to Polish-Ukrainian Problem.*

BRITISH EMBASSY
TO POLAND IN FRANCE

PARIS
NOVEMBER 6TH, 1939

Dear Strang,

I have read with interest your letter, C.17055/237/55, of October 31st, and Leeper's memorandum enclosed in it.

So far neither I nor Savery have worried the Poles about the Ukrainian question, or indeed about any of the larger political issues which they will have to face sooner or later. By the middle of this month we and, I hope, the Polish Government as well, ought to be settled in at Angers. Then, I think, Savery might begin to sound his friends in the Ministry of Foreign Affairs and also in other official Polish quarters as to their attitude towards both the Ukrainian and the Lithuanian questions, especially from the standpoint of a federalistic solution.

On the whole Leeper's suggestion that we should act through the Poles in the Ukrainian question seems to me sound. If we want the Polish-Ukrainian question to be settled on federalistic lines, we must do our best to make it appear to the Poles that this idea was originally theirs and not ours. The good old socratic method in fact — we are to be midwives of the political wisdom which is in them.

Leeper's views on the Ukrainian national movement seem to be much the same as those of Savery, who in a letter to Sargent, of October 6th wrote:

> *My own impression is that the Ukrainian national movement has taken root, that no efforts, not even those of Moscow, can extirpate it for good, but that it will probably not be sufficiently developed for a real settlement to be reached for another two or three generations.*

As to the question whether we should or should not have con-

tacts with individual Ukrainians, I do not think it desirable that
we should absolutely refuse to have anything to do with Ukrainians who present themselves to us. By adopting such a negative
attitude we might only drive waverers into one or other of the
enemy camps. But we must be very careful. In the first place we
must not take too seriously or show too great cordiality towards
persons who may be of no importance whatever. For instance,
Savery tells me that he has never heard of Dr. Solowij and does not
think that he can have held any *official* position of importance in
the Ukrainian national movement or political organization in
Poland.

Is Solowij a member of the UNDO? And, incidentally, who and
exactly what is Dr. Kissilevski?

To revert to the question of our contact with Ukrainians, I
think we must bear in mind that most, even of the Ukrainian
leaders, (a) are only just emerging from the status of "semi-
intellectual" and (b) have a decidedly oriental kink in their brains.
For instance, while we ought not to allow Ukrainians with whom
we talk to think that we are prepared to discuss political problems
with them behind the backs of the Poles and against the interests
of the Polish *raison d'état*, we want to be careful how we convey
those considerations and reservations. A few casual remarks to the
effect that we have been impressed by the vigour with which the
Poles have re-acted against their misfortunes and by the national
union which in the moment of danger at once came into being, and
has so far been maintained without any difficulty, − in short, the
suggestion, not put into so many words but clearly implied, that
Poland will come out of the present war a stronger State than
hitherto will probably have much more effect on the minds of
Ukrainian politicians than any amount of direct statements.

I shall write to you again on this subject in two or three weeks'
time.

Yours ever,

for H. M. Ambassador

W. Strang , Esq., C.M.G.,
Foreign Office

[sgd.] FRANK SAVERY

SOURCE: FO/371 23138
Public Record Office

11

Memo of Conversation between J. H. Watson,
British Embassy to Poland, and E. S. Carlton,
Concerning Polish-Ukrainian Rapprochement and
Possibility of Instigating Ukrainian Revolt.
Minutes by R. M. A. Hankey

22 JANUARY, 1940

I had an interesting conversation with Mr. Carlton this evening on the subject of the Ukraine.

Mr. Carlton is at present engaged in conversations with Poles and Ukrainians in order to try and persuade them to work together. His basic scheme is one that must have occurred to anyone thinking about the problem, namely how to get the two peoples to co-operate with each other in the territories now under Soviet control. Even if Galicia (which is by no means all the former Polish Ukraine) were to come into German hands the problem would not become less acute.

It is clear, to begin with, that the Allied Powers will not want, after the war with Nazism is over, to have to do more against Russia than is necessary. More especially, it will be much easier and cheaper for us to enable the Poles and Ukrainians to throw the Russians out of Eastern "Poland" than for us to have to do it by force ourselves. If the Poles and the Ukrainians will only co-operate, it should be possible to cut the few lines of communication between Russia and her newly won territories, and thus paralyze the mechanized forces on which she relies, but which cannot function without adequate supplies. The Poles seem satisfied that given Ukrainian co-operation the very few roads and railways could be cut and kept cut by perpetual sabotage. We would, when the time was ripe, supply small arms and other means of guerilla warfare. And whether or not we do anything ourselves against Russia, the effect would be sufficient to enable the territories to be recovered.

Here we come up against the problem of the Ukrainian people. It is fair to say that so badly did the Ukrainians consider themselves treated by the Poles that they all wanted Home Rule; and the vast majority were bitterly anti-Polish and anxious for an independent state. Realizing that they had nothing to hope for from Russia or the Democracies, they usually looked to Germany. And I have no doubt that a good many still do.

On the other hand I gather that the Ukrainian leaders are willing to co-operate with the Poles in order to gain freedom from Russia on the basis of the five south-eastern *Voivodships,* and of course, carte blanche east of the former "Polish" territories. This I heard in London before I left. Mr. Carlton has now discussed matters with leading Poles and Ukrainians, and he thinks that the Ukrainians would perhaps agree to co-operate with the Poles, provided H. M. Government gave a guarantee of a Polish promise. The promise would be that there should be complete internal autonomy (cf. no doubt Croatia, Slovakia) for a certain area, consisting of Volhynia, Tarnopol, Stanislawów, and part of the Lwów *Voivodship,* but leaving Lwów, the historic capital of Galicia, as a Polish town. The way would then be open for joint action when the moment comes.

This would involve serious concessions on both sides, and it somewhat surprises me that it should be possible. But, one must remember one great underlying thought   the whole programme of an expansion of the Polish-Ukraine into a Great Ukraine based on Kiev depends on Polish support, and Ukrainians know they need Polish friendship in order to make this possible. And there are many Poles who realize that a Great Ukraine is the only ultimate guarantee against the permanent and natural tendency of Germany and Russia to partition Poland. To exorcise this bogey it would be worth risking the loss of the South-Eastern territories to a greater Ukraine, which may never arise. That all is, unless Poland can be liquidated as a Power, and the Ukrainians can count on German support.

And that seems to me to be the point. How will this co-operation be possible if Germany acquires the lion's share of the "Polish" Ukraine? I do not think we can hope the Germans will treat the Ukrainians badly. At any rate not so very badly that they prefer co-operation with the Poles, and the promise of an autonomy under a Polish state after the war, to complete independence of Poland and the promise (which the Germans will, of course, continue to hold out to them) of a Great Ukraine. Nor must too much confidence be placed in the statements of Ukrainians here that the powerful Ukrainian bureaux in Berlin and Vienna cut no ice − of course, the people here say that. As long, however, as the Ukraine remains a purely Russian question I think it should be possible for the Ukrainians and the Poles to do a deal on the lines envisaged by Mr. Carlton. And in any case the shrewder Ukrainians know Germany is not going to win the war.

Anyway Mr. Carlton seems to have got prominent Poles and Ukrainians here to the point of co-operation provided H. M. Government will guarantee the Polish word. The difficulty seems to be the rôle of the French, who have never been able to grasp a state as any other than a centralized government with one great capital and unitary administration. According to Mr. Carlton the Polish Government in Angers do not seem to have thought very seriously about getting into touch with Ukrainians, and people coming out here from Angers have given him the impression that the French Government has been definitely cold shouldering any such approaches.

Mr. Carlton wishes to see his people again and on Friday he wants me to write semi-officially to someone in the Foreign Office and see whether they think there is any possibility of H.M. Government counter-signing a guarantee given by the Polish Government to the Ukrainian Bureau. If there is, Mr. Carlton thinks it will have to be announced more or less as a *fait accompli* to the French. And anyway most of the Poles with whom Mr. Carlton has come into contact here have been so anti-French in their attitude that a French guarantee would not be acceptable to either party. On Friday delegates will leave for Paris and Angers, however, to put the final plan, as evolved in discussions here, before the Polish Government and the Ukrainian Bureau in Paris.

The chief difficulty, I feel, is what will happen if the Germans take over Galicia. If we can get agreement between the Poles and Ukrainians before that happens, as opposed to actual revolt, it will be very much easier. In fact, once the Germans are in Galicia, agreement may not be possible at all.

[sgd.] J. H. WATSON

* * *

Minute

This is interesting and shows how the discussions, of which we wrote home recently, are progressing.

I do not like the idea of our putting up to Foreign Office as a ready-made idea at this stage the plan of a guarantee from H.M. Government, especially as it may get us in queer with the French. The Polish Government and the Ukrainians in Paris are in touch and have actually sent their delegates out here in order to size up the position and sound the Roumanian Government, as the Polish Ambassador has done. The next stage is for them to talk it all over in Paris.

According to M. Spitzmüller, the French First Secretary here, the French Government have not made up their mind. They have their sentimental feeling for a strong Russia, or at least a strong Power in the east. But they are disgusted with the present Russia, and are waiting to see.

Personally I agree with that attitude. If the Ukraine goes off at half cock, before we are ready, the whole thing may fizzle out, or if it succeeds the Germans will just take over the whole Ukraine. Unless I am wrong, we don't want a Ukrainian revolt before 1941 summer; then we will use it to down the Russians and Germans together. Meanwhile we can help the Poles and Ukrainians on tactfully towards an agreement, as we are doing.

I think we should send Mr. Watson's minute to Foreign Office with a covering despatch.

I am against the guarantee myself. We tried it in 1920-1924 and could not enforce it. East Galicia is outside our beat and always will be.

[sgd.] R.M.A. HANKEY

SOURCE: FO 371/24473
Public Record Office

12

Memorandum by E. S. Carlton, Department of Political Intelligence, 5 March 1940, Posing Solution to the Polish-Ukrainian Problem.

THE UKRAINE, WITH PARTICULAR REFERENCE TO
THE POLISH UKRAINIAN PROBLEM

5 MARCH, 1940

[........]
Reverting now to the main issue, it is clear that the whole position between Poles and Ukrainians was far from satisfactory because of the antagonism existing between Polish and Ukrainian races. This problem has long called for settlement and there has never before been such a moment when agreement is more vital to the joint interests.

Today Poles and Ukrainians in the occupied area are getting closer and closer together as a result of the state of adversity in which they find themselves under Soviet rule.

The only official representatives available who can discuss this question are the Polish Government and the Ukrainian Government in France. These are both essentially provisional and temporary institutions and any agreement arrived at between them should be in such a form as will be acceptable to the masses who will eventually decide.

Notes on the Polish Government and the character of its members have already been compiled so it now only remains to criticize the Ukrainian Government and Ukrainian Committee in France, and who claim to represent the interests of the Ukrainians.

[........]
The previous Government had consisted of:

President	Liwickij
Prime Minister	Prokopowycz
Foreign Minister	Smal-Stockij
War Minister	General Salskij
Minister	Jakowlew

The cohesion of this Government was broken up by the outbreak of war. The first, third and fourth persons mentioned may be
in Warsaw and the last named in Prague. In the event of the President being unable to act he has, however, the power to nominate a
successor who could form a government. Liwickij, therefore, sent
the necessary authority to Prokopowycz and a new government
was formed in Paris in December.

All the members of the former Government were collaborators
of Petliura, anti-German and anti-Communist and all of them were
from Russian Ukraine which they left two decades ago. They claim
to have liaison with the Russian Ukraine but their actual degree of
influence is questionable. Their influence in the Polish Ukraine is
undoubtedly small.

The Ukrainian Committee in Paris is composed as follows:

Chairman	Szulgin
Vice Chairman	Udowicenko
Vice Chairman	Solowij
Secretary	Kowenko
Secretary	Rudicew
Secretary	Col. Kowalskyj

The Committee has advisory functions to the Government. It
is obviously not sound that members of the Government should sit
in the Committee and it is understood that the Committee is to be
reconstructed so that the Government members will be replaced
by delegates from America in order to make same a more representative organ.

The activities of the Ukrainian Government appear to have
been financed by Ukrainians in America.

The strong character amongst all the foregoing is Szulgin, an
active worker and a good diplomat. The only member of the Ukrainian Committee who is at present in Roumania is Solowij who,
however, only joined the UNDO in 1935.

From the above it will be seen that the influence of these
Ukrainian representatives over the Polish and the Russian Ukrainian masses is small and for that reason they, like the Polish
Government, are definitely not competent to enter into any agreement of a fundamental nature. However, they are no doubt
respected by those who remember them and provided their activities are not contrary to the ideas of the UNDO and OUN leaders
there is no reason to assume that any commitments which they
enter into and which are of a conservative and moderate character
would be repudiated by the Ukrainian public at any rate in Poland.
The real leaders of the Polish Ukrainians are mostly in exile [........].

Of these Colonel Melnik is the strong character and his presence in Italy may be significant of Italian interest in this question. [........]

Mudryj is the strong character in [the UNDO] group with perhaps a runner up in the person of the writer "Kedren." In so far as religious influence is concerned, Archbishop Szeptycki, who is paralyzed, remains in Lwów where it appears he is isolated by the Russians. If Colonel Melnik and Mudryj could be drawn to Paris their presence would constitute a real representation of the interests of Polish Ukrainians.

METHOD OF SETTLEMENT

Proceeding now to the method of liquidating the Polish Ukrainian difference, the first point to be considered is whether this can be regarded as a purely local question or whether the question of a Greater Ukraine must be taken into account.

If this is to be regarded as a purely local problem, i.e. without regard to a Greater Ukraine, then the following factors must be taken into account:

The Ukrainian viewpoint is
- (a) that the Ukrainians in Poland should enjoy the full rights of Polish citizens; and
- (b) that the Poles cede to the Ukrainians part of their territory, i.e. that part in which the bulk of the Ukrainian minority is located.

The Polish viewpoint is that the Ukraine has no right to any former Polish territory, because
- (c) except for a few months in 1918, when the Ukrainians emerged as an accidental state, they have not existed as a separate entity for over 600 years;
- (d) that there is a very large Polish population in Galicia and Wolhynia [........] who would be the first to raise its voice if the district ceased to be part of Poland;
- (e) that the boundary between Poland and the Ukraine was fixed in 1920 by mutual agreement;
- (f) that the Polish nation would raise every obstacle to the cession of part of their territory and especially the city of Lwów, which is one of the oldest Polish towns;
- (g) that for obvious reasons it is important for Poland to have a common frontier with Roumania.

It is not proposed to comment on points (c), (d), (e), (f), and (g).

It is a fact that the Poles who understand this question think along these lines and that they will "stick to their guns."

In regard, however, to point (a), equality of rights for Ukrainians appears not only reasonable but necessary, and it is judged that the Poles would concede this point. Point (b) cession of territory to form a Ukrainian state — is, however, considered to present grave objections because:

  (h)   the formation of a small state consisting of two or three provinces which could not defend its own independence is unsound;

  (i)   Poland would be that state's bitterest enemy and generally speaking that state would have the character of a tasty morsel to be snapped up by its neighbours, and encouraged in a chauvinistic attitude by Germany.

The question of *autonomy* for the Western Ukrainians has also been considered and it is generally maintained in Polish circles that here again there would be grave difficulties owing to

  (j)   inherent opposition of the Poles, and

  (k)   the fact that this would have the effect of gradually divorcing from Poland a people who are basically more akin to the Polish race than to any other race and who need Poland's support and could under a mutually agreeable arrangement secure a fair deal from the Poles.

The easiest way of resolving the problem would be to treat same on broader lines by coupling the Polish Ukrainian question with that of the Russian Ukraine.

It would, therefore, not seem unreasonable to approach this matter in the following way:

  (l)   All Ukrainians in Poland to enjoy the full rights and privileges of Polish citizens; and

  (m)   the Poles to give the Ukrainians all assistance in reopening Russian Ukraine. Poles living in the Russian Ukraine to be ultimately treated as of equal rights to Ukrainian citizens.

Eventually, perhaps some scheme could be devised whereby Poles in Russian Ukraine could be transferred to Poland in exchange for Ukrainians in Poland who would go to the Greater Ukraine.

Information recently received seems to indicate that the Russian Ukraine would not be averse to overthrow of the Soviet régime, and, if this is possible the organization of a Ukrainian State in that region would have a greater chance of successful being if entrusted to the Polish Ukrainian *intelligenz* who have visions of a great future in that field and would probably not be unwilling to emigrate. There is no reason why the Ukrainian *intelligenz* in Roumania could not also take part in the work under a similar arrangement with the Roumanian Government in regard to their own minority.

The important facts to bear in mind are:

1. That if the Greater Ukraine is to be successfully established as a separate state then the population there will need assistance from outside.

2. That if the Poles and the Roumanians are forced to cede territory to the Ukrainians the assistance in question will not be forthcoming from either Poland or Roumania.

3. Lastly, that if the Ukrainians will agree to settle along the lines proposed, then Poland's 35,000,000 people and the Russian Ukrainians' 34,000,000 would form one block the importance of which could not be denied, but which could never threaten the interests of the British Empire.

There is a further point of importance. The Ukrainian *intelligenz*, not without reason, distrust the Polish and Roumanian Governments, and would probably be only too ready to welcome British interest in the question.

It is not possible to foresee the reaction of Mudryj or of Colonel Melnik to the proposed solution, but there is no doubt that any scheme under British patronage would warrant the most serious consideration.

It is repeated that Colonel Melnik's presence in Italy may be significant of Italian interest in the matter.

If an agreement can be reached it would be exceedingly desirable, having regard to the exiled state or the main Ukrainian leaders, for the Poles in co-operation with the Ukrainian Government to institute a Polish-Ukrainian Committee in Lwów which would propagate the decisions and direct propaganda for the furtherance of good relations between the two races.

Further the goodwill of the Ukrainians could be secured by the formation of a Ukrainian legion in France. The Ukrainians have always desired an army and this would have a great propaganda value in Polish, Russian and Roumanian Ukraine and also in America.

In so far as preparing the Russian Ukraine is concerned the establishment of a radio broadcast station in, say, Greece or on a ship designed solely to transmit to the Ukrainians, would be a useful method of contacting 34,000,000 people who have little liaison with the outside world.

Reverting once again to the purely Polish-Ukrainian problem it is submitted that settlement of this now will not only avoid a continuation of the present unsatisfactory state but will enable preparation to be made for a joint rising of Poles and Ukrainians at the opportune moment.

[........]

[sgd. E.S. CARLTON]

SOURCE: FO 371/24473
Public Record Office

13

Letter from F. Savery, British Embassy to Poland, Angers, to R. Hankey, 8 April 1940, Commenting on E. S. Carlton's Analysis of Polish-Ukrainian Relations.

BRITISH EMBASSY
TO POLAND

ANGERS
APRIL 8TH, 1940

Dear Robin,

Many thanks for your letter of March 23rd and also for kindly sending me a copy of Carlton's report on Polish-Ukrainian relations and of your despatch No. 120 also of March 23rd.

Carlton has obviously put a great deal of hard work into his study of the Ukrainian question, and I have read his memorandum with much interest. I am afraid, however, that after reading it through three or four times I still do not feel quite sure what solution, or alternative solutions, he proposes.

Does he envisage:

a) the creation of a Greater Ukraine, i.e. a Ukraine stretching eastwards from the Zbrucz but not necessarily including any territory which formed part of Poland on September 1st, 1939, or

b) a Ukrainian Piedmont consisting of Eastern Galicia and perhaps Polish Wolhynia as the nucleus of a future Great Ukraine, or

c) the grant of local autonomy to those parts of Poland in which the Ukrainians form the majority of the population.

As regards (a), I am, as I have said, more than once in the past, very sceptical as to the possibility of so far smashing up Russia, Soviet or Czarist, and keeping her permanently in a condition of such impotence as to permit the creation of an independent Greater Ukraine which would last more than a few years. I still think that the Russians will not be able, however hard they try, to annihilate Ukrainian separatism. The Ukrainian people will continue to produce writers and even scientists who refuse to throw in their lot whole-heartedly with Russia, or to write their books in Russian. I am also quite prepared to believe that the Ukrainian peasants will continue to despise the Russian peasants and soldiers, but I am not prepared to believe that Russia will ever acquiesce for long in the loss of the black earth belt or the Donietz Basin.

Suppose, however, that the present war should develop in such a way that Russia disintegrates, at any rate temporarily, we should be confronted with two alternatives. Is Poland to cede part of her "Ukrainian territories" to the Great Ukraine or not?

If she has to cede, say, her share of Wolhynia and about half of Eastern Galicia, it would surely only be because she meant to form a close alliance with the Ukraine in order to protect herself against Russia, but is it not more than probable that she would thereby involve herself at once in very bad relations and after a few years in a war with Russia? Surely in the reconstruction of Poland we must try to reduce as far as possible the points of friction between her and Russia. If, on the other hand, Poland does not cede a good deal of her "Ukrainian territories" to the Great Ukraine, she will be condemned in advance to have bad relations with the new State.

As regards solution (b), surely no-one wishes to increase the number of *small* States in Eastern Europe?

This leaves us only solution (c) — the grant of local autonomy to those parts of Poland in which the Ukrainians form the majority of the population.

If we can be quite certain that a Great Ukraine to the east of the Zbrucz will never arise, much of the danger for Poland which would otherwise attend this solution might disappear, but, in judging Polish reactions towards it, we must, I think, bear in mind that, however satisfactory their condition might be with autonomy inside Poland, the majority of the Polish Ukrainians would certainly want to join the independent Ukrainian State if such were to arise.

Hitherto the East Galician Ukrainians have not been honest in their demands for autonomy. Some six or seven years ago I wrote that at no moment since 1918 had there been among them a majority, or even a considerable minority, prepared to accept autonomy inside Poland as a solution, if not in *saecula saeculorum*, at any rate for two or three generations. It was only, I think, in 1935 or 1936 that the UNDO abandoned its fundamental opposition to all

Polish Governments. As a result mainly perhaps of the failure of the Polish Government to produce a positive policy, but in part also of the fact that they abandoned the demand for independence Mudryj – a man, in my opinion, of value as a statesman – and the other older leaders of the UNDO lost much of their influence over the rank and file of the party.

All the reports which reach me through Polish channels suggest that, thanks to Soviet tyranny and incompetence, there has been a remarkable "rapprochement" between the two races in Eastern Galicia since September, 1939. If that is really the case, there might be some hope of devising a scheme of "autonomy" for that part of Poland which would safeguard the rights of the Polish minority.

This is a very important consideration which must not be ignored if we accept the first point of Carlton's proposed solution – namely, that all Ukrainians in Poland are to enjoy the full rights and privileges of Polish citizens. This sounds very nice – and it also suggests that there has been something very wrong up to now as regards the situation of the Ukrainians in Poland. The Ukrainians had some real "wrongs" to complain of, but very often they cultivated those "wrongs" for the good of the national cause. In the matter of employment in the Polish Civil Service or Army, they never gave the Polish State a fair trial. They set out from the principle that Ukrainian Civil Servants must only be employed in the districts inhabited by Ukrainians. They would have had far less difficulties to contend with if they had admitted that, as Polish citizens, they might be employed in any part of the country to which their superiors thought fit to send them.

For the moment I would rather not go into details of possible exchanges of population, etc. as the ethnographical statistics which are being prepared for me in Paris have not yet been completed.

Before closing this letter I will just throw in one or two remarks on questions raised by Carlton's memorandum. I do not think that the so-called "Petliuran Government" in Paris counts at all with the Ukrainians in Eastern Galicia. It is almost entirely composed of émigrés from the "Great Ukraine," and has practically no connection with the Ukrainian population in Eastern Galicia. Further, as Carlton hints, it has really been so long in exile that it has very little connection with any part of the Ukraine at all.

I was very much interested to read that Melnik is now in Italy. You may remember that in the spring of last year the Italians established a career consular post at Lwów and the first incumbent of it, Caracciolo, who had previously been Vice-Consul at Los Angeles, told Holiday that he was being sent to Eastern Galicia to watch the German policy in the Ukrainian question. Holiday said that Caracciolo, though 100 per cent fascist, was very strongly anti-German and made no disguise of his conviction that the Germans wanted watching in this question. The fact that Melnik is now in Italy suggests that the Italians are still maintaining this point of view.

I am sending a copy of this letter to Makins.

Yours ever,

[sgd.] FRANK SAVERY

SOURCE: FO 371/24473
Public Record Office

14

T. Philipps to T. C. Davis, Department of National War Services, 13 April 1941, on Ukrainian-Canadian Political Attitudes toward the War and Allied Position on Ukrainian Independence.

APRIL 13, 1941

Dear Judge,

The enclosure is an accurate estimate. It is an under-statement of one of the parts of the picture which I have ventured to emphasize for 4½ months. This has been clear enough since the time when you were good enough to suggest I should accept the invitation to me from the Ukrainian Church for unity. Owing to the march of events on the continent of Europe, this situation will probably begin now to deteriorate here. It arises from the inevitable re-kindling in Canada of European nationalisms. Under the threat of calamity to their Old Countries and to their brethren in it, old Anglo-Canadians as well as new Ukrainian-Canadians are more than ever before looking back anxiously over their shoulders towards the lands where their race was bred. These are among the oldest and deepest of human emotions. Any counter-mysticism has also to be partly in the realm of the emotions, for Canada.

Dr. Archer says the Ukrainians are confused about the issue in E[astern] Europe. Most of *us* are too. We still cannot tell their 40 million kindred in Europe what we will do for them when we win. By caution, we do not even tell them that we should like them too to be able to throw off dictatorship, tyranny and enslavement. Our sauce is for geese but not for ganders. But Hitler is promising and showing them something quite definite. Whatever the Germans offer Ukrainians, it will be better than what they suffer now. So the months pass, until a day something will "surprise" us.

[........]

[sgd.] T. PHILIPPS

SOURCE: RG 44, Volume 36
Public Archives of Canada

15

Report of T. Philipps to Department of National War Services and Royal Canadian Mounted Police on Hemispheric Defence with Specific Reference to the Immigrant European Populations in the Americas, 13 May 1941

CONFIDENTIAL   *COPY*

[13 MAY, 1941]

HEMISPHERE DEFENCE. FOREIGN-BORN EUROPEAN POPULATIONS IN THE AMERICAS

1. At least half this war has to be won in the mines, ship-yards and defence-industries of North America.

2. Besides the Negroes, at least a third of the heavy Labour in these industries is of Eastcentral European origin.

3. The Communazis have long been exploiting their discontents. They have been also urging them that now is the time, before war-discipline, to seize their place in the sun by threats of sabotage and strikes. Moreover, the Communazis have virtually taken over all Europe and, therefore, hold as hostages these peoples' kindred (for good, *they* say). Combined with bribery, this provides the means of powerful pressure on the foreign-born population of the whole hemisphers.

4. Nearly a third of the population of the US is "foreign-born." When the war broke out, their old-nationalisms were re-kindled and the respective European foreign-born groups got together throughout the Americas. Even Englishspeaking America, that is US and Canada, has therefore a year and a half's start to catch up. (Germans, Italians, Hungarians, Ukrainians and unnoticed Syrians etc. exist in sporadic blocks from Canada to Argentina. This includes the large groups in Brazil and Chile where the writer saw them in 1938). As a result of the war in Europe, the assimilation of Europeans in North America is being arrested at a time of the nations' danger when national solidarity is most essential.

5. No country in the world has among its citizens such massive human branches of the tree of Europe from which in the end the Communazis have to be dislodged. Whatever the Federal Government does for or against the European-born communities, in the US, cannot be without repercussion and influence among the great groups of the same origin across the borders, both in Canada and in South America and in Europe. None of these proposed activities can be neutral. More particularly north of the border, in the other part of English-speaking America, any such US activities will be either a hindrance or a help to Canada, and thus to Canada's allies in Europe.

6. However illogical it may seem, among Europeans to be anti-Nazi does not necessarily mean to be pro-British. Even Jewish Germans, who are anti-Nazi, are not necessarily anti-German.

7. From information at its disposal, the US Department of State regards the foreign-born war-position as pressing. An outside man, with special knowledge of the Near East, has now been called in, as a matter of urgency, to organize and operate a specialized administrative unit to deal with problems arising directly from the foreign-born population. The unit may in the end fit into a Civil Defence Department under Mayor LaGuardia. Apart from Public Security of the Interior, its scope will include these peoples' considerable influence (and External Relations) with their ex-compatriots within the hemisphere and in Eastcentral Europe. In any case, the Communazis' exploitation of the cupidity or discontents of Eastcentral Europeans is calling for specialized attention. Apart from the bewildered or restless element which lends itself passively, it is only a small but active minority who constitute quislings and a danger.

8. Excluding the Germanic groups, Canada's foreign-born communities, and their Churches, are in a position to render valuable service to the Allied Cause, to Hemisphere Solidarity and to Public Security. They can influence, in favor of the Administration's policy, their very numerous kindred both in Europe and throughout the Americas. In wartime, blood is a bond. Many of these peoples' sons, especially in the case of the Ukrainian Canadians, are already serving in Britain. The fathers and mothers of these families are only too anxious to lend their aid to follow-up by seeing to it that nothing should prevent or even retard the essential weapons and supplies getting to them overseas. In addition to indications of sabotage and strikes, they can often forewarn of the nature and direction of Communazi activities being exerted on their kindred group across the borders. But, in Canada, there ex-

ists as yet no specialized unit to make the foreign-born feel full partnership, or to get and to organize their more positive coopera- tion in this valuable specialized work.

[sgd.] TRACY PHILIPPS

Atlanta University, Ga.

Part I

USA

1. On my way back from fulfilling a series of educational engagements in the southern States, I visited Washington. Senior members of the State Department, whom I already knew from Eastern Europe or met socially now, kindly asked me to the Department to make contacts with their staff and to compare notes on the general position of the Eastcentral European peoples. They were also good enough to invite me to examine with them their immediate plans for dealing with problems arising from their foreign-born citizens in case of war.

2. Before accepting the invitations, I consulted the view of the Counsellor of the Canadian Legation, for whom I subsequently summarized my useful exchange of views with the Department of State.

3. The following is a brief precis of the US situation as presented to me. The 1930 Census, which is a ten-year-old underestimate, shows 38 million US citizens of foreign-born white stock. This is nearly a third of the total population. Of the 38 millions, 13 millions are foreign-born and 25 millions have either one or both parents born abroad. Of these, some 90% are, so far, to be regarded as "loyal". In addition to the 38 millions, there are about 5 million recently registered aliens.

4. Of the several problems touching the foreign-born, two are regarded as increasingly affecting their morale and loyalty in the event of war:

Sabotage and Strikes

(a) The Germans, through other nations' diplomatic im- munities or side-trade channels, will exploit their new successes by threats or promises to the foreign-born whose relatives remain helpless overseas.

(b) Increasing discrimination against skilled foreign-born because of their foreign names, even in non-defence industries, is in places already restricting defence production and beginning to deloyalize many of the loyal.

5. (a) Unless a positive activity is promptly organized direct by the Federal Government, a state of war is likely to inflame the already smouldering suspicion of the American-born and to create a reaction of hot resentment which can rapidly undermine many of the foreign-born. Those of the latter who are unjustly rejected may be provoked to heed agents locally chosen by Hitler from among their old compatriots. A high proportion of the Eastcentral European elements are Labour in mines, shipyards and the now vital heavy industries.

(b) It is, therefore, the vast majority of the foreign-borns, namely farm-men and workmen, who need to be the first object of our care. The higher educated professional people already realize what their kind can expect from Hitler. Apart from the normal conflict of interests between town and country, there is often a mutual suspicion between the manual and the professional elements. The foreign-born manual element often inherits a feeling of being exploited and regards the professional class as one of the exploiters. The two classes sometimes oversimplify it into seeing each other respectively as near-Communists and near-Capitalists, even within the same foreign-born group. It does not, therefore, at all follow that the manual class can best be reached through the professional class of any given group. Nevertheless, in wartime, blood tells.

(c) No two racial groups can be treated in the same way. "The Germanic" foreign-born (especially those between the ages of sixteen and forty) with either parent born outside North America, and all who have been part-educated abroad, are unavoidably recommended for treatment on a special restrictive basis. It is possible to overestimate their Nazism. But it is dangerous to underestimate their Germanism, especially on a rising tide. It has to be remembered that the other is daily crackling in every language, audible enough here, with Hitler's contention that he has stabilized currencies, torn down Customs barriers and virtually federated Europe. To the workers of the world, he swears that he has freed the tired non-German masses from conscription, mobilizations and long years of fear and tension, and that he has given to "the common man" of all Europe work without war! Whether he is or not believed, prestige is a conjuring trick in which nothing succeeds like success.

[sgd.] TRACY PHILIPPS

Part II

CANADA

1. The matter is one of hemisphere defence within the wider issue of self-defence of the American and English-speaking peoples. The immediate objectives are four:

(a) To get and to maintain the full and positive support of our foreign-born citizens for the following purposes:

(1) Closer consciousness of national solidarity. Canadianization.

(2) Reinforcement of national defence (civil and military) in all fields of the war.

(3) Modernized maintenance of our democratic form of government, not so much as a fixed form of government, but as a moral concept of human relations.

(4) Internal public security.

(b) Of equal importance. To spread among old-established citizens an appreciation of the contribution to the Nation being made by the newer comers. In this, the Canadian Clubs, Service Clubs, Chambers of Commerce, the Churches and all educational organizations can render valuable service to the Nation.

2. (a) Neither in Canada nor in the United States is there any one department or section of the Government whose primary responsibility is the handling of the problems arising from foreign-born citizens (chiefly Eastcentral Europeans) who, in the United States, constitute nearly a third of the total population.

(b) In the United States, the Federal Government is feeling the need of creating a Federal organism to take over and specialize in the work as a matter of urgency, now regarded as long overdue. Their government organizations most closely concerned are the Department of Justice because Foreign Immigration is a section of it, and the Department of State (i. e. Foreign Affairs) because the foreign-born long remain internally foreign in feeling and in activities overseas. Both in Canada and in the States, the Department of Justice would find itself embarrassed to have to take responsibility for the specialized problems of citizens of Eastcentral European origin (who are notoriously suspicious of Police) because of the Department's executive responsibility for prosecutions. But the strong interest of the Department of Justice, for the purposes of Public Security, must be taken for granted as obvious. In Canada, some of the larger organizations of foreign-born communities, such as Ukrainians, are already in the habit of looking to External Affairs for advice and guidance. This has arisen from the sympathetic understanding of their old-national problems which they have been fortunate to find among certain members of that Department.

3. (a) This war has, from its outset, been rekindling all nationalisms. Therefore, in North America, the assimilation into the English-speaking body-politic of the solid blocks of Europeans from Italy and Eastcentral Europe is being unavoidably retarded at a moment when it is particularly desirable that the process of assimilation should be hastened.

(b) The positive work of active assimilation should clearly start from the date of the prospective citizen's approval by the Immigration Department of whose initial act this work is a logical and indispensable extension.

4. *Suggested structure of organization.* Although in wartime it may be temporarily a matter of Civil Defence, it is suggested that a small new specialized unit be formed as a link between External Affairs and the Immigration Division of the Ministry of Mines-and-Resources. Few people would wish to maintain that immigrants and their loyalty are not among the most precious human resources of any rich and lightly-populated country. All the essential records of the foreign-born population are to be found already in this Ministry. Still fewer would wish to deny that so long as these foreign-born communities are still foreign in tradition and feeling, and still unemancipated from an external political outlook whence springs the roots and reasons of their apparently curious conduct, men with experience of their old background (which is an External Affair) are best placed to offer useful advice to those who have to assimilate and administer these new elements of the Nation.

5. (a) Each of the few racial groups large and foreign enough to need attention will have to be treated separately in proportion as they are, in fact, still separate in sentiment. Their un-Canadianism and their racial separatism would only be a base from which to work *away*, towards Canadianism. If this proposed new administrative unit is not clogged by committees or paralyzed by papers, it could consist only of a small number of travelling specialists from these groups, not more than two for each foreign-born community. Each, in turn, would be the central office to keep Ministers in touch with facts and feelings in the field, while the other is out-and-about to keep the people in direct touch with the facts of the war and the feelings of the Dominion Government. The object of the travelling would be to insure, all the year round, a direct and living contact with "the common man" in the heart of the

mass of the people, both among factory-Labour and in out-Districts. If the keystone of the work is made a personal and direct living touch with the relatively simple and imaginative foreign-born communities to whom background and personality still count far more than among people of Western European stock, it is clear that the most important point will be the choice of the character and personality of the few specialists concerned. Their selection will call for great care and judgment. These men would forge the links and weld the joints which can build the foreign-born communities into conscious Canadianism as more positive (instead of negative) British subjects and as contributing-parts of the democratic English-speaking world.

(b) Newspapers, films, radio, public speeches, foreign-language press, pamphlets, etc. would be adjuncts to set out the real situation in their old countries which are now subjects of obscurity or misrepresentation. They can help also to explain the reasons and objects of the relative policy of the Dominion which is so often misunderstood by these communities who now feel themselves objects of suspicion or neglect. The Bishops and Synods of the respective churches should be among our most valued allies. They can, if they will, powerfully reinforce our work by dotting the i's and crossing the t's of Christian brotherhood towards National unity.

(c) For the purposes of presentation to foreign-born communities, much will depend on the name of the label of the new work. It is suggested that a combination of the ideas underlying "Extension Department of the Immigration Division" or "Citizenship Department, European Section," linking External Affairs with Immigration (and Public Security) might afford the Public the proper presentation.

6. *Decentralization.* Provincial and local units. Much of the executive responsibility can be devolved upon existing local organizations. Consolidated central bodies for each racial community should be formed where they do not yet exist. Such bodies should be as small as possible. A great deal of work is capable of decentralization, much as the Department of Agriculture has been able already to decentralize their activities into the Provinces. At Washington, the Department of State has called in an outside man, with special long experience of the Near East, to create and operate a positive and new administrative unit as a small independent section of the Office of Emergency Measures. A State Department man, with East European experience, is his associate in a less positive (Foreign Policy) sense. I have had the advantage

of both their views, with which I find myself in general agreement.

7. *A National Advisory Panel of Assimilated Foreign-born Citizens.* For consultation when needed and to give a sense of responsibility and partnership, a number of foreign-born persons of wise and mature judgment, including, of course, manual men, could be got together as a National Consultative Council of foreign-born citizens. Such a council may have, at first, to function by *groups* of nationalities. They should be chosen solely on personal merits and not to represent any organizations.

8. There may be people who may think that all such suggestions are retrograde steps in exactly the wrong direction. Such persons would probably suggest that it was only necessary to issue authoritative orders to all the foreign-born communities that they must just become Canadians immediately, and leave it at that. If such old-British subjects exist, they probably do not realize that the inhabitants of North America are no exception to general rules of life and world currents. As the nations of Europe melted before Hitler, they fed the river of old European nationalisms which had already started to flow again strongly here on both sides (and across) the border. Such a river cannot be confined or dammed without danger. The reality of its existence cannot be ignored. It is, therefore, best to turn it to account and to canalize the current so that it shall not break out here and flood or disintegrate the Nation's fields. With care, this rising flood can be harmonized and harnessed with our own. It can then help generate the Nation's power. If it can be fused, the current can be Canadianized and be utilized to enrich and reinforce the Nation in the process.

9. Whatever is done or happens among the foreign-born communities in the States has an influence on their old-compatriots in Europe and a direct repercussion on the corresponding community which extends across in Canada. These foreign-born citizens do not forget that the agreements which gave rise to the war status and creation of both Czecho-Slovakia and Jugo-Slavia were negotiated by foreign-born committees formed in North America. Those precedents are not without significance now. When the war broke out, the foreign-born communities of the Americas got together among themselves and eliminated the border, throughout the hemisphere, long before the American Governments subscribed to a hemisphere policy. The foreign-born communities got a year and a half start. That start is something with which we now have to catch up. Owing to the present difference in (belligerent) status, the countries concerned cannot adopt identical measures to meet a nearly identical problem among similar immigrants. Although,

therefore, the measures cannot, even if it were desirable, be identical, it is important that, between Canada and the States at least, the gears of the two organizations, now being simultaneously created, should be constructed on such parallel lines that the teeth of the two gears can instantly engage automatically, with ease and silence, and work together so soon as the United States find themselves at war. It is with this in mind, and after exchange of views in Washington with those directly concerned, that this plan is now submitted without delay.

[sgd.] TRACY PHILIPPS

SOURCE: MG 30 E350 Vol. 2
Public Archives of Canada

16

Memorandum of Conversation between L. W. Henderson, Assistant Chief, Division of European Affairs, US Department of State, and Prof. A. Granovsky, 3 July 1941, on the Latter's Representation Requesting Official Anglo-American Support for a National Ukrainian State.

DEPARTMENT OF STATE

MEMORANDUM OF CONVERSATION

JULY 3, 1941

Professor A. A. Granovsky of the University of Minnesota and President of the Organization for the Rebirth of the Ukraine called upon me today.

He said that it was the hope of American citizens of Ukrainian origin in this country that the American and British Governments would take advantage of the present international situation in order to declare themselves in favor of an independent Ukraine. He advanced arguments which he has used on previous occasions in favor of the independence of the Ukraine and took the position that an independent Ukraine would restore the lost balance of power in Europe and would add to that continent a strong democratic state.

I told him that there was no possibility at the present time that the Government of the United States would take a stand with regard to the independence of the Ukraine and added that it would be useless for him to talk to officials of this Government on the subject.

The Professor said that he wished to emphasize the fact that he and the Ukrainian groups with which he was connected were just as much opposed to German control of the Ukraine as they had been in the past to Polish or Russian control. Both he and his group had been attacked unfairly as being Nazi sympathizers because they favored the granting of an opportunity to some forty millions of people to govern themselves. The fact that Germany might desire to create a puppet Ukrainian State did not mean that advocates of liberty for the Ukrainians were pro-German.

He asked if in the opinion of the Department of State his organization should disband. I said that the Department did not express opinions as to the desirability or undesirability of the existence of organizations of the type which he represented.

Before leaving, Professor Granovsky made another plea that the American Government should make no commitments which might later make it difficult for it to advocate or recognize an independent Ukraine.

[sgd.] L.W. H[ENDERSON]

SOURCE: M1286 Reel 5
State Department Records
US National Archives

17

*L. W. Henderson, Assistant Chief, Division of
European Affairs, US Department of State, 24 July
1941, Describing Ukrainian-American Attitudes
towards the War and Responding to Demands for
Increased Surveillance of Ukrainian-American
Community.*

DEPARTMENT OF STATE

MEMORANDUM

24 JULY, 1941

Mr. Dunn:

We cannot initial this instruction. It is our feeling that the instruction together with the attached memorandum is likely to
prove prejudicial to persons of Ukrainian descent in this
hemisphere. We have been endeavoring to keep in touch with the
various Ukrainian movements in this country for a number of
years. In our opinion, Ukrainian emigrés in the Western Hemisphere, at least those in the United States and Canada, are as a
rule hard-working, inarticulate persons. For the most part they are
more interested in making an honest living for themselves and
their families rather than they are in engaging in politics. The
Ukrainians on the whole are a peasant race. Such intelligentsia as
they have produced in Europe during the last hundred years have
tended gradually to be absorbed into the Russian, Polish or
Austrian middle or upper classes. They have, therefore, been
without outstanding leaders in Europe. In the United States there
are a relatively small number of Ukrainians to be found among the
professional classes. Some of these delve into local and international politics in a sort of amateurish way. Their efforts to organize
any kind of real political blocks among the Ukrainians have met
with little success. Most of these Ukrainian political leaders are
rather harmless. They quarrel with each other. Leaders of one
group charge leaders of other groups with being communists,
nazis, socialists, etc. They have only one goal in common and that

is a movement in the direction of some kind of independence for the Ukraine. There is violent disagreement with regard to the extent of independence, to the type of a Government which the Ukraine should have, to the international orientation which a Ukraine state should have, etc.

Naturally patriotic Poles and Russians become very much incensed at any talk of Ukraine independence and are quick to charge that any person of Ukraine origin who is in favor of an independent Ukraine is a Nazi. It would be unfair towards a rather decent element of our population to accept such charges at their face value.

I think there is little doubt that the *Hetman* group, which is extremely small in number, would be willing to work with Hitler. I am sure that the majority of the members in the United States of the ODWU are not pro-nazi or pro-German.

There may be a few terrorists among extreme Ukrainian nationals. Of course Poles and Russians will exaggerate their number and violence. It is perhaps advisable that we instruct our missions in the other American Republics to keep a watchful eye on developments in the Ukrainian national movement, particularly in view of the apparent endeavor of Hitler to organize a puppet Ukraine state. I feel, however, that such an instruction should be drafted in a manner which would not throw discredit or suspicion upon all persons of Ukrainian origin who would like to see the area which they consider their motherland to be independent. Ukraine and the Ukrainians may some day in spite of their present inability of self-expression become a real force. It would be unfortunate for us to drive that force into the camps of the Nazis by misunderstanding or misinterpreting. There are less than a million persons of Ukrainian origin or descent in the United States.

The nationalities situation in Eastern Europe is extremely complex. We should, therefore, exercise care in sifting out information which may come to us relating to the reflections of that situation in the Americas.

[L. W. HENDERSON]

SOURCE: M1286 Reel 5
State Department Records
US National Archives

18

*S. Welles, Under Secretary of State, Washington, 23
August 1941, to American Diplomatic Officers,
Concerning Ukrainian Nationalist Groups and the
Need to Orient Ukrainian Nationalist Sentiment
toward a pro-American Position.*

DEPARTMENT OF STATE

STRICTLY CONFIDENTIAL   WASHINGTON
AUGUST 23, 1941

POSSIBILITY OF INCREASED COOPERATION
BETWEEN UKRAINIAN NATIONALISTS AND NAZIS
IN THE OTHER AMERICAN REPUBLICS

*American Diplomatic Officers in
the other American Republics*

Sirs:

Reference is made to reports which the Department has received from time to time from several of the missions of the United States in the other American republics concerning Ukrainian nationalist groups, particularly with respect to their reputed close cooperation with the Nazi organization in those countries. For your information in this connection, there is transmitted herewith a copy of an excerpt from a memorandum, dated June 19, 1941, entitled "Ukrainian-Nazi Movements in United States and South America," which the Department has received from a source believed to be reliable.

In view of the fact that the recent outbreak of hostilities between Germany and the Union of Soviet Socialist Republics, which has resulted in an attack by Germany upon the Ukraine, may be assumed to exercise an effect upon Nazi-Ukrainian relations in the other American republics, you are requested to report fully to the Department the conditions which prevail in this respect in the countries to which you are accredited.

It has been suggested that, although the Ukrainian nationalists have seemed to find their outlet in pro-Nazi activities so
far, they are not necessarily in sympathy with Germany today and
could conceivably be directed into a pro-United States stand if
some imaginative positive policy were pursued toward them. For
this reason it is emphasized that the utmost delicacy and care be
used in any action taken by you in this regard, and you are requested to submit your comments as to the possibilities of shifting
the Ukrainian nationalist sentiment to a position more favorable to
the United States.

Very truly yours,

For the Secretary of State:

[sgd.] S[UMNER] WELLES

SOURCE: M1286 Reel 5
State Department Records
US National Archives

19

Canadian Department of External Affairs Memorandum to Prime Minister W. L. Mackenzie King, 14 April 1942, Discussing Proposed Anglo-Russian Treaty with Specific Reference to Territorial Commitments in Eastern Europe and Canadian Policy.

MEMORANDUM

14 APRIL, 1942

PROPOSED ANGLO-RUSSIAN TREATY

Negotiations concerning recognition by the United Kingdom of the 1941 frontiers of the USSR have reached a stage where it appears that the United Kingdom Government is prepared to accede to the Russian demands.

In the course of negotiations extending over some five months the United Kingdom Government has had two related objectives: to satisfy the Russian Government without making definite commitments on post-war frontiers, and to avoid any conflict between its own policy and that of the United States. Neither of these objectives has been reached.

During November 1941 the nature of Russian policy began to become apparent. Stalin was urging a declaration of war on Finland, Hungary and Roumania; and when the British Government tentatively suggested sending General Wavell and General Paget to Russia to discuss military co-operation, the reply was that such a visit would not be useful unless there were discussion and agreement on (a) an understanding between the two countries on war aims and post-war organization of peace, (b) mutual military assistance against Hitler.

In view of this answer it was decided that Mr. Eden be sent, together with high military and other experts, on what had now become a mission of the highest diplomatic importance. The character of the pending conversations was partly forecast in an exchange of telegrams. Mr. Churchill explained that every aspect of co-operation in the war could be discussed; and that post-war reorganization could be taken up at the end of the war, with the particular object of keeping Germany from breaking out a third time. In reply Mr. Stalin welcomed the mission, discussion of an agreement on common military operations, and emphasis on security. He added that

> *difference of State organization between Soviet Russia on the one hand and Great Britain and the USA on the other hand, should not and could not hinder us in achieving a successful solution of all fundamental questions concerning our mutual security and legitimate interests.*

Early in December the United Kingdom Cabinet examined the line to be taken by the Foreign Secretary in Moscow. In the conclusions reached great emphasis was laid on maintaining agreement with the United States. It was recognized that Clause 2 of the Atlantic Charter ("They desire to see no territorial changes that do not accord with the freely expressed wishes of the peoples concerned") made difficult any conclusions on post-war territorial settlement. The Cabinet felt that an Anglo-Russian public declaration, similar to the Atlantic Charter, would be desirable. A draft was drawn up, which pledged collaboration in war and in the peace settlement. In territorial questions, policy was to be based on the Atlantic Charter.

On December 7 the United Kingdom declared a state of war with Roumania, Hungary, and Finland.

Such was the background of the Moscow Conference. On December 16th and 17th Mr. Eden had long conversations with M. Stalin. Two draft treaties were produced by the latter, one on mutual military assistance and the other on political collaboration during and after the war. It was thought that an agreement was in sight, when Stalin suggested a secret protocol embodying joint views for a settlement of post-war frontiers. As the conversations developed it was seen that Stalin, on the one hand, was chiefly interested in committing the United Kingdom to definite frontiers for the USSR, while Eden worked for a second Atlantic Charter.

Both Mr. Eden at Moscow, and the Cabinet on his return, rejected either a public or secret agreement committing them to defined boundaries. There were several arguments against such a course, but the chief ones were the Atlantic Charter itself and the pledge at the Atlantic meeting that the United Kingdom had no secret commitments respecting post-war settlements.

The United Kingdom Government had kept in touch with

Washington over the Russian question, and Eden had secured
Russian consent to his informing the us Government of the
Moscow discussions. The British Ambassador in Washington was,
consequently, requested to explore the matter informally with
President Roosevelt. He was to explain Stalin's position that the
Baltic States had been added to the ussr by plebiscities, and the
portions of Finland and Roumania by duly negotiated treaties. The
United Kingdom Government believed that Stalin's demands
tested the sincerity of their avowed desire to work with him during
and after the war. A plain refusal might bring a deterioration in
Anglo-Soviet relations, and in the collaboration of Great Britain,
Russia and the United States.

But could the demands be accepted without doing violence to
the Atlantic Charter and raising a crop of demands from other
quarters? If not, one of two alternative offers might be made.

(1) To support Russian demands for strategic bases, but leave
the future of the Baltic States to the peace conference.

(2) Promise to support at the peace conference a Russian demand for control of the foreign policy and defence of the Baltic
States.

The President rejected both the Russian proposals and the
British alternative, and decided instead to seek a direct agreement
with M. Stalin. The United Kingdom Government preferred tripartite discussions in London, thinking it inappropriate that they
(with whom the ussr sought a treaty) should be left out; but the
President saw Litvinoff, through whom he sent a message to
Stalin. He could not, he said, consider a secret treaty, nor any treaty with regard to definite frontiers. Public opinion would not allow
it. The United States would, however, support − after the war −
Russian efforts to achieve security.

The approach was failure, since the only reply was that the
Soviet Government had taken note of the President's communication. In passing on the reply to the United Kingdom Government,
Maisky said that they had not asked the United States Government for their point of view, and so considered the President's
observations as for information. Maisky went on to say that he
hoped the United Kingdom Government would explain to the
United States that there was no question of a secret treaty and
that the United States was not being asked to join in any agreement (as the President had apprehended). He added that he hoped
the United Kingdom Government would make it plain to the
United States that in the interests of the war effort the United
Kingdom Government considered it should now conclude the trea-

ty with the USSR.

The latter remarks were given as the Ambassador's personal opinion, but obviously were intended as a Russian desire that a decision be quickly reached. The United Kingdom Government accepted them as such and reconsidered the whole matter. The question, they agreed, could not be allowed to drag on, and further negotiations would not be helpful. Lord Halifax was, therefore, directed to speak to the President on the following lines (Dominion's Office telegram of March 31):

(1) The American position is appreciated, but "this country, as a European Power for whom cooperation of a victorious USSR after the war will be essential, cannot afford to neglect any opportunity of establishing intimate relations with Stalin." That can be done only by negotiating a treaty recognizing Russian claims to the 1940 frontier (other than with Poland).

(2) We hope that the President will realize that he has been consulted at all stages; and that, if he cannot approve of the projected treaty, will understand our reasons, and "abstain from any overt action which would indicate that there is any divergence between us." British public opinion would not forgive any failure to establish co-operation with the USSR.

(3) Security is not for the USSR the whole question, which has also "a psychological character which derives from the fact that for twenty years the Soviet Government has not been in relations of equality or confidence with any of the Great Western Powers."

(4) The USSR is bearing the brunt of the fighting. The limitations of British assistance make it all the more necessary not to refuse a political concession.

THE PROPOSED TREATY

The treaty is apparently intended to contain the following territorial terms:

(1) The inclusion in the USSR of Estonia, Latvia and Lithuania. In July 1940 the assembly of each State, after an election under Communist auspices, passed resolutions applying for admission into the Soviet Union.

(2) The inclusion of Bessarabia and northern Bukovina.

A Russian ultimatum to Romania in June 1940 led to Romanian agreement to the transfer.

(3)   The frontier with Finland to be as under the treaty of 1940. Finland would thus lose a part of the Rybachi Peninsula in the north; the Salla region in the centre; and, in the South, islands in Viipuri Bay and the Gulf of Finland, the Karelian Isthmus, and a strip to the north of Lake Ladoga.

Note: Stalin agreed to leave the future frontiers of Polands as an open question.

UNITED KINGDOM POLICY

It is evident from the foregoing that the United Kingdom Government is prepared to negotiate a treaty; and as the general terms have already been accepted by both parties it seems probable that negotiations would be successful.

In spite of all efforts, it has not been possible to establish agreement amongst the three principal allies on this major political question. The British have consistently sought to find an alternative to the Russian proposals, but — having found none that was acceptable — have felt it necessary to adopt the Russian policy. The arguments for and against that decision may be summarized thus:

For

(1)   By creating confidence it will further Anglo-Russian military co-operation.

(2)   Acceptance will compensate for the small scale of British military assistance.

(3)   Anglo-Russian *entente* will be necessary in the peace settlement and post-war period.

Against

(1)   The treaty conflicts with the general British policy of avoiding commitments on territorial questions before the peace conference.

(2)   It conflicts (in spirit if not in letter) with the Atlantic Charter.

(3)   It may endanger Anglo-American co-operation.

(4)   There may be similar demands by others of the United Nations.

(5)   It will lend to the destruction or weakening of certain small nations, and perhaps later of others.

Canadian Policy

This government has been kept fully informed by the Dominions Office and the High Commissioner both of the progress of negotiations and also of the reasons for the various British moves. So far no reply has been requested and no comment has been offered. It is none the less obvious, however, that the proposed treaty is of major importance to Canada.

Some facts of the situation are:

(1) *Estonia, Latvia. Lithuania.* The Canadian Government has taken no action to rescind our recognition of these States. Whether or not the vote of their assemblies to join the USSR be considered as taken under duress, it was an act of the duly constituted government of the day. Technically at least, there is an argument for letting them remain within the USSR. Furthermore, neither the earlier history of these districts nor their short existence as independent states altogether suggests that they can or should be sovereign states.

(2) *Roumania.* By act of the Canadian Government, a state of war has existed with Roumania since December 7, 1941. It is more evident here than in the case of the Baltic States that the cession of territory was a forced one. On the other hand, it must be remembered that Bessarabia has changed hands a number of times, and that the wishes of its inhabitants have never been clearly declared.

(3) *Finland.* A state of war with Finland also has existed since December 7. The first Russo-Finnish war can only be regarded as an act of aggression by the former, though the Russians may argue that subsequent events have shown that it was a justifiable defensive aggression for protection against Germany. In any event, Finland is now giving aid to Germany, and all indications are that she is committed to the German cause. At the opening of the parliament on February 3, Ryti, in his presidential speech, spoke of relations with Germany as close and cordial. His personal wish was that Finland should whole-heartedly enter Germany's new order. Russia, he said, if left as today, would always be a danger to Finland. It is stated that anti-British propaganda has recently been remarkably successful in Finland.

Under these circumstances the possibility of inducing Finland to make a separate peace with the USSR seems remote. Efforts, however, have been and are being made by both the United Kingdom and United States Governments to that end, and the two Governments are cooperating in their actions. A Dominions Office telegram of April 1st reports that

> *His Majesty's Ambassador has been authorized to take a*
> *suitable opportunity to suggest to the Soviet Government*
> *without arousing their suspicions that Finland might*
> *possibly be persuaded to cease hostilities in return for*
> *something like the 1939 frontier and a guarantee of essential*
> *supplies of food and care.*

If peace between Finland and Russia were established on that basis, both the military and political problems would be simplified. It is very doubtful, however, whether Finland is free to act, given the presence there of German troops.

(4) *Atlantic Charter.* Canada adhered to the principles of the Atlantic Charter. Even in the general form in which it is expressed, the second of the principles may be interpreted as in opposition to such intergovernmental decisions on the transfer of territories as are envisaged under the projected treaty. On the other hand, it is no more easy to reduce to fact and machinery "the freely expressed wishes of the peoples concerned" than it was "self-determination" twenty-five years ago.

MAJOR CANADIAN INTERESTS

From the Canadian point of view two considerations stand out: maximum efficiency in the conduct of the war, and Anglo-American-Canadian comity. The United Kingdom Government is convinced that, under the circumstances, the first consideration requires a treaty with Russia; but have realized from the first the threat to Anglo-American co-operation involved in following a policy different from that of the United States. In communications between them both the British and American Governments have emphasized the pressure of public opinion. The same factor must be taken into account by the Canadian Government when deciding its policy.

CANADIAN OPINION

(1)   Closer association with the USSR would be criticized in Canada by those who, while admitting the military value of the Russian campaign, are so influenced by anti-communist opinions that they would object to more intimate political relations. Such a point of view would probably be most marked in the Province of Quebec.

(2)   Opposition to the treaty would also be based on the ground that it destroyed certain small nations and might open the

way for further absorption by the Great Powers.

The Atlantic Charter has given the impression that such territorial changes would not be made. The Canadian minorities immediately affected – Roumanians, Estonians, Latvians, Lithuanians, and Finns – would suffer disillusionment; while others from small states, such as Poles and Ukrainians, would be apprehensive of the extension of the principle to their homelands. Amongst some of these groups there are divisions, so that some elements would support any move of aid to Russia, but on the whole the effect would probably be bad.

If a separate peace were made by Finland some of the cause of criticism would be removed, since the Russian claim to Finnish territory is based on a war of aggression.

(3)   There would be objections to following a policy different from that of the United States, especially if the policy of the latter were represented as based on higher principles. On the other hand, the alternative of following a policy conflicting with that of the United Kingdom would be at least equally open to criticism.

(4)   The importance of aid to Russia is increasingly recognized; and while the public has not had any cause to think of aid in political terms, a careful explanation of the reasons for such a course should create a sympathetic reception. A great deal would depend on the way in which the question was represented to the public. In the past there has been confusion of thought arising from the over-emphasis by some writers on the co-operation of the English-speaking peoples, with little regard for Russia or China. It will have to be appreciated that the peoples who have borne the brunt of the land fighting cannot be ignored politically.

CANADIAN POLICY

If the treaty is signed by the United Kingdom it will be because the pressure of the war has forced that course, and because no alternative could be found. The Canadian Government will welcome it no more than will the United Kingdom Government. None the less some Canadian policy with regard to it will have to be adopted.

There are three alternatives:

(1) to stand aside,

(2) to oppose the treaty,

(3) to support and adhere to it.

As to (1): This course, which presents certain obvious advantages, would be in line with that which the United States will probably take. It could be defended on two grounds: (1) that Canada has taken no part in the formation of the policy leading to the treaty, (2) that Canada is a party to the Atlantic Charter. This negative attitude, however, has the weakness that it means avoiding a responsibility which — however objectionable from some points of view — must be taken by some of the United Nations. Apparently none of that responsibility is to be shared by the United States, and it is to be feared that Anglo-American relations will become more difficult as a result. Canada's aloofness may underline these difficulties and the divergence of us-British policy on this issue.

There are many international issues decided in London, where Canada can remain uncommitted and formally aloof, without causing any particular attention or provoking any controversy; without, in short, advertising lack of unity within the Empire. It is extremely doubtful, however, if a Treaty with Russia in present circumstances, and in the terms proposed, is one of these issues.

As to (2): Open opposition to the Treaty can, I think, be ruled out, though the Government can, if it sees fit, point out its dangers and disadvantages to London.

There remains (3). Support and adherence. This would take one of two forms:

(a) Signature of, or formal adherence later to, the treaty. In this event (particularly in the case of signature) it would seem proper to have some part in the negotiations, directly or indirectly.

(b) An expression by the Canadian Government of its agreement with the policy of the treaty.

In favour of this course are:

(a) Anglo-American differences over the Treaty, would be reduced if the Dominions supported it.

(b) The value of the Treaty, which may be of vital importance in the winning of the war, would be greatly enhanced if Canada and the other Dominions supported it.

If alternative (1) is adopted — the non-committal course — every care should be taken to ensure that Canada's attitude does not serve to weaken the positive advantages of the Treaty. To this end, the following steps should be taken.

(1) The Government should state its position in such a way to make it as difficult as possible for the enemy to exploit that position. The necessity of, and the purpose and advantages of the Treaty — as a Russian-United Kingdom Treaty — should be emphasized.

Every effort should be made to influence American opinion to the most favourable point of view possible. It is essential that the American Government should (in the words of the British instructions to Lord Halifax) "abstain from any overt action which would indicate that there is any divergence between us." This is an opportunity for Canada to prove her traditional claim to act as interpreter between the United Kingdom and the United States.

Finally, it might be desirable to ascertain the views of the other Dominion Governments.

The Anglo-Russian treaty may well prove to be one of the decisive actions of the war. It calls for the most urgent consideration. If it is held to be unavoidable — and there is every reason to believe it to be so — its value should not be reduced, nor its dangers underlined by any action of ours.

Source: rg 2 Series 18,
Vol, 43 File U-5
Public Archives of Canada

20

*Memorandum from G. de T. Glazebrook
to N. Robertson, Canadian Under Secretary of
State for External Affairs, Enumerating Reasons
for Supervision of Foreign Groups in Canada,
2 July 1942.*

JULY 2ND, 1942

MEMORANDUM FOR THE UNDER SECRETARY

POLICY TOWARD FOREIGN GROUPS

There are in Canada a large number of persons of foreign origin. Many of these, such as the early German immigrants, are sufficiently assimilated not to create any problem. Others, whether of Canadian or foreign nationality, have retained or revived a self-conscious nationalism. These latter are of varying sizes and at different stages of organization. Some distinction must be drawn between those who are British subjects and those who are not; but the distinction is not absolute, as is shown, e.g., in the case of the Ukrainians.

In dealing with foreign groups, however, it will be necessary to distinguish between British and foreign nationals to the extent that the former have the rights of other Canadian citizens.

It will also be necessary to distinguish between (a) nationals of states whose governments or provisional governments are recognized by Canada and (b) alien enemies and persons adhering to non-recognized states. For practical purposes the Free French should be included in the former category.

The reasons for supervision of foreign groups are:

1. There are amongst them individuals convicted or suspected of hostile actions. These are interned, or are under observation by the RCMP.

2. Other individuals or groups are of concern to the Department for one or more of the following reasons:

(a) Because of suspicion of the motives of individuals or

groups. There are, e.g., good grounds for regarding Otto Strasser with suspicion. He is opposed to Hitler for obvious reasons, but has he changed his political views? Is he still a National Socialist, though the leader of a faction that has been put out of power? His correspondence, which is considerable, shows a strong anti-Russian colour and a thin veneer of liberalism.

(b) In some cases the factional quarrels (which are common in the Free Movements) not only destroy most of the value which — from our point of view — the movement might have, but tend to spread beyond the movement itself. The dissensions amongst the Free Austrians provoked disagreement with the Czechs (besides wasting the time of the Canadian Government and Parliament).

(c) There is a danger that divergences in political and social policies may weaken the co-operation of the United Nations. An aspect of this problem that affects Canada is the policy of the groups representing the Russian borderlands. Amongst all these peoples there is some degree of opposition to communism, and they have territorial ambitions that involve a corresponding loss to the USSR.

PRESENT POLICY

Free movements are permitted to exist in Canada, but are, for the following reasons, given no recognition.

(a) Uncertainty that the group commands or can command support of the anti-Axis population in the home country.

(b) A belief that it is unwise to make any commitment in respect of either the particular group or the future of the country concerned.

(c) Because of dissensions within the Free movements.

(d) To make Canadian policy consistent with that of the United Kingdom and the United States.

COMMENT

The wisdom of the policy of non-recognition cannot be doubted; but it covers only the negative side of the question, omitting any means of control of the activities of the Free Movements. While there are objections to unnecessary suppression, it may be suggested that there is a wide divergence between the liberty allowed to dubious groups such as Strasser's and the vigorous control of the Japanese in Canada.

It is the aim of the Governments of the United Nations to encourage, as far as possible, all opposition to the Axis powers. It is

possible to agree on an anti-Nazi and anti-Fascist stand, but not to
pursue far the distinction between democracy and authoritari-
anism.

A more immediate problem is the relations of various foreign
groups to the USSR. There are those of the Right who denounce
communism, and others of the Left who — if they do not openly
support communism — at least advocate more aid to Russia, etc. A
recent development is the so-called *Pan-Slav* movement.

While there is no division of opinion in Canada in regard to the
Axis, there is a considerable difference on the USSR. It is, therefore,
advisable to keep a close watch on the foreign groups in this
respect, particularly those with extreme views. It is difficult
enough to keep Canadian opinion on an even keel without additional interference with the trimming.

Suggested Modifications in Policy

As far as possible, it will be desirable to maintain a common
policy toward all Free Movements (except, perhaps, the French).

To suppress one or more of them would be difficult to defend,
and probably do more harm than good. It is almost equally difficult for the Government to dictate who should or should not be
leaders.

The direction given by the Government might be by "unofficial" pats on the back, or equally unofficial warnings.

For official policy the following lines are suggested:

(1) To adopt the principle that Free Movements or similar
groups must not conduct any propaganda which, in the view of the
Canadian Government, is calculated to be damaging to the cause
of the United Nations. There could be particular reasons given for
a ruling, e.g. that Strasser's writings were anti-Russian, or that the
Hetman group was pro-Nazi, but the Government would be in a
much stronger position if it refused to give specific reasons. Once
the Government had laid down such a ruling, any group need be
tolerated only so long as it was considered to be doing no harm.

(2) To insist that all the correspondence, incoming and outgo-
ing, and all published material, be voluntarily submitted for censorship. Some of the correspondence is caught now, but under the
existing censorship much must go through.

A breach of this rule, if discovered, would be a cause for removal of privileges.

How could these proposals be carried into effect?

A first step might well be to find out, informally, how such a plan would be regarded by the United States and United Kingdom authorities. There is a particularly close relationship between the problems of foreign groups in Canada and the United States. A discussion with some of the UK representatives in New York might settle both points. Thought should also be given to the loss of intelligence information by the general imposition of censorship.

If these preliminaries are satisfactorily cleared up there remains the question of how to inform the Free Movements of the conditions to be imposed upon them. It is understood that there are objections to official correspondence with them. There is also the further difficulty that, in some cases, competing groups claim to represent the free movement of a particular country. I would suggest, however, that it would be possible to draft a form letter which would not commit the Government to recognition of a particular organization, but merely inform its officers of the rules thereafter to apply to such organizations.

[sgd.] G. DE T. GLAZEBROOK

SOURCE: RG 25 G1, Vol. 1896
File 165, Part III
Public Archives of Canada

21

*Foreign Nationalities Branch, Office of
Strategic Services Report, 26 September 1942,
Describing the Effects of Foreign Influences on
Ukrainian-American Public Opinion.*

SEPTEMBER 26, 1942

The masses of the 750,000 Ukrainians in the United States have been law-abiding and loyal. Although being often as not poorly informed on actual political developments at home and abroad, the Ukrainian immigrant has seemed, for the greater part, to accept the democratic traditions of his adopted country. Numbers of Ukrainians have continued, quite naturally, to retain an interest in European Ukrainian affairs whether in Galician Poland, the USSR, Rumania, or Czechoslovakia. Often, indeed, this interest has served as the basis of constructive and charitable activities. The *Defense of the Ukraine* society, for example, aided in the acquisition of two buildings in Lwow (Poland) for use as educational and recreational centers, founded an organization *Samosvita* (self-education) for the publication and distribution of books to the peasants, and provided financial aid for the establishment of educational centers for peasant women. Ukrainian workers in the United States helped their relatives in the old country buy land from their Polish landlords.

At the same time, the identity of the American Ukrainians with their homelands was both variable and confused. The long-standing rivalry of the Greek Catholic Orthodox faiths in European Ukraine reflected itself in religious organization in the New World. Soviet religious attitudes and practices caused still further schism: many of the Orthodox Ukrainians refusing to recognize the Metropolitan Sergei at Moscow and others failing to recognize any other. Religious affiliations, often ran parallel with, [and] often cut across political ideologies. Not all Greek Catholics, for instance, showed orientation to their western Catholic near-relatives. Nor did the Orthodox faith of other Ukrainians necessarily direct them toward pro-Russian sympathies, although earlier Russian propaganda had not failed to make full use of this religious identity.

The political scene was dominated by the recollection of the age-old interest in Ukrainian self-determination. The American Ukrainians had come themselves or had relatives who had come from territories long subjected to non-Ukrainian rule. Numerous Ukrainian elements had long aspired, some of them by the use of any means available, to the creation of an independent Ukraine including Ukrainian areas of Russia, Poland, Rumania, and Czechoslovakia. Others had, like their European fellows, cast their lot with these respective States, and devoted their efforts to the achievement of maximum economic and political security within this framework. The majority in America probably normally regarded these problems with interest, but with secondary attention.

The Ukrainians in the United States, like other recent immigrant groups, have scarcely had the time to attain complete assimilation on the one hand or complete coordination of their organized life on the other. Low economic status has not, moreover, been conducive to the development of an extensive, educated mass population. As a result, the average Ukrainian American has looked for guidance and encouragement to his priest and to whatever leaders appeared on the scene: especially to those of his trade union.

Ukrainian organization in the United States has in the past shown considerable talented leadership. Economic problems here and political events abroad have, however, for some time, brought to the fore a particularly egregious, fanatical type of Ukrainian nationalist. With the growth of widespread propagandistic and subversive activity originating in Europe, new "emigrants," "visitors," and "fellow countrymen" increasingly made their appearance. Certain sections of Ukrainian organizations began to maintain closer relations with "friends," "sympathizers," and governments abroad.

The Second World War has brought to the center of the stage this element which hitherto, in the United States, had stayed largely in the wings. Certain developments signified its appearance in a more active role. In 1938 a Communazi Ukrainian Club was organized. In the same year Danilo Skoropadski, son of the first rated *hetman* visited the United States and had the pleasure of seeing the *Sichova Organisacia* revamp itself as the *United Hetman Organization*. "Delegates" from Germany "visited" American Ukrainian organizations. Ukrainian Americans received, and in several instances, accepted invitations to visit in Berlin and Vienna, and broadcast speeches introduced by none other than Dr. Goebbels. It is reported even that the president of a Ukrainian-American society was able to travel unmolested in Carpatho-Russia at a time of German domination when virtually no foreigners were permitted there. Simultaneously, in 1938, the European press began to feature articles about a *Greater Ukraine*. German leadership in a so-called Ukrainian movement had long been conspicuous.

Individual organizations were accused by their opponents of being undisguisedly pro-Nazi. The *United Hetman Organization* and the *Organization for the Rebirth of the Ukraine* were stamped as such organizations. The first of these ceased activities in March, 1942, only to reappear recently as the *League of Americans of Ukrainian Descent* [........]. The *Organization for the Rebirth of the Ukraine,* still in existence, may or may not be clearly pro-Nazi. Claims have been made that the *Providence Association Ukrainian National Association,* the *Ukrainian National Aid Association,* the *United Ukrainian Organizations,* and others were at least temporarily brought under the influence of the first two. Changes, originating in one quarter or another, have been made linking most of these directly with the *Ukrainian Nationalist Organization* led by Col. Andrew Melnik.

There is evidence that the democratic Ukrainian elements found themselves, to say the least, confused by the political activities represented by their organizations. The question of a *greater Ukrainia* became almost of necessity a question of *greater Ukrainia for whom?* Indeed, so thoroughly had the quest for the *free Ukrainia* become intermingled with entangling political policies that the primary nationalistic aim seems often to have been lost sight of. Personal recriminations and intrigue assumed a prominent rôle in the activities of Ukrainian organizations with the press serving as a frequently employed medium by which to make charges and to counter them.

The extent to which individual Ukrainians are carrying on subversive activities is a matter for the FBI and has been investigated by this agency. Whatever the actual extent of such anti-democratic activity – and there are indications that it has been considerable – it seems to be a danger only to the extent that it seeps down into the larger mass of American Ukrainians, introduces confusion, and interferes with American war efforts.

[........]

From the American standpoint it is probable that the Ukrainian must be appealed to chiefly on [an] economic level if he is to be weaned away from possible anti-democratic beliefs; the position of the priest in the Ukrainian community — still important — has lost its status of a decade or two ago. For a considerable segment of the Ukrainian-American population, the trades union, the factory, or his group of labor-associates serve increasingly as the milieu in which and the means by which his attitudes are formed.

Within the Ukrainians organizations operate, of course, on an unknown scale, the propaganda of the Third International. There are indications that the *Ukrainian American League*, a section of the *International Worker's Order*, and the *Ukrainian Working-men's Association* have been exposed to increased communist propaganda of late. In certain areas, at least, it is said that this influence has won over also certain of the former Social Democratic and Social Revolutionary elements. While pro-communist leanings have certainly not penetrated to masses of Ukrainians, they have, however, made significant inroads.

Not to be confused of necessity with pro-communism, is, on the other hand, the increased sympathy toward fighting Russia, even on the part of formerly violently anti-Soviet groups. This attitude is a cautious one: not incomparable to that held by many Americans, it recognizes the urgency of the war situation, is willing to admit the vital contribution of the Soviets, but, at the same time, continues to be unwilling to accept the communist ideology.

It should be realized that among considerable sectors of nationalistic Ukrainian organizations, the democratic principle has little offensive value. A pessimism pervades this group. It has not seen thus far, the establishment of democracy in Europe for its own people, it is sceptical of Democracy's honesty in the matter of national boundaries, and would not be surprised to find *Ukrainia* become again a buffer for political rivalries. By false logic, numbers of Ukrainians have been propagandized to the absurd conclusion that what the Democracies have failed to do, the New Order will accomplish. For some time the belief was widespread among Ukrainians both in Europe and in America that Hitler would grant autonomy or even freedom to all Ukrainian territories. The "sell-out" of Carpatho-Russia to Hungary, the establishment of *Gauleitern* rather than Ukrainian governors in occupied Galicia and Russian Ukraine has done considerably to alter this view.

The revival of propaganda has again tipped the balance, however, by throwing its weight on the thesis that Hitler's plans for the "independent Ukraine" have been tactically delayed, but not altered. Once again, accurate news on the actual situation in occupied Ukrainian lands is not available to the average Ukrainian. Organized German propaganda is thus able to fill him still with false notions of German benevolence and interest for the well-being of Ukrainians.

    [........]

SOURCE: RG 226, Entry 100
Box 96, UK 101-110
US National Archives

22

W. S. Greene, Chargé d'Affaires ad interim, *Legation of the United States of America, Stockholm, to US Secretary of State, 16 December 1942, Quarterly Report on Nazi-occupied Ukraine Describing Political Conditions and Growing Nationalist Insurgency.*

LEGATION OF THE
UNITED STATES OF AMERICA

No. 1232

STOCKHOLM, SWEDEN
DECEMBER 16, 1942

POLITICAL CONDITIONS IN THE UKRAINE IN OCTOBER 1942

The Honorable
The Secretary of State
Washington

Sir:

I have the honor to refer to despatch No. 1108, dated November 3, 1942, entitled *Political and Educational Conditions in the Ukraine in September 1942,* and to enclose a similar memorandum prepared by the Legation's Special Reporting Section covering the month of October 1942.

[........]

This report, which follows the outline given on its first page, may be briefly summarized as follows.

The chief characteristics of the situation in the Ukraine seem to be: (1) the predominant position being established for the Reich Germans and to a lesser extent for the so-called German *nationals;* (2) the great efforts being made by German propaganda to induce the Ukrainians to *collaborate;* and (3) the apparently growing resistance of the latter.

An important decree was published in the period under review providing for the return in *usufruct* to German nationals belonging to sections 1 to 3 of the German *racial list* of agricultural and other real estate, houses, business establishments etcetera. In carrying out this decree, consideration is to be given to the value of property said to have been stolen or destroyed by the Bolsheviks.

The provisions of this decree contrast significantly with the corresponding situation in the Ostland (i.e., the three former Baltic States and White Ruthenia), where the problem of *denationalization* of property is much simpler, as it has only to go back over a short period of the recent Soviet occupation, as compared with the Ukraine, where property has been *nationalized* for a longer period. The reason for this difference in German policy is presumably the result of different conditions in the Ukraine and in the Ostland. In the latter area, the Germans probably feel that the local population is more dependable, from their point of view, whereas the Ukrainians are less likely to collaborate with the Reich and thus the Germans are faced with the necessity of endeavoring to build up a local group on which they can rely. Hence they are tackling a problem there which is much more difficult than in the Ostland.

Nevertheless, it is clear that this and other similar discriminatory legislative enactments will serve to increase the hostility of the Ukrainian people toward the New Order. This situation is not helped by German references to the *Herrenvolk* idea and to Germany's "historic mission" in the east.

Further decrees issued during the month of October 1942, which tend to strengthen the position of the Germans vis-à-vis the Ukrainians include the following: (1) the introduction of the German Hunting Laws in the Ukraine, which mean in effect that the Ukrainians will no longer be permitted to hunt in their own country; and (2) *Reich* German forest officials have been authorized to use their weapons against persons suspected of illegal hunting or of stealing firewood from the so-called closed forests.

The memorandum also includes information about other developments intended to solidify the German position in the Ukraine, such as choosing pupils from the German population for the *Langemarck* studies, organizing new tours of the *Reich,* and the establishment of a home for German nationals at Nikolayev.

In this connection, it is worth noting that even the German-controlled press indicates the difficulties in bringing back all German *nationals* into the fold of *German national consciousness,* as so many of those in the Ukraine have been residing there for a long time.

It seems probable, on the basis of all available information, that the economic position of the Ukrainians has deteriorated under the German occupation, due to the increasing shortage of general consumption goods, and that this situation, coupled with the obvious steps being taken to establish a preferential status for *Reich* Germans and German nationals, seems likely to prevent any great collaboration on the part of the Ukrainians.

Nevertheless, the Germans are continuing their efforts in this direction, not only by a great volume of radio and press propaganda and by frequent addresses by officials, but also by more subtle methods which include the organization of tours of Germany for "deserving" Ukrainians (such as former *kulaks*) and the sending of Ukrainian "deserving" workers back from Germany on holiday trips to the homeland, where they are given an appropriate reception.

In this connection, the Swedish daily *Aftonbladet* for November 5, 1942, contained an interesting article by Gunnar Mullern, formerly its Berlin correspondent (1939-1941), in which he claims that the Germans are at last realizing the necessity of treating the Ukrainians better, in order to improve the morale of this *civilian garrison* in the *fortress of Europe.* This idea makes interesting reading against the background of the Legation's telegram No. 3088, dated November 2, 5 p.m., although it appears, from all available evidence, that thus far there have not been many signs of such a change in German policy. Mullern cites as examples the reintroduction of a certain degree of local government run by the Ukrainians and efforts to secure collaboration by the local clergy, although it appears to the Legation that such steps differ but little from similar developments in the Ostland. Whether or not such a change in German policy has in fact occurred should become more evident in the coming months.

Apart from the Ukrainian *self-government,* in which it is true that certain lower administrative posts have been given to Ukrainians, the other most important organization from the point of view of possible *collaboration* seems to be the Ukrainian Militia, a police force which the Germans are endeavoring to develop from the local inhabitants. Thus far this organization has, however, apparently not been entrusted with greater responsibilities than the maintenance of order in the city of Kiev, including the control of traffic and market conditions.

The German-controlled press of the Ukraine made further mention of *guerilla* activities in the month under review, from which it is apparent that this form of warfare is still going on. In this connection the memorandum contains extracts from an interesting report obtained by the Legation from a private source (transmitted by airgram No. A 59, November 6, 1942), which suggests that even members of the local German-appointed administrative bodies take part in these guerilla activities, and that effective German control does not extend much beyond the towns and lines of communication. For this reason the Legation's informant believes the Germans are getting even less supplies from the Ukraine than they did in 1918.

The memorandum closes with a few items about education. [........]

Respectfully yours,

[sgd.] WINTHROP S. GREENE

Chargé d'Affaires ad interim

SOURCE: M1286 Reel 4
State Department Records
US National Archives

23

Transcript of Conversation Between Marshal Stalin and British Foreign Secretary A. Eden, 17 December 1942, Regarding Territorial Changes in Eastern Europe.

RECORD OF A MEETING BETWEEN THE FOREIGN SECRETARY AND
M. STALIN, DECEMBER 17th, 1942, MIDNIGHT

MR. EDEN. You have probably seen the work we did this morning on the Agreements.

M. STALIN. Yes, the work is very interesting but I am more interested in the question of the future frontiers of the USSR. Have you yet been able to get any decisions from your government?

MR. EDEN. No. Nor have I tried to get any. I have not telegraphed for this purpose and with the Prime Minister on the High Seas there is no responsible person who could state the views of His Majesty's Government on the matter. I have telegraphed the Prime Minister an account of our interview last night and I have told him I would bring back your suggestions as to the future frontiers of Europe and that I would discuss them in London and then communicate again with you through diplomatic channels.

M. STALIN. You will remember that last night we talked of the possibility of doing something as regards the frontiers of the USSR apart from the general question of Central and Western European frontiers. The Soviet Government is very interested in this question because during the time of the Chamberlain Government in the earlier negotiations they broke down on this very question of the Baltic countries and Finland and we want to know what is the position on this matter of the present British Government.

MR. EDEN. Of course, I was not a member of the Chamberlain Government at that time so I cannot tell what went on in the Government. I do, however, fully realize that you want security on your North Western frontier and also I bear in mind that two have signed the Atlantic Charter. I am afraid it is impossible for me to give you any decision on this question because that decision must be a decision of the British Government. All I can do is to report to them what your views are and then communicate, as I have promised, with you again through diplomatic channels.

M. STALIN. Is it really necessary on this question of the Baltic States to have a Government decision? Surely this is absolutely axiomatic. We are fighting our hardest and losing hundreds of thousands of men in the common cause with Great Britain as our Ally and I should have thought that such a question as the position of the Baltic States ought to be axiomatic and ought not to require any decision.

MR. EDEN. You mean the future of the Baltic States at the end of the war?

M. STALIN. Yes. Would you support the entry of these three States at the end of the war into the Soviet Union?

MR. EDEN. The present position is that we do not recognize the independent existence of any of these states. They have no diplomatic status with us but we are committed to the United States of America not to bind ourselves as to any decision upon European frontiers before the end of the war without consultation with them. I am, however, prepared to seek a decision from my Government on this issue and also consult the Americans upon it as soon as I get back to London. I think it is most desirable that all three Governments should come to an agreement on this question.

M. STALIN. In that case I am afraid there will be great difficulty in coming to any agreement on these proposed treaties.

MR. EDEN. This is really quite a new issue which you are raising. You will remember that the Prime Minister has long since stated publicly that we cannot acknowledge, during the war, any changes of sovereignty that have been made since the beginning of the war.

M. STALIN. Last night I put forward the question of your recognizing at least the post-war frontiers of the USSR. We might re-occupy the Baltic States in the near future and how are we to know that in that event Great Britain will not deny to us these frontiers?

MR. EDEN. The Prime Minister made his statement that we would not recognize changes made during the war while Germany was advancing and that statement was really to the advantage of the USSR. The statement was made publicly to the whole world and it is quite clear that I cannot now decide this issue though, as I have said, I am prepared to take it up when I return to London.

M. STALIN. If you say that, you might well say tomorrow that you do not recognize the Ukraine as forming part of the USSR.

MR. EDEN. That is a complete misunderstanding of the position. It is only changes from the pre-war frontiers that we do not recognize. The only change in the Ukraine is its occupation by Germany, so, of course, we accept the Ukraine as being part of the USSR.

M. STALIN. This seems to be just the same position as was taken by the Chamberlain Government on the question of the Baltic States, and in that event it is difficult to come to any terms on these agreements.

MR. EDEN. I can only say that I am sorry if that is so. Our position is perfectly clear. The Americans have asked us not to agree to any altered boundaries in Europe but I am prepared to put the question up to my Government and to the Americans and then to give you the answer. I cannot give you that answer now without consulting the Americans. If you wish for it and attach great importance to this point then I will try and get a favourable answer for you upon it. There is this difference between the present and the earlier negotiations which I should like to make plain. At the time of the earlier negotiations the Baltic States were free and independent states. Since that time those States have ceased to exist as independent States and, therefore, *de facto* the situation is now a completely different one.

M. STALIN. Where is the evidence of that? You still have their representatives in London.

MR. EDEN. We don't accept them as representatives. We neither accept notes from them nor allow them diplomatic status. The USSR is in fact recognized as having the *de facto* sovereignty of the Baltic States.

M. STALIN. That seems to be a very curious situation.

MR. EDEN. I agree it may seem curious but I don't really think that this is a very important political question. The present position is that there are no independent Baltic States and that in fact they do form part of the USSR. I am prepared to get an answer for you on your question if you wish for it from the British Government.

M. STALIN. I am surprised and amazed at Mr. Churchill's Government taking up this position. It is practically the same as that of the Chamberlain Government.

MR. EDEN. I have tried to explain to you what the difference is. The Baltic States have now ceased to exist as independent states and they are in fact part of the Soviet Union. Do you want me to say that they are recognized *de jure* as part of the USSR?

M. STALIN. We are in the midst of the greatest war of history and I think these nice formulas about *de jure* and *de facto* etc. are rather out of place. According to our Constitution the three States form part of USSR. This is the result of a plebiscite in which the great majority of all the inhabitants voted in favour of coming into the USSR. If the USSR retained these three republics in their constitution does the British Government have any objection?

MR. EDEN. Of course, we cannot take objection to what the Soviet Government do or do not put into their Constitution.

M. STALIN. If so, and the British Government does not have any objection then some method of saying that should be found.

MR. EDEN. My difficulties, and I want to be perfectly frank about this, are two-fold. Firstly, the Prime Minister has stated publicly that we could not accept any territorial changes made during the war. It may be that this particular change is an exceptional one and if you wish it I will consult the British Government on that basis and let you have their answer. Secondly, under the Atlantic Charter we have pledged ourselves to take into account the wishes of the inhabitants. It may be that in this case they have been taken into account but that is a matter that we must check up on before we arrive at a decision.

M. STALIN. Yes, they were taken into account before the war.

MR. EDEN. But not before our war started with Germany.

M. STALIN. Then I think we shall have to postpone the signing of the two treaties.

MR. EDEN. That, of course, is for you to decide. I should like to meet you but I cannot do so without consulting my Government and the USA. I should not have thought that that was any good reason for not signing these Agreements which will be of value to both our countries and which offer greater possibilities for the future of our arriving at an Agreement upon this question of frontiers and certainly do not in any way prejudice it.

M. STALIN. It is not only the question of the Baltic States but of the whole of the Western Frontiers of the Soviet Union.

MR. EDEN. I should like you to understand my position in this matter. I promised President Roosevelt, and it was nothing to do with this present visit of mine, indeed before the Russian Government came into the war, not to agree to any changes in the European boundaries without consultation. You will agree that if I had made such an agreement with you you would expect me to keep it. There is nothing in these proposed Agreements which in any way prevents my putting the question of your Western boundaries up to the USA.

M. STALIN. I think that the whole war between us and Germany began because of these western frontiers of the USSR including particularly the Baltic States. That is really what the whole war is about, and what I would like to know is whether our Ally, Great Britain, supports us in regaining these Western frontiers.

MR. EDEN. We in this war are fighting for lots of peoples frontiers. As you know we went to war because of the aggression against Poland but we have never tied ourselves down to any particular frontiers, as you will remember we stated [that] clearly in the Polish-Russian negotiations. If, however, you wish us to agree to some specific boundaries now I will try to get it done but I cannot do it now myself as I am bound by my promise to America.

M. STALIN. We are bound by the provisions of our Constitution.

MR. EDEN. Of course, you are and we have no objection whatever to that, but we are not bound by your Constitution. Up to this point I have not agreed to any frontiers anywhere in Europe. I didn't hear of these frontiers which you now propose until I came here last night and I cannot agree to them until I have consulted both my own Government and America.

M. STALIN. This attitude of the British Government towards our frontiers is indeed a surprise for me so I think it will be better to postpone the proposed Agreements.

MR. EDEN. There is nothing new at all about our attitude. We should expect, if we were to sign these agreements, to consult with you on questions of European boundaries such as, for instance, the French boundary and the question of Alsace and Lorraine and that is one of the things that this Agreement says.

M. STALIN. Tomorrow, perhaps, our troops might occupy the three Baltic States and then perhaps at the Peace Conference you would take an objection to that occupation.

MR. EDEN. If you were to do so no one would be more delighted than myself.

M. STALIN. I don't understand.

MR. EDEN. This is the position. In your view and according to your Constitution the three states now form part of the USSR. In our view at the moment they are neither within it nor without it. If you wish us to come to a decision upon this I can consult the American Government.

M. STALIN. Great Britain and the USSR are now Allies and as I understand it an Ally must support an Ally. If anyone were to come to me and ask me as to the desirability of touching the Irish Free State I should tell him to get out. If Great Britain wanted air and military bases in Belgium and Holland I should certainly give my support to it, because it affected the safety of Britain and raises the question of their security.

MR. EDEN. This is not a question of loyalty but we have committed ourselves to America as I have stated, and the Prime Minister has made a public statement to which I have referred. I am sure that you would not respect me if I were to go back upon my arrangement with President Roosevelt. I can get a decision upon this point before the Soviet troops occupy the Baltic States even if they continue doing as well as they are doing now.

M. STALIN. If you cannot give us your support on this question of our Western frontiers, which is the main question for us in the war, perhaps it would be best to postpone these agreements and to fall back upon our agreement of July last.

MR. EDEN. That is the matter for you to decide. From the point of view of Anglo-Soviet relations there would undoubtedly be a great disappointment in our country and in the Dominions. Nothing in these agreements in any way weakens the claims that you have put forward as regards frontiers.

M. STALIN. We too have our public opinion here and they would certainly be horrified if they learnt that Great Britain was not prepared to support us on the question of our frontiers in the Baltic States.

MR. EDEN. There is certainly nothing of that sort in the agreements nor is it in the least necessarily the position.

M. STALIN. If our people were to learn that after their sacrifices Great Britain, our Ally, was reluctant to support the claim of the USSR that the Baltic States in fact form part of the USSR then they would certainly regard these treaties as scraps of paper.

MR. EDEN. I don't think that that is a fair way of putting it. I had never heard of these western boundaries until I got here and I cannot agree to them without first putting them to my own Government and to the Dominions and to America. But that does not in the least prevent us being loyal allies or from doing all we can to help you to defeat the Germans.

M. STALIN. You were in general informed of the two questions of importance. Military collaboration and post-war reconstruction including the question of frontiers. If the general question of European frontiers is a difficult one to decide upon at least that of the Soviet frontiers is in a different category.

MR. EDEN. I have always, as you know, been very strongly in favour of promoting good relations between our two countries but there are limitations to the power of a Minister in our country and I cannot commit the country to your propositions without consulting my own Government, the Dominions and the USA.

M. STALIN. I am far from blaming you for your attitude and I know very well of your desire to improve relations between our two countries. I would not like to blame the British Government but I am surprised that upon this question our Allies cannot give us their support.

MR. EDEN. Let me take the case of Canada and the question of the frontier between Poland and Russia. Canada has sent us hundreds of thousands of soldiers to help in the war and if they were to hear tomorrow that I had agreed upon the Polish-Russian frontier without any consultation with them they would have every right to the strongest complaint. No Minister who did a thing like that could survive for 24 hours.

M. STALIN. I certainly do not want to demand the impossible from you and I fully realize the limitation of your powers but I am addressing myself to the British Government and I am genuinely surprised. I thought that the Atlantic Charter was directed against those people who were trying to establish world dominion. It now looks as if the Charter was directed against the USSR.

MR. EDEN. No, that is certainly not so. It is merely a question of your putting forward certain views as to your frontiers and of my being unable to give you an immediate reply and asking you to allow me time to get the answer.

M. STALIN. Why does the restoration of our frontiers come into conflict with the Atlantic Charter?

MR. EDEN. I never said that it did.

M. STALIN. When you gave your pledges to America we were not then Allies of yours and our relations were very different. At that time the British and French Governments were contemplating giving help to Finland against the Soviet Union. Now you are at war with Finland.

MR. EDEN. And we did that in order to please you.

M. STALIN. Yes, I understand that but the position is now changed.

MR. EDEN. If you were asking for the frontiers which existed in 1939 before the war broke out between us and Germany there would be no difficulty at all but now you are asking for frontiers which differ from those of 1939 in various places. I have taken a note of that and will report it to my Government, but I cannot see how these Agreements that [we] proposed to sign will make it any more difficult for us to give you the answer that you want.

M. STALIN. It makes it look as if I should have to come cap in hand.

MR. EDEN. Not at all, I don't understand that. These are documents of perfect equality and don't represent the conferring of anything by either party upon the other.

M. MOLOTOV. We are talking of common war aims, of what we are both fighting for. On one of these important aims, our western frontiers, we have no support from Great Britain.

MR. EDEN. It is not a question of support or lack of support. For the first time last night I heard the details of the boundaries which you thought you ought to have. It is a technical question as M. Molotov will realize in his position as Foreign Secretary of the consents that we must obtain. No English Foreign Secretary for the last two hundred years could have done what you are asking me to do.

M. MOLOTOV. It is a question of the decision of the British Government and not of yourself.

MR. EDEN. If the Prime Minister and myself were both here we still could not give you that decision. It is a question of our meeting the demands of the USSR. We are fighting as a family with our Dominions and we must consult them.

M. STALIN. Last night when we were discussing the question of the whole map of Europe it was obviously new and a complicated matter and I did not insist upon your accepting our views, and agreed that they should be referred to your Cabinet but the Western frontier of the USSR is in a different category and should surely be an easy matter as between allies.

MR. EDEN. I agree, of course, that it is in a different category but it is still a question of frontiers in Europe and of some complication since these run from Finland and the Baltic States in the North to Rumania in the South. I cannot say more than that, I will report the matter to my Cabinet. How could I agree, for instance, to the Polish-Russian frontier without saying a word about it to the Poles first.

M. STALIN. The Polish frontier remains an open question and I do not insist upon settling that now. What I am most interested in is the position in Finland and the Baltic States and in Rumania. With regard to Poland, I hope that we shall be able to come to an agreement between the three of us. Generally speaking our idea is to keep to the Curzon Line with certain modifications. But it is very important for us to know whether we shall have to fight at the Peace Conference in order to get our Western Frontiers.

MR. EDEN. I am certainly hoping not. As to Poland we shall always, of course, be glad to do anything we can to help in reaching an agreement. We want to agree to the frontiers before the peace conference but we have not yet reached that point and it seems to me to be not unreasonable to ask you to let me consult the necessary persons on these very important proposals.

M. STALIN. I fully appreciate your position, that you cannot give me any definite answers.

MR. EDEN. I am sorry to appear difficult. I certainly don't want to be but under our constitution that is my position.

M. STALIN. I fully realize that.

[........]

SOURCE: FO 181/963
Public Record Office

24

Letter from G. de T. Glazebrook, Canadian
Department of External Affairs, to A. J. Halpern,
British Security Co-ordination, New York,
30 March 1943, Replying to British Requests
for Exchange of Intelligence on
Ukrainian-Canadian Organizations.

SECRET
BY SAFE HAND

OTTAWA
30TH MARCH, 1943

Dear Halpern,

With reference to your letter of March 24th and previous correspondence concerning Ukrainians, I am now forwarding copy of a secret report which we have received from the Royal Canadian Mounted Police in regard to another Ukrainian organization. This is the Ukrainian-Canadian Association which was formed amongst the Communist and Leftist Ukrainians following the German invasion of Russia, and which held a national Convention in Winnipeg last June. It is, of course, in violent opposition to the Ukrainian National Federation and is also hostile to the Ukrainian-Canadian Committee in which the UNF have played a very influential part. You will see from the RCMP report that the enmity amongst these organizations has led even to violence. In the absence of any well organized moderate opinion amongst Ukrainian-Canadians, leadership seems to be falling into the hands of one or another of these extremist groups. Both are nationalist but the Ukrainian-Canadian Association holds that Ukrainian nationalism has been achieved within the framework of the Ukrainian-Soviet and that it lacks only the inclusion within the Soviet of the Western Ukrainian territories in Poland and Czechoslovakia. The other organization, of course, regards Ukrainian nationalism as attainable only on the dismemberment of both Russia and Poland. There is here the material for much embarrassing conflict though it is not clear how strong a following either of these organizations actually has. Most Ukrainian-Canadians are probably more interested in Canada than in Europe, and give their support one way or the other to the local Ukrainian organizations depending on a general interest in radical reform or alternatively on a general sympathy for Ukrainian nationalism.

Yours sincerely,
[sgd.] G. DE T. GLAZEBROOK

A. J. Halpern
British Security Co-ordination
Room 3553, 630 Fifth Avenue
New York, USA

Source: RG 25 G1, Vol. 1896
File 165, Part III
Public Archives of Canada

25

N. A. Robertson, Canadian Under Secretary of State for External Affairs, to J. G. Grierson, Wartime Information Board, 17 May 1943, Recommending New Policy Initiatives in Dealing with Ukrainian Canadians.

PERSONAL AND CONFIDENTIAL

OTTAWA
MAY 17TH, 1943

Dear John,

Glazebrook has spoken to me of his conversations with you about Soviet complaints of the activities of the Ukrainian-Canadian Committee and its constituent organizations. Prior to the Moscow despatches which have been carried in last week's Canadian press, I had had a word on the subject with the Soviet Minister, who spoke of the Ukrainian Nationalists as Fascists and enquired why our Censorship authorities could not suppress newspapers which, in effect, advocated partition of the territory of an ally. He had in mind, particularly, the memorandum submitted to the Government in March last by the Ukrainian Canadian Committee, in which a plea was made for Canadian support of the Ukrainian claim to self-determination. Ironically enough, the occasion of this Ukrainian memorandum was the unfortunate declaration of Polish policy of February 25th which provoked the Soviet counter statements and the subsequent suspension of diplomatic relations between the USSR and Poland.

The Ukrainian question has been, for a good many years, a source of irritation in our relations with Poland, against which Ukrainian irredentism has been primarily directed. It now looks as if it may become an even more troublesome factor in our relations with the Soviet Union. One important aspect of this question is its treatment in the Canadian foreign language press, Ukrainian, Polish and Russian. I have felt for a long time that we should be receiving prompter and more objective summaries of political comment in the foreign language press than have been made available by the Press Censors service and the Translation Division of the

Department of National Revenue. I am hopeful that the new arrangements under which the preparation of these press summaries
will be concentrated under the Wartime Information Board will effect a real improvement in the present position which will be of use
to the Press Censors and to this Department, as well as to WIB. The
latter, I think, has a special and positive responsibility in relation
to the foreign language press which, in the past, has been worked
over and interfered with from time to time by three or four different agencies of the Federal Government, none of which has ever
been given any clear directives in policy and none of which has
really been properly equipped in respect of personnel or authority
to do durably useful work in this field.

I think the first thing to be done is probably to take an inven-
tory of the various Government agencies which have been monkey-
ing with the foreign language press and bring them together in an
examination for discovery which will establish what had been attempted and accomplished and where matters now stand. For this
purpose, I think you would want to have present representatives
of the Department of National War Services, including the Committee on Education in Canadian Citizenship and the Press Censors, the RCMP and the Department of Justice (reference to preven-
tive or punitive measures taken under the Defence of Canada
Regulations), the Department of the Secretary of State, insofar as
the assets of illegal organizations, including newspapers, are still
in their custody, and, of course, this Department which takes an
extra-curricular interest in a good many questions not specifically
enumerated in the Statute and/or Order-in-Council setting it up.

I think the step suggested is the first one to be taken. It will be
followed, I hope, by the concentration of contact with the foreign
language press under the Wartime Information Board, which I
would expect to work in very close consultation with this Department on any aspect of relations with the foreign language press
which might directly or indirectly affect Canada's relations with
other countries. This assumption of responsibility by WIB will, of
course, require some strengthening and stiffening of your staff, as
the work to be done is technical and treacherous, and the experts
are apt to have axes to grind.

To revert to the particular, the Ukrainian question in Canada
is difficult and delicate. There were, before the war, five or six
Ukrainian organizations, organized and divided according to the
political, religious and social interests and attitudes of their
members. The major line of demarcation, however, was between
the various Ukrainian nationalist movements on one side and the

Ukrainian Communist associations on the other. In the period immediately before the war, the Ukrainian Nationalists were pretty ardent Municheers, whose hopes had been raised by the temporary separation of Carpathian Ruthenia from Czechoslovakia. It is from this period that most of the "evidence" of Fascist sympathies on the part of the Ukrainian Nationalists dates. It was a very brief spell of self-delusion which did not last much longer with the Ukrainians than with the other people who believed we had secured peace in our time, for the Ukrainian hopes, built upon the Munich settlement, were dashed, very promptly, by the Hungarian annexation of the Carpathian Ukraine. When the war broke out the Ukrainian Nationalists by and large gave the Canadian war effort their good and loyal support. The Ukrainian Communists, on the other hand, following the party line, opposed it. A great deal of water has run over the dam since then and now Ukrainian Communists are themselves staunchly supporting the general war effort. The background of controversy, however, is still pretty recent and can be inflamed again, as we have seen in these last weeks. I think there is an important job of work to be done by the Wartime Information Board in this field and I think it is one which will have to be planned pretty carefully, taking all the relevant factors into consideration.

Yours sincerely,

[sgd.] N. A. ROBERTSON

SOURCE: RG 2 Series 18,
Vol. 43, File V-15-2
Public Archives of Canada

26

Report by F. Savery Prepared for the British Foreign Secretary, A. Eden, 24 January 1944, Characterizing Minorities Situation in Eastern Poland.

24 JANUARY, 1944

MINORITIES IN EASTERN POLAND AND
THE SLAV MINORITIES IN GENERAL

In dealing with this part of the question one must consider two possibilities – a Poland with her eastern frontier following the old Riga line and a Poland shorn of much of her eastern territory.

2. The first alternative would leave inside Poland a very large Ukrainian Minority with a developed national consciousness and a very uneasy conscience as regards its behaviour towards the Poles under both the Soviet and the German occupations, a smaller, though still fairly large, White Russian [Byelorussian] Minority with a much less developed national consciousness and – probably – a less uneasy conscience as regards war-time sins against the Poles; a small but extremely bellicose Lithuanian Minority which has probably taken its share in the efforts of the Lithuanian nation as a whole to get rid of the Polish element in the Wilno region; and a large number of Jews who differ in many respects from the Jews of Galicia and Central Poland and have generally been less loyal to the Polish State or, at any rate, have had less close and friendly relations with the Poles.

3. If Poland recovers her eastern territories, she will certainly have to accept as citizens of the Polish State all the prewar inhabitants of those provinces, whatever their attitude towards Poland and the Poles may have been during the war. There will be far more Ukrainians and White Russians and probably far more Lithuanians, too, in the Soviet Union than on Polish territory. Is there any possible way by which the Polish Government can prevent these national Minorities from becoming nursery gardens in which the Soviet Government, appearing as the champion either of the proletariat or of the Orthodox Church can rear up trouble-

makers for the Polish State?

4. It is, I think, conceivable that once again, as between 1926 and 1939, the White Russians might succumb to the prestige of polonism and begin to assimilate themselves spontaneously — often by way of the Roman Catholic Church of the Latin rite. It is, however, much less likely, in my opinion, that this will happen if, in the new Poland, the upper-classes lose all influence and the country is run by and for the peasants and workers. The White Russian [Byelorussian] peasants regard Poles of the squire class, including priests, as beings of a superior, if not always very agreeable, order: I do not think that they have the same feelings as regards Poles of the same class as themselves. It is, I imagine, quite certain that the Soviet authorities would run propaganda on the other side of the frontier and the poverty of the whole Wilno region, where there are no industries, the land is not as a rule very fertile and the climate everywhere very hard, is so great that it is not easy to counteract propaganda based on appeals to the stomach.

5. The situation as regards the Ukrainian Minority in Poland is, I think, even more difficult. There is no doubt that the Polish element in Eastern Galicia, where it used to be economically very strong, will be much weaker — both, economically and numerically — after the war than it was in 1939. The same will be the case in Wolhynia and Polesia where even before the war there were very few Poles. Stalin once said to Sikorski that the Soviet Union and Poland would have to take common measures to put a stop to the Ukrainian nuisance. With a whole continent behind him in which to execute, starve or exploit those who impede his policy, Stalin is in a position, if he wishes, to get rid of any Minority inside the Soviet Union. Poland has no Siberia at her disposal and she is also inhibited by the possession of moral principles like our own. Whatever Stalin may do to his Ukrainians and however many settlers from other parts of the Soviet Union he may bring in to change the ethnic character of the population of the Ukraine, the Polish Government will have to leave their Ukrainians to live in their old homes. Personally, I do not see how they will be able to avoid giving them a far-reaching autonomy. The Ukrainians will not be contented and loyal citizens of a Polish State unless they can make their weight felt in its general policy — it may be doubted whether even in that case they would be really reliable citizens, but let that pass for the present. If they have a voice in the conduct of the Polish State, they will certainly interest themselves in the fate of their fellow-Ukrainians outside Poland. If they do this, it is not certain that they will involve the Polish Govern-

ment in troubles with the Soviet Government. I am profoundly sorry for the Ukrainians of Eastern Galicia who have, I am sure, no desire to live under the Soviet rule – whatever may be the feelings of the Ukrainians of Wolhynia and Polesia – but it seems to me that if Poland is to avoid chronic trouble with the USSR, the Ukrainian population of Poland must be so small that not even the morbidly sensitive Bolsheviks will regard it as a potential danger. Is it carrying cynicism too far to suggest that, if Poland has a very small Ukrainian Minority and especially if that Minority consists of Orthodox and not of Greek-Catholic Ukrainians, the Russians will do their best to make use of it, as they did of the "dissidents" of the 18th century, to interfere in the internal affairs of the Polish State?

6. Let us now take the second alternative – that the new Poland will be shorn of much of the eastern territory which the Polish State possessed between 1921 and 1939. To begin with the north, she will perhaps lose everything or nearly everything east of the Curzon Line. That will, however, leave outside Poland not only the very numerous Poles who live scattered all over the country to the east of Bialystok but also the solid mass of Poles in and around Wilno. These Poles of the north constitute a most valuable element. Pilsudski was one of them, so was Mickiewicz. It is not quite absurd to say that they stand to the Poles of Galicia somewhat as the Scots do to the people of southern England. It is possible, I am afraid, that these Poles, who are profoundly attached to their corner of Poland and are as immovably obstinate as a granite mountain, may refuse to leave their homes even if they have the offer of new lands in some other part of Poland. I hope, however, that that will not be the case. I look upon East Prussia as the predestined home of these Lithuanian Poles and for that reason, as well as on other grounds, I consider it indispensable that the Poles be allowed to turn out the German inhabitants of that province when it is handed over to them.

7. Moving southwards along the Curzon Line where it follows the River Bug the Minority question is much less troublesome until the old Austro-Russian frontier is reached near Sokal. According to the 1931 census there were at that time in the Lublin *voivodeship* 210,000 persons belonging to the Orthodox Church, constituting 9.9 per cent of the total population as against 1605,000 Roman Catholics (75 per cent of the total population). When the Congress Kingdom of Poland was established in 1815, it included two districts – Podlachia and Chelm – in which the Slav inhabitants were, in the main, Uniates of the Greek-Catholic rite

like the East Galician Ukrainians and not Roman Catholics of the
Latin rite. The Uniate Church in these, its last, strongholds on
Russian territory was suppressed by the Imperial Government
about 1878. By that time, however, the peasant population,
especially in Podlachia, had developed a Polish national consciousness. As soon as they had a chance — in 1905, when the Imperial Government issued a *ukase* under which, for the first time,
Russian subjects were allowed to leave the Orthodox Church —
very many of the inhabitants passed over to the Roman Catholic
Church, which they joined in its western, Latin form. From then
onwards, the population of Podlachia was, in general, scarcely
distinguishable from the rest of the Slav population of Congress
Poland: that is to say, the overwhelming majority was completely
Polish. According to the 1931 census there were about 18,000 Orthodox as against 83,000 Roman-Catholics in the Biala *powiat* and
hardly any Orthodox at all on any other part of former Podlachia.
The Czarist Government must, I think, have come to realize the
hopelessness of the struggle in Podlachia, but they continued right
down to 1914 their efforts to strengthen the Orthodox element in
the Chelm region and to detach it from Congress Poland. It was
the action of the Austrian representative at Brest-Litovsk in sur-
rendering that region to Russia which contributed more than
anything else to break the loyalty of the Galician Poles to the
Habsburg Monarchy. The settlers whom the Czarist Government
planted in the Chelm region were, I believe, often "Great Russians"
rather than Ukrainians but they tended to become ukrainized
through contact with the autochtonous Ukrainians. Needless to
say, the Czarist Government had also built plenty of Orthodox
churches and chapels. Many of these were permanently closed and,
so far as I could judge, the lack of services in them was not generally felt as a hardship in view of the considerable number still open
and in use. The fact was, that the churches had, in many cases,
been a missionary effort and were not required for the needs of the
local population. None the less it was immediately felt as a
grievance when in, I think, 1938 a very ill-advised general in command in the district set to work to dismantle some of them. I
should like to add that his action was strongly reprobated by most
Poles of my acquaintance, including several priests.

    8. The 1931 census furnishes statistics of population according
to both mother tongue and religion. According to the former there
were in the Lublin *voivodeship* about 74,000 persons speaking
Ukrainian as their mother tongue as against 1,814,000 Polish-
speakers. The statistics of religion give 210,000 Orthodox as

against 1,605,000 Roman Catholics. My experience was that the use of the Polish language had made considerable progress in the Chelm district between 1919 and 1939 and it would not surprise me if by 1939 20 per cent of the Orthodox population of the *voivodeship* could fairly be described as Polish-speaking. At the same time since 1939 the Germans have been fostering the Ukrainian movement and the Orthodox religion in the Chelm region, and I dare say that in consequence a certain number of persons who in 1931 honestly described themselves as Polish-speaking have been brought back, at any rate temporarily, into the Ukrainian fold. Leaving out of consideration the 18,000 persons of that faith in the Biala district in the north, the Orthodox in the Latin *voivodeship* are to be found along the Upper Bug (districts of Wlodawa 33,000, Chelm, 35,000 and Hrubieszów 49,000) and then westwards in the districts of Tomaszów (33,000) and Bilgoraj (21,000). Hrubieszów is the only one of these districts in which the Orthodox are anything like as numerous as the Roman Catholics – 49,000 as against 63,000. North and north-west of Tomaszów and Bilgoraj, in the districts of Zamość and Janów the Orthodox dwindle to a very small minority. A few years before the outbreak of the present war, when the economic crisis was being very acutely felt in the rural districts of Poland, a curious episode occurred. The country folk of some villages in, I think, the Tomaszów district, held meetings at which cries of *Long live Stalin* were heard. Such meetings were only held in Ukrainian, i.e., non-Catholic, villages. The neighbouring Polish villages, where the economic situation was just the same, took no part in them. As was explained in the preceding paragraph, what is roughly called the Chelm region has always greatly interested the Russians, who in the past have certainly tried to separate it from ethnographic Poland. There are, I think, some signs that during this war, too, the Soviet Government have tried to stake a claim on the left bank of the Bug, where the population contains a Ukrainian element. Before the Ribbentrop-Molotov line was laid down the Soviet forces did, in fact, occupy some territory to the west of the Bug. Some of my Polish informants have told me that in the matter of parachutists and guerilla bands the Russians are more active in the eastern and south-eastern parts of the Lublin *voivodeship* than anywhere else in the General Government.

9. We now come to Eastern Galicia. Let us suppose for the moment that Lwów remains inside Poland. That means that, unless they can be got rid of by exchange or deportation, there will be quite a lot of Ukrainians in that part of Poland – mainly in the

districts between Lwów and the River San but also in the hilly
districts at the south-eastern extremity of the Cracow *voivodeship*, where the so-called *Lemki* live. At the same time it is most
unlikely that the Polish-Russian frontier in Galicia will be fixed so
far to the east that Tarnopol and Trembowla not to mention
Skalat, which lay on the old Austro-Russian frontier, will be inside
Poland. According to the 1931 census those three districts *(powia-
ty)* had about 200,000 Poles out of a total population of 315,000.
Unfortunately, as regards the Tarnopol *voivodeship* I have no
"confessional" statistics by which to check the statistics based on
mother tongue. Needless to say a very large number of these
200,000 Poles belong to the working class — generally peasants
and their families. I see no possible solution of the "minority question" in Eastern Galicia likely to be satisfactory for Poland in the
long run short of an exchange of population on a large scale. I
think that in all probability the Polish peasants from Eastern
Galicia would rather take up new holdings in Central Galicia (between Lwów and the San) than live under the Soviet régime. But
how about the Ukrainians who now live in parts of Galicia which I
am assuming will be preserved to Poland? Will they have the least
desire to expose themselves to the tender mercies of the Soviet
Government? Most probably not, I should say. And if they do not
want to go, shall we and the Poles be able to square it with our con-
sciences to put compulsion on them and to drive them out of
Europe into Asia? All the same, for the reasons set out in
paragraph 5 above I consider that the presence on Polish territory
of a Ukrainian minority so large that it has to be given a voice in
the policy of the Polish State will always constitute a serious
menace to good relations between Poland and the Soviet Union.

10. If, of course, Lwów cannot be saved for Poland and if the
future Polish-Russian frontier in Galicia follows the Ribbentrop-
Molotov Line, there will be very few Ukrainians left in that part of
Poland — less, I should say, than in the Lublin *voivodeship*. But in
that case what is to happen to all the Poles from Eastern and Central Galicia? If they are saved from Siberia, where are they to find
a home in Poland? East Prussia will presumably accommodate the
Poles from the lost provinces of the north-east, Wilno, &c., but
surely there will not be room there for the Poles of the south-east
as well? Much of Central and South-Western Poland is very dense-
ly populated for an agricultural country — with, in general, a not
very fertile soil. It is all very well to talk of the industrialization of
Poland in general by means, presumably, of foreign capital. The
ultimate solution will probably be found on those lines, but it is

very difficult to see how the dispossessed Poles from Galicia east of the Ribbentrop-Molotov Line are for some years to come to be fed, kept alive and given suitable work to do if the whole Polish population, which hitherto formed perhaps the most numerous element in Eastern Poland taking that part of the country as a whole, is to be forced to live in already almost over-populated ethnographic Poland.

Source: FO 371/38012
Public Record Office

27

British Foreign Office Minutes on Speech by O. Bogomolets, 8 February 1944, Regarding Ukraine's Postwar Relations with Poland and Czechoslovakia.

Minutes

3RD FEBRUARY, 1944

M. Bogomolets states that the very possibility of friendly relations with the Polish Government in London is excluded. "A new democratic Poland" will soon make possible friendly relations between that country and the Ukraine.

The speech would seem to foreshadow a direct approach by the Ukrainian SSR [........], to a "democratic Polish Republic" for the inclusion in the Ukraine of areas west of the 1939 frontier; to be followed in due course by a direct approach to the Czechoslovak Government.

In point of fact, Mr. Grechukha, another Ukrainian Deputy to the Supreme Soviet of the USSR, on the following day called upon the Government of the USSR and Stalin to "help our Ukrainian brothers" inhabiting the territories of the "Kholm area, the Grubeshov, Zamosc and Yaroslav and other western areas, to enter into the fraternal family of the peoples of the Soviet State."

[sgd. _____]
Central Dept.

*

The possibilities of endless confusion from Byelorussia and the Ukraine mixing themselves up in the Polish problem are all too obvious. It is too soon yet to say what part the republics will play, but the Ukrainian claim to areas west of the Curzon Line is ominous. We should, of course, try to deal exclusively with the central Government in Moscow, but if we are asked, and agree, to exchange ministers with the Ukraine, it will be difficult to ignore them entirely. It may be equally difficult to exchange *ministers with the Ukraine until we know what its frontiers are to be. But for the moment we can carry on as we are doing, and scale these fences when we come to them.*

[sgd.] C. F. WARNER

*

It does not seem fantastic to read into this that the Ukrainians are thinking in terms of a Polish-Czechoslovak-Ukrainian-Byelorussian bloc of like-minded democratic Slav republics, directed against Germany and coming somehow (one must assume) under the umbrella of the Soviet Union.

[sgd.] O. SARGENT

*

All this shows how unwise this Polish Government is not to come to terms over Curzon Line. I fear that they are doomed.

[sgd.] A. E.

SOURCE: FO 371/43311
Public Record Office

28

British Foreign Office Research Department Memorandum on "Liberated Ukraine," 29 March 1944, Discussing Ukrainian-Russian Relations and Ukrainian Nationalist Resistance Movement.

LIBERATED UKRAINE

MOSCOW AND THE UKRAINE

Great attention has been paid to Ukraine affairs in Moscow during the past year, but this has become even more marked since the liberation of the territory of the Republic. Meetings of Ukrainian representatives have been held at regular intervals in the capital, and long descriptive articles about the sufferings of the Ukraine under the occupation have appeared frequently in the Press. On the 2nd June it was announced in *Izvestia* that the second part of a four-volume history of the Ukraine was nearing completion. The work was to reveal "the centuries-old struggle of the Ukrainian people against social and national oppression." Two themes have throughout predominated in Soviet publicity on the Ukraine, both clearly directed to countering German propaganda, which had possibly made a certain amount of headway — the indestructible friendship of the Ukrainian and Russian peoples, which had been of inestimable benefit to both throughout their history, and the union of the Ukrainian lands in one State, the age-long dream of the Ukrainian people, which had only been realized at long last under the Soviet régime. Both were well illustrated in an article in *Krasnaya Zvezda* (4 Sept.) written at the start of the victorious advance: "Two years of war have shown that the attempt of the Hitlerites to wrest the Ukrainian people from the friendly family of Soviet peoples has completely failed." The article went on to describe the nightmare of German slavery still hanging over many Ukrainian towns, mentioning Lvov alongside Poltava, Kiev, Odessa. Concrete expression was given to the conception of Ukrainian-Russian unity by the institution of the Order of Bogdan

Khmelnitsky on the 11th October, followed two days later by the renaming of Pereiaslav as Pereiaslav-Khmelnitsky. Khmelnitsky, a turbulent seventeenth-century Cossack nobleman, who fought Poles and Russians alike, but finally decided to cast in his lot with Moscow, sealing the decision by the Treaty of Pereiaslav in 1654, has always been a favourite hero of the Ukrainian nationalist and separatist movement. The *Pravda* editorial discussing the new Order described the name of Bogdan Khmelnitsky as "indissolubly linked with the struggle of the Ukrainian people for liberation from the foreign yoke and with the fraternal union of the Ukrainian and Russian peoples." The article also stressed the second theme, that through the unity of Ukrainians and Russians under Stalin the Ukrainians, after their stormy and divided history, had at last been united in a single State.

From the outset of the Soviet-German war, when the Red Army had to leave Western Ukraine after nearly two years of occupation, it has been made quite clear that the USSR was in no way renouncing her claim to those territories, though the issue was soft-pedalled for a time after the conclusion of the Soviet-Polish agreement of 1941. A new periodical *Ukraina*, which first appeared in Moscow in July, 1943, showed on the cover a map of the Ukraine "which had recently become united under Marshal Stalin, in accordance with the wish of the people for many centuries." Lvov, Stanislav and Cernauti were all included within the Ukrainian frontiers. The same points were raised and a similar map shown in the February, 1944, issue of *Bolshevik*. In January, 1944, it was announced by the chairman of the Soviet Government Committee for Geological Affairs that "the Soviet Carpathians" would be prospected in the course of 1944.

Though claims to Western Ukraine have been thus plainly formulated, the area of the united Soviet Ukraine has not been clearly defined. Carpatho-Ukraine appears definitely to be excluded and to be destined to return to Czechoslovakia, despite the strongly philo-Russian pronouncements of many of the representatives of that area in the United States. There has been very little reference to it in the Soviet Press beyond sporadic reports of partisan activities, but, with the approach of the Red Army to the Carpathians, an appeal was issued (on the eve of the anniversary of Hitler's march into Prague) by leading Czechoslovaks in the USSR to the population of Carpatho-Ukraine, urging them to prepare to welcome the Red Army and not to allow the Germans to convert the Carpathians into a fortified line against the advancing Soviet troops. From numerous references it is plain that the Ukrainian districts of

northern Bukovina and northern and southern Bessarabia, included in the 1940 frontiers, are intended once again to form part of the
Soviet Ukraine. The ambiguity occurs in the districts claimed from
Poland. Grechukha, in his speech to the Supreme Soviet of the
USSR (*Pravda,* 8 Feb.) acclaiming the constitutional changes, asked
that the Soviet Government, when fixing the boundaries between
the Ukraine and its western neighbour, should include not only the
districts joined to the Soviet Union in 1939, but also the Kholm
district, Grubeshov, Zamosc and Yaroslav, which were inhabited
by Ukrainians. Khrushchev, in his Kiev speech, put the position
even more strongly, and added Tomashov to the districts west of
the September, 1939, frontier and of the Curzon Line claimed by
Grechukha. He maintained that

> *for good-neighbourly relations to be established between
> neighbouring States it is necessary that the State boundaries
> should coincide as far as possible with the ethnographic boun-
> daries. Then there will be no ground for misunderstanding
> and disputes of any kind.*

He repeated the contention, put forward by Grechukha, and indeed
by every writer dealing with the subject in the Soviet Press, that
Western Ukraine had been incorporated into the Soviet Union in
1939 in accordance with "the unanimous desire of the population
expressed by the National Assembly at Lvov." It was only their
"addled neighbours" the Poles who were trying to encroach on the
legitimate rights of the Ukrainian people.

Ukrainian Nationalists

The situation actually found by the advancing Soviet troops in
the Ukraine is apparently one of considerable complexity, especially in Wolhynia. The Wolhynian Ukrainians have never been so
acutely nationalist as their brethren in Galicia, and the Germans
do not appear to have attempted to raise bands of Ukrainian
troops there, parallel to the ss divisions from Galicia, of which four
were said to have been formed and to have left for the Front by
November, 1943. On the other hand, many of the Galician Ukrainians have felt that they had been defrauded by Germans of their
promised independence and have consequently been forming nationalist partisan detachments, and with them nationalist partisans in Wolhynia are now co-operating, their ranks swollen by
some refugees from the Ukraine proper. These bands, who declare
that they are fighting for "free, non-Soviet Ukraine," have been
combating Poles, Germans and pro-Soviet partisans (either local
inhabitants or parachutists) impartially. Some of these partisans

appear to be willing to co-operate to a limited extent with the Russians, both with partisans and, since the January advance, with the Red Army troops. The situation is in many ways similar to the state of the Ukraine as a whole in 1917-20, but no personalities to rival Petliura or Makhno seem so far to have emerged. There is no evidence of the presence on the spot of any of the well-known nationalist leaders such as Melnik to direct operations. Soviet sources themselves testify to the strength of the nationalist movement. Shortly after the Red Army had crossed the Wolhynian frontier, *Pravda* (21 Jan.) published a letter to Marshal Stalin from the people of Sarny, cursing "the German occupationists and their hated underlings the Ukrainian Nationalists" who had been doing nothing against the Germans, and had been murdering Red Army officers and men, guerrillas and "honest Poles," as well as their fellow Ukrainians who were actively fighting for the liberation of their country and the unification of all the Ukrainian peoples in one Ukrainian Soviet Republic. Fierce reprisals were promised against these "hirelings of gory German Fascism."

Khrushchev, in his speech to the Ukrainian Supreme Soviet already quoted, castigated "the enemies of the Ukrainian people, the Ukrainian German Nationalists" even more vigorously and in greater detail. He said that he was in possession of documents definitely exposing the black treachery and loyal service to the Germans of these "adherents of Melnik, Bandera and Borovetz, known as Taras Bulba." [........] Bandera, a younger and even more militant man, set up a Ukrainian administration in Lvov when the Germans entered, but was forced to flee on the following day and has not been heard of since; unfortunately no further evidence is available on the modern descendant of the picturesque Taras Bulba: Khrushchev described "leading Ukrainian circles" as having attempted to form a National Rada in Kiev when the Germans arrived, though the German authorities had soon suppressed its activities. According to him, the organizers were not local Ukrainians, but outsiders who had come in with the German supply trains. With their retreat the Germans had apparently become even more anxious to collaborate with these nationalists, and Khrushchev gave an account of conferences organized by Borovetz with the German High Command, with specific reference to a meeting held on the 13th January between representatives of Ukrainian organizations known as SUN and UPA and the Gestapo Chief and garrison commander at Kamen Kashirsk. One Antoniuk, commander of a UPA detachment, had come to a similar arrangement for the supply of arms with the Germans in the previous

December. In the name of his Government Khrushchev promised an amnesty to those members of UPA and the similar organization UNRA who had become members of these bands by accident, been drawn into them by deception, or were mobilized by force. If they severed all connections with the Hitlerites of SUN they would receive forgiveness for all their mistakes. Ruthless punishment was promised to all who continued the struggle against the Soviet partisans and the Red Army.

[.......]

Koch, *Reichskommissar* of the Ukraine, in his New Year message for 1944, delivered from the safety of East Prussia to the Germans still in the Ukraine, himself admitted that Ukrainian nationalists had to some extent been fighting against the Germans. He referred to the death of many of his *Verwaltungs-führer* at the hand not only of Soviet partisans, but of national Ukrainian bandits, whose persistent efforts to secure independence only proved their political immaturity. He went on to assert that

> *no efforts of Ukrainian chauvinists could influence the Führer's decision. ... Nothing but the effective, whole-hearted support of the German* Führung *can prove that this historically poor people deserve emancipation.*
>
> *Those immature Ukrainian leaders who fled to the woods in order to harass the Germans instead of fighting the Bolshevik bandits were ruining their own cause, because every square inch of Ukrainian territory abandoned by the German grenadiers would fall to the Bolsheviks, not to Ukrainians or Englishmen.*

[.......]

SOURCE: FO 371/43314
Public Record Office

29

*British Embassy, Moscow, to Northern Department
of the Foreign Office, 12 May 1944, Commenting on
Khrushchev's Reference to the Ukrainian Separatist
Movement in a Speech to Supreme Soviet of
the Ukrainian SSR.*

BRITISH EMBASSY

Moscow
12TH MAY, 1944

Dear Department,

Your unnumbered letter of March 30th about Khrushchev's
speech to the Supreme Soviet of the Ukrainian SSR on March 1st.

2. We are sorry to say that we have no additional information
either about Borovetz or about SUN. The Soviet press usually sees
fit to ignore the existence of separatist movements and we were
surprised by the frankness of Khrushchev's speech. Indeed, we
thought it best to send our telegram to you on the subject (No. 739
of March 18th) in cypher lest our interest be misunderstood. For
the same reason it is difficult for us to make enquiries, but we
shall, of course, keep our ears cocked and let you know if we hear
anything.

Yours ever,

CHANCERY

*Northern Department
Foreign Office*

Source: FO 371/43315
Public Record Office

30

A. J. Halpern, British Security Co-ordination, New York, to G. de T. Glazebrook, Canadian Department of External Affairs, 16 August 1944, Commenting on Political Attitudes and Future Orientation of Ukrainians in North America.

BRITISH SECURITY CO-ORDINATION

16TH AUGUST, 1944

BY SAFE HAND
PERSONAL AND CONFIDENTIAL

Dear Glazebrook,

I have just received from the [US] Office of Strategic Services a report on *The Ukrainians in Canada,* copy of which I enclose herewith. I should be extremely glad to have your Department's comments on it.

[........]

The author of the report admits that the connection between the Canadian and American Ukrainians is a very close one. In the States there is, in my mind, not the slightest doubt that the pro-German Ukrainian organizations (and all the Ukrainian National organizations in the USA) are, or have been, either directly or indirectly influenced by Berlin, [but] have suffered a tremendous setback. More and more people have come to the conclusion that a strong united Ukraine has only one chance for survival as an independent cultural and national entity, and that this chance lies in its union with Russia.

The OUN tendency is on the wane, and the American Ukrainians insofar as they will not be entirely absorbed by American culture, will have to orientate themselves towards Russia. Apparently *tertium non dat* − I wonder whether there is a similar evolution in Canada.

I am also enclosing copy of press notes prepared by the Office of Strategic Services *The Ukrainian-American Press in the middle of July, 1944.*

Yours ever,

George de T. Glazebrook
Department of External Affairs
Ottawa, Canada

[sgd.] A. J. HALPERN

SOURCE: RG 25 G1, Vol. 1896
File 165, Part IV
Public Archives of Canada

31

Secret and Controlled Report, Research and Analysis Branch, Office of Strategic Services, 16 December 1944, Presenting Arguments against Recognition of Legal Status of Soviet Republics.

OFFICE OF STRATEGIC SERVICES
RESEARCH AND ANALYSIS REPORT

No. 2670   16 DECEMBER, 1944

THE ROLE OF THE UNION REPUBLICS OF THE USSR
IN THE CONDUCT OF FOREIGN AFFAIRS

Copy No. 3

Summary and Conclusions

1. The amendments of 1 February, 1944 to the constitution of the USSR gave to the Union Republics the right to enter into direct relations with foreign states, to conclude agreements and to exchange diplomatic and consular representatives. The amendments also provide that the central government shall establish a "general procedure" to govern the relations of the Union Republics with foreign states. Finally, the People's Commissariat for Foreign Affairs was transformed from an All-Union to a Union-Republican commissariat.

2. By virtue of these amendments, the Union Republics acquired concurrent jurisdiction with the central government in the field of foreign affairs. However, the Union Republics did not receive co-equal or co-extensive jurisdiction. The constitution of the 1927 indicates the subordinate and limited role of the Union Republics in the contours of foreign relations.

3. The Union Republics are limited first by the fact that they are not sovereign states, but instead form the constituent parts of a highly centralized state. They are restricted from exercising autonomy in most governmental functions. For example, a Union Republic is subject to the control of the central government in the

formulation of its constitution, in the legislation of its laws and decrees, in the operation of most economic affairs, and in the administration of finances, defense, law enforcement, and foreign affairs.

4. The Union Republics are further limited by the fact that the transformation of the People's Commissariat from an All-Union to a Union-Republican commissariat does not abolish the ultimate control of the central government over the conduct of foreign relations.

5. The Union Republics are also limited by the provisions of the constitution of the USSR which restrict the Union Republics from dealing with most subjects of foreign relations.

6. The Union Republics are limited by the new amendments themselves, which provide that the Union Republics must conduct their foreign affairs in accordance with the "general procedure" established by the central government. In addition, the amendments give to the Union Republics the right to conclude "agreements," whereas the central government has the right to conclude "treaties." This difference in terminology permits the inference that the Union Republics do not have the competence to conclude political pacts.

7. The Soviet Union may attempt to maintain that the Union Republics, by virtue of the amendments, are now *sui generis* among political entities. However, the international status of a Union Republic will not be decided so much by the legal arguments advanced to deny or to justify its claim to sovereign statehood, as by any recognition that is accorded by foreign states to the Union Republic. The establishment of diplomatic relations between a Union Republic and a foreign state would provide the Russians with a strong rebuttal to any charges that a Union Republic does not constitute a 'state.'

8. The application by a Union Republic for membership in an international organization conceivably could be denied on two grounds: (a) that the representation of both a Union Republic and the central government (the USSR) would be an unjustifiable duplication; (b) that a Union Republic would be unable to carry out its international obligations without the permission and the assistance of the central government of the USSR.

SOURCE: OSS Research and Analysis
Reports, No. 2670, M 1221
US National Archives

32

Note Prepared for the Yalta Conference by B. E. Pares, Northern Department, British Foreign Office, 23 February 1945, Dealing with Ukrainian Minority in Poland. Includes Minutes.

NORTHERN DEPARTMENT

23 FEBRUARY, 1945

POLAND'S UKRAINIAN MINORITY

1. The problem of Poland's eastern frontiers presents not simply a Russo-Polish issue, but a triangular situation in which Poland's national minorities constitute the third party; and the record of Poland's relations with the most important of those minorities – the Ukrainians – has been anything but a happy one. It would perhaps be unfortunate if our strong concern for Poland's interests were allowed to obscure these facts.

2. In what was the Austrian Crownland of Galicia before 1918, the Austrians allowed the Poles a general ascendancy over the Ukrainians, but at the same time kept that ascendancy sufficiently within bounds to enable the Ukrainians of Eastern Galicia to make considerable progress – educational, social and economic. Moreover, in the decade before the war of 1914-18 both the Austrian authorities and a number of Ukrainian political movements were exploiting the state of extreme social tension which even then existed between the Ukrainian peasantry and the local Polish landlords. On the collapse of the Austro-Hungarian monarchy in 1918 an Ukrainian Government was set up in Lwow, which shortly afterwards proclaimed the union of East Galicia with the Russian Ukraine.

3. But the Ukrainians were driven out of Lwow by Polish forces in November, 1918, and out of the rest of East Galicia by the middle of 1919; and the efforts of the Principal Allied Powers to secure Polish acceptance of an autonomous Statute for East Galicia foundered on the *fait accompli* of Polish military occupation. Nevertheless, in recognizing Poland's annexation of the ter-

ritory by its decision in March, 1923, the Conference of Ambassadors did insist upon the Polish Government recognizing the necessity for an autonomous régime and for applying the provisions of the Polish Minorities Treaty.

4. Without attempting to assess precisely how far, or with what justification, successive Polish Governments fell short of fulfilling the moral obligations thus laid upon them, we are bound to note that even the very modest project for East Galician autonomy proposed by the Poles in 1922 (and regarded by the British Government of the day as inadequate) was quietly shelved; that by 1938 the number of Ukrainian elementary schools had fallen from 3,600 in 1918 to 420; and that, in contravention of the Polish Minorities Treaty and of the Polish Constitution of 1921, the Ukrainian language was never recognized as the second official language in East Galicia. Nor can it be forgotten how, in 1930, the serious agrarian and cultural grievances of the Ukrainians gave occasion for a widespread compaign of arson and sabotage, provoking in turn such severe measures of repression by Polish troops in 1930-31 (the "Pacification") that in January 1932 the Council of the League administered what, in diplomatic language, amounted to a rebuke. By 1938 even the most moderate Ukrainian political leaders had despaired of obtaining any effective guarantee of minority rights and, repudiating the *modus vivendi* reached in 1935, submitted in December an Ukrainian Home Rule Bill which was rejected out of hand by the Speaker of the Polish Diet.

5. To turn to more recent developments, we find the Germans, during their occupation of East Galicia in 1941-44, fostering Ukrainian hostility towards the local Polish population and employing Ukrainians as police and militiamen to perpetrate throughout Poland some of the worst brutalities that have been recorded. And in fact, feeling between Poles and Ukrainians now runs so high that, according to information received during the past few weeks, there has been a spontaneous movement of Poles living east of the Curzon Line into the areas administered by the Lublin authorities, in anticipation of the officially organized transfers.

6. If it should be objected that the Ukrainian minority as a whole would prefer to remain in Poland rather than to be incorporated in the Ukrainian SSR, it can only be said that we know of no evidence of their entertaining such a preference. The only other possible alternative – namely, the creation of an independent Ukrainian State – is the goal for which certain extremist Ukrainian nationalist organizations have worked but these movements owed much of their strength in the pre-1939 period to the fact that

they were fostered and financed by the Germans for their own ends. In any case, the creation of an independent Ukrainian State would at this late stage in East European history be quite inconceivable; the only practical possibility of uniting all Ukrainians in a single political unit lies in the incorporation of the Western Ukraine with the Ukrainian Soviet Republic.

[sgd.] E. PARES

* * *

Minutes

These minutes appears to have lain unprized for some months. Since they were written the matter has been to a large extent taken out of our hands by the Russian announcements in E. Poland.

[sgd.] T. BRIMELOW

*

Yes. Publicly, the troubles of the Ukrainians, now reunited at last in their own state, are at an end. Any manifestations of discontent will in future be the work not of Ukrainian patriots, but of fascist brats, black reactionaries and enemies of the people. Thanks to the brotherly protection of the Great Russian people the centuries-old problem has now found a complete and just solution, and the enclosed minutes on past events can be consigned to the limbo of forgotten things.

[sgd. _____]

SOURCE: FO 371/47788
Public Record Office

33

D. C. Poole, Associate Public Liaison Officer, United States Delegation to the San Francisco Conference, 14 May 1945, Regarding Conversation with Representatives of the Ukrainian Congress Committee on the Ukrainian Situation in Europe.

UNITED STATES DELEGATION

MEMORANDUM

14 MAY, 1945

TO:

Secretary of State

This morning a delegation of American citizens representing the Ukrainian Congress Committee of America called this morning and presented the attached memorandum on the Ukrainian situation (to which their names are appended).

I received this memorandum on your behalf and said that in due course it would come to your attention. It is respectfully recommended that the document be referred to the Eastern European Division of the State Department.

In the interval between the two wars the cause of Ukrainian nationalism became emeshed with the German drive eastward and one or two of those who called this morning have records which are not too clear in that regard. However, what has passed need not be reminded always too vividly and it is my impression that the four gentlemen who called this morning are patriotic Americans and that they are now disposed to present the cause of Ukrainian nationalism in a reasonable way. The attached memorandum hardly goes beyond asking that this Conference should include a Bill of Rights in the proposed World Organization.

During the conversation this morning the delegation remarked that the United States was the champion of oppressed peoples and that they felt confident of American official interest in the cause of Ukrainian nationalism. I answered that the interest of the people of the United States in all who felt themselves to be oppressed was well established in history but I pointed out that it would not serve anybody's interest to create an impression that the United States government was the unreasoning champion of the discontented. It was necessary above all at this time to work out a friendly accommodation with the USSR. Nothing should be done to disturb that effort. The delegation professed to agree.

[sgd.] DeWitt C. Poole
Associate Public Liaison Officer

Source: RG 226, Entry 100
Box 98, UK 351-360
US National Archives

34

*D. Wilgress, Canadian Ambassador to the USSR, to
N. A. Robertson, Canadian Under Secretary of State
for External Affairs, 25 May 1945, on Ukrainian
Canadian Committee's Protest over Repatriation of
Ukrainian Political Refugees to the USSR.*

Memorandum   MAY 25, 1945

With reference to the attached telegram from the Ukrainian
Canadian Committee and the representations which you received
from Dr. W. Kushnir, I do not think it would be advisable for us to
intervene on behalf of the prominent Ukrainians who are likely to
fall into the hands of the Soviet authorities as a result of the occupation of Germany.

It might be advisable to send a telegram to the High Commissioner for Canada in London asking him to ascertain from the
United Kingdom authorities what policy is being followed regarding the handing over to the Russians of Ukrainian nationalists
found in the British zone of occupied Germany. The receipt of such
information from Mr. Massey might assist us in answering further
enquiries or representations which we may receive from the Ukrainian Canadian Committee.

It would be prejudicial to our relations with the Soviet Union if
we were to make representations to the United Kingdom
authorities that prominent Ukrainian nationalists should not be
handed over to the Soviet authorities. The Soviet Government
regard these people as "Fascists" and our interest on behalf of such
men would be understood as an unfriendly act towards the Soviet
Union. From the purely strict legal point of view it is also no
business of ours what happens to these Ukrainian nationalists,
although this could not be very well used in reply to representations submitted to us by the Ukrainian Canadian Committee.

[sgd.] D.W. WILGRESS

SOURCE: RG 25 F6, Vol. 1022, File 139
Public Archives of Canada

35

Memorandum to the Canadian High Commissioner to the UK from J. W. Holmes, Canadian Department of External Affairs, 16 November 1945, Explaining British, American, and French Policy Regarding Repatriation of Displaced Persons to the Soviet Union. Includes Comment by S. M. Scott.

MEMORANDUM TO THE HIGH COMMISSIONER

16 NOVEMBER, 1945

REPATRIATION TO THE USSR OF DISPUTED PERSONS

At the Crimea Conference two separate Agreements were made with the Soviet Union concerning the repatriation of each other's citizens. One Agreement, signed by the countries of the British Commonwealth, was dated February 11th and the text may be found in Dominions Office telegram D. No. 273 of 12th February, 1945. At the same time an identical Agreement was signed between the United States and the Soviet Union. According to this Agreement the British countries and the USSR agreed that "all Soviet citizens liberated by Forces operating under British Command, and all British subjects liberated by Forces operating under Soviet Command" would be repatriated. The chief intention of this Agreement was to make certain that the Soviet Government did not hold up the repatriation of British subjects on the grounds that Soviet citizens were being detained by the United Kingdom.

Although under the terms of this Agreement a very considerable repatriation has taken place on both sides, differing interpretations have caused a good deal of trouble. The matter was the cause of some considerable argument at the meeting of the Council of Foreign Ministers in London. The difference in interpretation concerns the meaning of the phrase "all Soviet citizens." A Soviet memorandum to the Council of Foreign Ministers referred to the failure of the other Allies to repatriate persons from the Baltic States, Western Ukraine, and Western Byelo-Russia "in accordance with the Yalta Agreement". The United Kingdom in a memorandum stated clearly that they did not recognize the Soviet Government's claim that these persons were Soviet citizens, and, therefore, did not regard them as liable to compulsory repatriation under the Yalta Agreement. The United Kingdom Government would return to their homes persons from these territories who expressed a wish to return, but persons who declared themselves unwilling to return would, as hitherto, be kept in camps to which the Soviet repatriation authorities would not be allowed access.

Although the question raised involved nationals of the former Baltic States, the chief discussion revolved around persons from the former Polish areas east of the Curzon Line. Mr. Molotov made it clear that his Government considered that the United Kingdom and United States had agreed at Yalta that Polish territories east of the Curzon Line should become a part of Russia. Mr. Bevin and Mr. Byrnes, however, insisted that although the three heads of Government had expressed their view that the eastern frontier of Poland should follow the Curzon Line, until this cession of territory had been recognized officially by their respective Governments they could not regard the former inhabitants of these areas as Soviet nationals. Mr. Molotov complained that no question had been raised at Yalta by the British or Americans concerning the meaning of the term "Soviet citizens."

United Kingdom policy is, briefly, to interpret the term "Soviet citizens" to mean people who lived in the Soviet Union as its boundaries existed on September 1st, 1939. All citizens of the pre-war Soviet Union, whether they wish to return or not, are sent back to the USSR. However, those who in September, 1939, were resident in territories which were not at that time part of the Soviet Union, are not forced to return to the Soviet Union if they do not wish to do so. With regard to those persons who were citizens of the pre-war Soviet Union the United Kingdom has maintained that they were bound by the terms of the Yalta Agreement to use constraint in repatriating them to the USSR. In their directives they have instructed their military authorities to do everything possible to persuade such persons to return. They do not sanction the use of handcuffs or extreme measures of force, but it is the policy of the military authorities to surround the persons concerned with soldiers, and in general to make such a display of force in the background that the persons will consider resistance to be futile.

The United States policy, on the other hand, has been somewhat different although they are bound by an identical Agreement

with the Soviet Union. General Eisenhower has maintained that no
force must be used in sending any persons back to the Soviet
Union. The Americans make a distinction, also, with regard to
Soviet citizens captured in German uniform. They maintain that it
is the uniform rather than nationality which matters, and they
treat all persons captured in German uniform as prisoners of war.

Out of the United States attitude towards persons in German
uniform has arisen one of the most embarrassing problems, and
one in which it seems to be the view of the United Kingdom
Government that the Soviet Government has some cause for complaint. There are in Italy at the present time a number of officers
and men who served with the Germans under the traitor, General
Vlasov. It is the view of the United Kingdom Government that
these persons should be forcibly repatriated to the Soviet Union.
They are, however, the responsibility of the Allied Commander-in-
Chief in Italy, who accepts orders neither from the United
Kingdom Government nor from the United States Government,
but from the Combined Chiefs of Staff in Washington. In the
Council of Foreign Ministers, when this matter was raised, Mr.
Byrnes told Mr. Molotov that he would have no sympathy with
any of Vlasov's men who were in the hands of the United States
authorities. He promised to take this matter up again with his
military authorities. The question has been referred to the Combined Chiefs of Staff in Washington. According to the understanding of the Foreign Office Mr. Byrnes has not yet been able to
secure an agreement. There seems to be a difference of opinion as
between Mr. Byrnes and the United States Service authorities.
The United Kingdom are pressing for a decision which will result
in the forcible repatriation of these men to the USSR.

One matter which has caused considerable difference of opinion is the question of the right of Soviet representatives to visit
persons whom they consider to be Soviet citizens, but whom the
United Kingdom and the United States do not. It is United
Kingdom policy to separate from those whom they recognize as
Soviet citizens those who are classified as "disputed persons." They
have refused to allow Soviet representatives to visit the latter. It is
their policy to give the Soviet repatriation authorities full information about, and unimpeded access to, camps and points of concentration of Soviet citizens as recognized by the United Kingdom
Government in accordance with the terms of the Yalta Agreement.
As for the disputed persons, the Soviet repatriation authorities are
only allowed to interview them outside the precincts of the camp.

Citizens of the former Baltic States, that is, Latvia, Lithuania

and Estonia, are treated as Soviet citizens for purposes of repatriation only if they so desire. In other words, although the question of
the recognition of the Baltic States is a separate issue from that of
the recognition of the cession of Eastern Poland to the USSR, persons whose homes of origin are in the Baltic States are treated in
the same way as those whose homes of origin were in Poland east
of the Curzon Line. At the Council of Foreign Ministers Mr.
Molotov showed little concern over persons from the Baltic States
as he said that that matter had been virtually settled in practice.

The question of French policy is one which cannot be very
clearly ascertained from London. The Foreign Office do not seem
to be entirely sure of the policies which are being followed in the
French zone or in France. They were recently assured, however, by
a representative of the French Ministry of Foreign Affairs that the
French were keeping in step with the United Kingdom on this matter. At the Council of Foreign Ministers Mr. Bidault was chiefly in-
sistent upon securing reciprocity with the Soviet Union with
regard to Alsatians who had been found in German uniform and
whom the Russians had been reluctant to repatriate.

The question of the Polish-Soviet Agreement on repatriation
and nationality which was concluded on 6th July was raised at the
Council of Foreign Ministers. At that time Mr. Bevin pointed out
to Mr. Molotov that the United Kingdom's only knowledge of this
Agreement was what it had read in the press reports. Mr. Molotov
agreed to provide copies of the Agreement. It was not until very
recently, however, that this text was made available to the United
Kingdom. It was found to rest on the assumption that persons
coming from territories which had been ceded to the Soviet Union
by Poland became Soviet citizens on the incorporation of these territories into the USSR, but provided that they might opt for
withdrawal from Soviet citizenship before November 1st, 1945, if
they so wished. One Article in the Agreement extended application
of this provision to Poles at present outside the territories in question. After seeing the Agreement the United Kingdom Government decided that they were under no obligation to recognize the
Agreement or the assumption on which it rested as applying to
persons coming from ceded territories who were outside those territories at the time of their recent incorporation into the Soviet
Union, that is in 1944 and 1945. (There seems to be great difference
of opinion over the interpretation of this Agreement, and a special
memorandum will be prepared on the subject after further discussions with the Foreign Office.)

In view of the fact that the particular question of concern is

the repatriation of Ukrainians to the Soviet Union the policy of the
Polish Government in this regard is not irrelevant. According to
the Polish Agreement with the Soviet Government, the Ukrainian
population to the west of the Curzon Line is to be allowed to opt for
transfer to the territories east of the new frontier. Although many
of these Ukrainians wish to remain in Poland the Poles are determined to remove them in order to realize their aim of a
homogeneous Polish state. It is the understanding of the United
Kingdom Government that Ukrainians are being forcibly expelled
to the Soviet Union or else being made to opt under duress for
transfer.

[sgd.] J.W. H[OLMES]

* * *

17TH NOVEMBER, 1945

*My observations upon this memorandum are I fear purely academic. I
don't think the United Kingdom negotiators at Yalta had in mind any forcible deportations except of* bona fide *Russians captured in German
uniforms. I don't believe they envisaged the possibility of enforced return
of uninterned persons at all. And I don't read the Agreement as calling for
enforced return of anybody. It is clear from the surrounding documents
that the Russians had uninterned civilians in mind, and they did not succeed in writing it into the document. I do not think the Agreement calls for
compulsory return of Russians captured in German uniforms (the
Americans are right). The British yielded in practice on this point partly
because they did not care much, partly because their camps were over-
crowded and chiefly because the Russians would not help our boys until
theirs were on the boats.*

*However, Yalta is a long way off and maybe the Foreign Office did not
tell me all they were thinking.*

*When the Agreement was made Canada's only concern in this par-
ticular regard was that non-British persons in our uniforms should get
home. For awhile we supported the principle that nationality followed the
uniform. However, the fear arose that if we began debating nationality no
agreement would be reached at all. Hence the vagueness of the present
text.*

[sgd.] S.M.S[COTT]

SOURCE: File 8296 - 40c
Department of External Affairs
(Canada), Historical Division

36

War Office Report on Ukrainian Nationalist Movement and Resistance in Ukraine, 13 December 1945. Minutes by T. Brimelow and B. Miller

13TH DECEMBER, 1945

GENERAL

Historical Background (1917-39). The collapse of the Russian Empire early in 1917 and the defeat of the Central Powers in November 1918 were in each case followed by the setting up of Ukrainian Governments in the areas thus liberated, which, for a short period at the end of 1918, bid fair to unite the Ukrainians in one state. The campaigns of the Poles and Bolsheviks in the next two years, however, left the Ukrainian people once more divided between three foreign rulers in Poland, the Soviet Union and Czechoslovakia.

In Poland, the Ukrainians retained a considerable liberty of organization, particularly in the social, cultural and economic fields, and Polish East Galicia continued to be the main centre of Ukrainian nationalism. Political unity of the Ukrainians in Poland was largely achieved, both in the parliamentary field and also in the shape of the OUN (Organization of Ukrainian Nationalists), a paramilitary secret society formed in 1929. This latter body carried out sabotage and assassination directed against the Polish administration, as it was later to do against the Soviets in 1944-45. Ukrainians had largely looked to Germany for support in establishing their aim of an independent Ukraine, and after Hitler's rise to power the OUN came strongly under Nazi influence.

The Ukrainians in Czechoslovakia, in the Carpatho-Ukraine, were comparatively backward and not actively nationalist, though here also irridentist forces received support from Germany. The settlements of 1938-39, which distributed the Ukrainians of these regions between Hungary and the Soviet Union, caused considerable disillusionment among the OUN as well as other Ukrainians of similar leanings who had counted on Germany for support.

In Soviet Ukraine an extremely liberal policy towards Ukrainian nationalism was followed at first, in spite of the abolition of the separate diplomatic service of the Ukraine SSR. From 1930 onwards, however, Ukrainian separatism, in conjunction with the discontent caused by Soviet agricultural policy, became a serious danger to the Soviet Union. This was substantially aggravated by the advent to power of Hitler in 1933. Ukrainian nationalism became an object of attention by the GPU, and simultaneously the movement was undermined by the policy of industrialization which brought large numbers of Russians into leading administrative positions in the Ukraine and greatly increased the economic dependence of the Ukraine on the rest of the Soviet Union.

The arrests and trial of Ukrainian nationalists in the Soviet Union from 1930 onwards offered *prima facie* evidence of attempts to form Ukrainian separatist bodies inside the Soviet Ukraine, and also of the connections of Ukrainian individuals with the OUN and foreign powers. There is evidence that, during the period of German occupation of the Ukraine, the OUN had branches throughout the Ukraine which worked in the utmost secrecy, (including, of course, secrecy from the Germans). No evidence is at hand, however, of the activities of the OUN or of any other separatist organization in the Soviet Ukraine before the war.

Wartime Developments (1939-41). During the years 1939-44 the movement appears still to be suffering from disorganization as a result of the assassination of the leader of the OUN, Colonel Konovalets, and the manifest failure of his pro-Nazi policy. (One group, led by Andreas Melnik, split away from the OUN and in 1942 had almost become a part of the Soviet partisan movement).

On 28 July 1941, the OUN leadership in Lvov issued a proclamation of Ukrainian independence; the arrest by the Germans of the OUN leader, Stefan Bandera, which followed, led to further disintegration. The organizations which emerged, the Taras Bulba Movement and the UPA *(Ukrainska Povstanska Armiya* — Ukrainian Insurrectionary Army) were, however, not mutually hostile and the latter eventually largely absorbed the former.

THE TARAS BULBA MOVEMENT (1942-44)

Origins. Was led by Borovets, a prominent member of the OUN, who before the war had been engaged in literary activity against Polish and Soviet authorities. In 1940 he started to organize partisan and other disruptive activity in the part of Poland which had been occupied by the Soviet Union. During the German advance in 1941, he disarmed the Soviet authorities in the town of Sarny and later handed over the town to the Germans.

At his own suggestion Borovets was then entrusted by the German forces with the task of forming a special police force, the *Poliska Sitch,* to mop up Red Army stragglers in the forests of North Volhynia. He accomplished this task and had several successful engagements with Red Army units, his force having at one time a size of 2 thousand men. Negotiations for further "operations" and expansion, however, broke down and the *Poliska Sitch* was disbanded by the Germans. In February 1942 Borovets started negotiations for its reconstitution but without success.

Thus Borovets saw himself frustrated in his aim of building up under German auspices the nucleus of a future Ukrainian army. In the meantime with the introduction of the German civil administration in the Ukraine, it had become clear that, far from independence, the Ukrainians could expect little but exactions and repressive measures from the Germans. In the summer of 1942 Borovets took to the forests with some of his men, and adopted the name of "Taras Bulba."

Partisan Activities. Activity by Bulba bands is reported from September 1942 onwards, and included the following:

    (i)   battles with Soviet partisans
    (ii)   attempts to dislocate the German civil administration, e.g. redistribution of requisitioned grain, raids on state farms, liberation of prisoners.
    (iii) raids on German units and posts, with a view to getting supplies, in which, however, the shedding of German blood is said to have been avoided.

These operations took place mainly in the region Pinsk-Luninets-Sarny-Rovno-Lutsk-Kovel, that is to say roughly the Southern half of the Pripet Marshes.

Organization, Strength and Membership. No evidence is available of any form of rigid organization in the Bulba movement. German estimates of the armed strength of the movement during the years 1943-44 vary between 5,000 and 20,000. A statement of June 1943, which may possibly emanate from Bulba himself, gives the strength as 40,000 men organized in 15 camps. It is likely that the active strength was in fact limited by the supply of equipment.

Armament. This consisted mainly of machine guns, machine pistols and rifles, though anti-tank guns are also mentioned. Sources of supply are raids on German units, actions against Soviet partisans, deserters who bring their own weapons and deception of Soviet planes carrying supplies to Soviet partisans.

The movement recruited its members exclusively from Ukrainians but included amongst them those of every political leaning. The original nucleus of the movement consisted of deserters from the German auxiliary police formations and other Ukrainians who had come into conflict with the German civil administration. Later, however, Bulba was able to institute a compulsory call-up in parts of Volhynia and Polesia, the German administration being permanently effective only at focal points.

General Policy. The principal aim of an independent Ukraine was to be achieved, either after the mutual exhaustion of Germany and the Soviet Union, or alternatively by developing partisan activities to such an extent that Germany would be forced to modify her Ukrainian policy. As regards political conditions in the planned "independent Ukraine," the movement appears to have had no policy at all. This vagueness of policy may have been deliberate, with a view to enrolling the largest possible number of supporters; it was, however, to prove a weakness when competition developed between the UPA and the Bulba movement.

During the German occupation of the Ukraine the movement preserved an attitude on the hand of willingness to negotiate with the German Army and on the other hand of hostility to the German civil administration and Soviet partisans. There are, however, isolated reports of temporary non-aggression agreements between Bulba and Soviet partisan groups during actions against the German civil administration.

Later History (1942-44). Attempts by the Germans to induce Borovets to give up his illegal existence and to join them in fighting Soviet partisans lasted from October 1942 to April 1943. In these negotiations Borovets characterizes the German administration in the Ukraine as "plundering" and the *Reichskommissar* himself as a "bandit." In his final letter to the chief of the *Sicherheitsdienst* in Rovno he threatens reprisals against German military objectives and lines of communication for any further German acts of barbarity against the Ukrainian civil population. A further meeting between Borovets and German agents took place in June 1943, at which it appeared that he was willing conditionally to negotiate with the German forces, but nothing seems to have come of this.

By this time the UPA in Volhynia had become a substantial force, and increasing penetration of the Taras [Bulba] movement by UPA members was taking place; in addition the movement is reported to have been losing members to the Soviet partisans. In

November 1943 Borovets found himself so much weakened as to swallow his objections to negotiations with the German *Sicherheitsdienst* (Security Service). His offer, details of which are not known, was referred by Himmler to Hitler and turned down. In January 1944 Borovets was in the custody of the German *Sicherheitsdienst* in Warsaw under safe-conduct. Early in 1944 Borovets reappeared as the head of a new organization, the UNRA, Ukrainian National Revolutionary Army, which was active in the same region as, and presumably largely identical with, the Taras Bulba [Movement]. Like that organization it considered itself an inter-party organization, and tried to recruit followers from Ukrainians of all political views. A propaganda leaflet suggests that the UNRA was hostile to the UPA, and was sympathetic to, or possibly even included, the radical Melnik group. Information as to its activities and organization is extremely scanty. Nevertheless the fact that the UNRA and the UPA were the joint objects of an appeal to come over to the Soviet side, issued by the Supreme Soviet of the Ukrainian SSR, indicates that the UNRA must have been of some importance.

The unification of Ukrainian parties which took place in June 1944 is reported to have included the UNRA and the Melnik group. Partisan activity, directed mainly against Soviet line of communication, and directed by Taras Bulba, is reported in the Polish region as late as December 1944.

THE OUN-UPA MOVEMENT (1942-45)

Origins. At about the same time as Borovets attempt in 1941-42 to train up the nucleus of a future Ukrainian Army under German auspices, another section of the OUN leadership was seeking, with greater success, to achieve the same end by sending its members to join the German Army as volunteers. It appears that a large part (perhaps 50%) of the personnel of the German SS division "Galicia" fell into this category. The eventual military leader of the UPA, Shukhevych, is said to have served as a captain in this division. The setting up of the UPA Movement began in mid-1942, but the nucleus of trained fighting men arrived only in the winter of 1942-43, in the shape of mass desertions from German SS volunteer divisions, which desertions continued at intervals throughout 1943. By the middle of 1943 the UPA was estimated to have 50,000 armed men in the region Kovel-Rovno-Zviahel; by the end of 1943 it had spread to Galicia and was able to undertake the clearing from the North slopes of the Carpathians of Soviet partisans with a view to using that region as a base. Immediately prior to the reoccupation of the Western Ukraine by the Red Army the UPA was in control of large areas between the Carpathians and the River Pripet.

Partisan Activities. Before the Soviet reoccupation of the West Ukraine the main activities of the UPA were recruitment and training. Its only practical achievements during this period appear to have been the expulsion from parts of the West Ukraine of Soviet partisans and Polish peasants. Many of the latter had been settled there by pre-war Polish governments and placards were put up in villages announcing the dates by which Poles had to remove themselves to the West side of the San River. Those who failed to comply had their houses burnt down.

The UPA was also antagonistic to the German civil government in the Ukraine, and to Polish partisans of all kinds. The extent of actual hostilities between the UPA and these bodies is, however, not known.

Hostilities on any substantial scale between the UPA and the Soviets date from April 1944, when UPA territory began to be reoccupied by the Red Army. The movement of the Soviet-German front across this region caused some disorganization in the UPA's activities, but in September 1944 95% of UPA units were reported to be behind the Soviet lines. The disappearance of the German civil administration in the Ukraine had by then removed the main obstacle to cooperation with the Germans. UPA activities included:

(i) Attacks on Soviet supply columns moving up to the front, both by road and by rail; some stretches of railroad were rendered unusable, and armed escorts for convoys moving by road were becoming essential.

(ii) Battles, apparently mainly defensive, against NKVD and Red Army troops.

(iii) Liberation of conscripts from the reoccupied areas.

(iv) Terrorism, directed mainly against officials of the Communist Party, the NKVD and the Soviet Government. One German intelligence unit regards it proved that General Vatutin's death was the result of such an attack at Shepetovka.

(v) Annihilation of Soviet parachutists.

(vi) Transmission of intelligence on the Red Army to the German forces

(vii) Assistance to German stragglers, including their passage through the Soviet lines.

(viii) Assistance to occasional German long-range recon-
        naissance groups.
(ix)   Extensive propaganda amongst the Ukrainian
        civil population and amongst Ukrainians in the
        R[eoccupied] A[reas].

Operations by the UPA against Soviet line of communication
and officials are reported up to and including March 1945, the date
of the latest available information, the operations covering roughly
the quadrilateral Kovel-Przemysl-Stanislavov-Kiev.

Organization. During the years 1941-44 the leadership of the
OUN-UPA movement was in the hands of Lebed (alias Maxim Ruben)
and Shukhevych (alias Klim Savur), the political and military
deputies respectively of Bandera, who himself was in German
custody in Berlin.

A report of November 1943 describes a combined headquarters of the movement, then situated in the town of Stydin, 45
km North of Rovno. With the staff of the UPA these were said to be:

(i)   Headquarters of the security service (a secret ter-
        rorist organization).
(ii)   Supreme party executive.
(iii)   Directorate of medical services.
(iv)   Supply department.
(v)   Training school for officers and NCOS.

In the same report the UPA itself was stated to be organized in
three divisions, each of 10-12 thousand men. These divisions were
divided into regiments and companies (termed *Sotni* or
"hundreds").

[........]

Strength and Membership. German estimates agree on a
strength of 40-50 thousand men for the UPA in the latter half of
1943, which towards the end of 1944 had risen to about 100,000. It
is not known whether at this latter stage the UPA forces were still
organized into divisions of about 10,000 men. There are many
reports about this time of UPA groups acting in strength of 2-5
thousand. This great increase of strength in 1944 is partly to be accounted for by the reoccupation of the West Ukraine by the Red
Army which had unwelcome consequences for a large part of the
population. The reoccupation of every village was followed within
a few days by a call-up of all men between the ages of 18-50 usually
conducted by an officer of the NKVD. Those who had collaborated
with the Germans were, according to the degree of their offences,
either summarily executed, sent to the interior for further in-

vestigation or sent direct to penal companies. The remainder, with the exception of certain party officials and those who had been with the partisans for more than one year, were sent to ordinary companies of reserve regiments. For the West Ukrainians these units appear to have been only a modified form of punishment company, where by bravery in the face of the enemy they might expiate their offences against their Fatherland in not having actively resisted the Germans. They were given 5-10 days training and were sent ill-armed and ill-clothed in the most dangerous parts of the front; casualties and desertions seem to have been heavy.

Originally the UPA had encouraged its supporters to present themselves for recruitment as the Red Army reconquered the W[estern] Ukraine, hoping thereby to utilize the training facilities of the Red Army for its own benefit, as it had used previously those of the German army. The use of the West Ukrainian recruits as cannon fodder caused this policy to be reversed. Cases were frequently reported in autumn of 1944 wherein UPA units attacked the guards of parties of recruits, the majority of whom were alleged to join the UPA after their liberation.

During 1944 a number of German stragglers joined the UPA. They were found in command of units and also in technical capacities. Units composed of dissident nationalities in sympathy with the aims of the OUN, e.g. Caucasian, are also reported as having fought with it.

Armament. Originally light and heavy machine guns, machine pistols, rifles. Later in November 1943 each division of 12 thousand men is reported to have at its disposal two 3 inch guns, four to six anti-tank guns, as well as mortars. In 1944 tanks are occasionally reported. [........].

Policy. As with Ukrainian Movements, the cardinal point in the policy of the OUN was the establishment of an independent greater Ukraine. Its political propaganda spoke much of civil liberties, and had a mildly socialist character; *Moscow* and *Berlin* were depicted as foreign imperialisms coveting Ukrainian wheat, while London came in for criticism as a stronghold of capitalism. After the unification of Ukrainian parties in June 1944, a more precise political programme was adopted.

The movement was uncompromisingly hostile to the German civil government in the Ukraine, the Soviet Government, the NKVD, Polish forces of both the London and Moscow groups, Poles living in the Ukraine, and the Vlasov movement. The movement was willing to negotiate, always solely with a view to its own benefit, with the German Army and Hungarian Army. The only non-Ukrainian body with whom the OUN appear to have been on good terms was the Serbian national partisans, with whom an agreement is reported to have been concluded in March 1944 not to assist Tito's organization.

As has been stated above, the OUN originally hoped to achieve its aim with German assistance but these hopes were repeatedly shattered. As in 1944 the impending defeat of Germany became increasingly obvious, there are reports of the OUN seeking support in England, and *vice versa*. All these reports lack confirmation; the most specific one of them states that Maxim Ruben, (alias Lebed), the political leader of the OUN, travelled to England *via* Spain in April 1944, presumably in order to canvas support.

Later History. Negotiations between UPA and the German Army units at a purely local level are reported from early 1944 onwards on a basis of mutual non-aggression and the exchange of German arms for intelligence on the Red Army. During negotiations on a higher level in June 1944, the UPA sought without success to make the agreement conditional on the German Army using its influence to improve the treatment of the Ukrainian population by the German civil administration. A final agreement, between German Army Group North Ukraine and the UPA leadership was made in August 1944, with the approval of the *Reichsminister* concerned and Himmler, the German civil administration in the Ukraine having ceased to exist. The UPA insisted throughout on negotiations with the Germans being kept secret, in order not to prejudice its propaganda inside the Red Army.

The policy of the German Army on the Ukraine question was reviewed late in 1944. The conclusion was reached that the Ukrainians did not constitute a separate nation, and that as the freedom of the national minorities depended on the defeat of the Red Army, all the forces of the dissident minorities should unite under General Vlasov. This decision represented a considerable victory for Vlasov, who had been putting forward this view for several years without securing German agreement; sympathy in the Ukraine for the German cause was, however, likely to be annulled by it.

SOVIET COUNTER MEASURES

Military Action. During 1944 military action by the Soviet authorities against the UPA is reported on an increasing scale. The troops used for this purpose were drawn in roughly equal numbers

from the Red Army and the NKVD; the direction of the campaign
against anti-Soviet partisans was, in rear areas, the responsibility
of the KGB. The number of troops engaged was estimated at one
time as about 40,000, of which the Red Army contribution would
naturally be drawn from the most reliable divisions. It is known
that Soviet Ukrainian partisan personnel were often employed for
this purpose under the control of the NKVD, after their zone of
operation had been re-occupied by the Red Army.

Deportation of Families. The removal (mainly to Siberia) of
families of known UPA members, as of other politically unreliable
persons, was widely carried out in the West Ukraine, and seems to
have been one of the most effective methods of undermining the
UPA movement. It does not seem, however, that these measures
were normally applied collectively to whole villages.

The policy of deportation of disaffected elements naturally
brings with it the danger of building up centres of resistance in the
reception zones. Mixed German-Ukrainian partisan activity in the
Soviet Far East was in fact reported in November 1944, from a
reliable source.

Pan-Slav Propaganda. A Pan-Slav movement was founded by
the Soviet authorities in August 1941, in order to turn to the advantage of the Soviet Union the fact that Germany either had
destroyed or was seeking to destroy all independent Slav states,
and to represent the Soviet Union as the protector of the Slavs.
Though not designed solely or even primarily with a view to the
Ukraine, this propaganda move appears to have had a wide
response there; this is no doubt partly to be accounted for as a
natural reaction on the part of the population of the occupied territories to foreign rule in the Ukraine and in particular to the Nazis'
estimate of themselves as *Herrenvolk* and Ukrainians as
asiatisches Untermenschentum (Asiatic sub-human).

Anti-Separatist Propaganda. Reference has been made above
to the appeal issued in early 1944, from the Supreme Soviet of the
Ukraine SSR to the members of the UPA and UNRA. A free pardon
was offered to those who deserted to the Soviets. In the same document the Soviet Union was represented as having achieved the
union of the Ukrainian people by its march into Poland in 1939.

Constitutional Changes. Early in 1944 the constituent
republics of the Soviet Union were granted the right to maintain
their own separate Ministries for defence and foreign affairs. There
can be little doubt that this measure was largely intended as a con-

cession to nationalist feeling in these republics particularly in the Ukraine.

RECENT HISTORY OF UKRAINIAN MOVEMENT

As mentioned above, in June 1944 the various Ukrainian resistance groups united into a Union for the Liberation of the Ukraine *(Spilka Vyzvolenia Ukrainy)*, from which there was constituted a Supreme Liberation Council *(Ukrainska Holovna Vyzvolna Rada)*. Under this, a shadow government was set up with ministries, supreme court, etc. It is not certain that this government had any but a nominal existence. There are, however, a number of reports of areas in the West Ukraine coming under the control of the Ukrainian resistance movement, during the winter of 1944-45. It is likely that the Soviet hold on this region at that time was concentrated on big towns and lines of communication.

The political programme put forward by this organization attempted to cater to both the peasantry and those of liberal and socialist leanings. This programme provided for civil liberties, and the socialization of heavy industry and transport, while for agriculture it was proposed to set upper and lower limits to the amount of land that an individual might hold.

FUTURE PROSPECTS

In World War II, as in World War I, the Ukrainian movement did not begin to attain the necessary unification and organization until it was too late for advantage to be taken of the mutual preoccupation of Germany and Russia. With the defeat of Germany and the disappearance of the operational commitments of the Red Army, NKVD and NKGB it cannot be expected that the UPA will be able to keep its forces in being for many months. Moreover, the UPA like all partisan movements was dependent in many ways on the whole-hearted support of the population of the territory in which it worked, and up to April 1945 there was every indication that policy of transporting UPA sympathizers to Siberia and elsewhere was being remorselessly carried out. When we add to these considerations the inevitable Sovietization and Russification of the West Ukraine under Soviet rule it will be seen that Ukrainian nationalism has little prospect of being anything more than a nuisance to the Soviet Union in future years of peace.

Appendix I

*The following data on UPA organization, tactics and supply
circumstances are given by a German reconnaissance group,
who spent a month behind the Soviet lines in
the Carpathians in Oct[ober]-Nov[ember] 1944.
Throughout this period the group received
guidance and hospitality from
the UPA organization:*

FRONTAUFKLARUNGSKOMMANDE 202   In the field
BEI HEERESGRUPPE A   22nd November, 1944

SECRET

Results of Observation of upa

[........]

I. *Organization.* The smallest tactical unit is the group *(Riy)*
strength one leader and nine men.

4 groups form a platoon (*Chota*),   4 platoons form a company *(Sotnya)*

3-4 companies form a battalion (larger tactical units were
not observed)

Specialist personnel are attached to a company for particular duties, e.g. scouts, liaison, supply and provost personnel.

The total strength of a company in the field may be 160-180
men.

The issue of orders takes place daily, mostly in the evening
through the csm.

Battalions work for the most part independently of one
another, liaison being maintained by couriers or despatch-riders.

In addition to the above combat units, there are so-called
"local" or "political" combat groups *(Mistsevi Boyovki)*. These differ from the regular troops by being resident in their zone of operations. Their strength does not normally exceed ten men. They
carry out police duties.

The leaders of the various upa units from group to battalion
are known as *Riyoviy, Chotoviy, Sotenniy* and *Komandir* respectively.

The official mode of address is *Druzhe* (comrade), e.g. *Druzhe Comandir*

Other ranks also address one another as *Druzhe*.

II. *Discipline*. The discipline is patterned on that usual in German units.

Relations between superiors and their subordinates are largely on a comradely basis.

A smart soldierly bearing is maintained.

Orders are carried out with precision.

Disobedience is severely punished.

For severe offences floggings are a common form of punishment.

Desertion is punished by shooting (deserters are sought out and arrested by police).

III. *Tactics*.

Meticulous selection of an opponent.

Only profitable actions undertaken.

Avoidance of open battle.

Preparations for a typical undertaking.

Thorough reconnaissance.

(a) through the civil population *(Tsivilna Rozvitka)* the results of which are often exaggerated and vague.

Hence, in addition –

(b) military reconnaissance, *(Viyskova Rozvitka)*

When these two types of reconnaissance agree with one another, a plan of attack is drawn up.

Duties are allotted and arrangements made in consultation with someone who knows the locality concerned.

Time and place for *rendezvous* are fixed. Approaches to the locality involved are watched. Telephone lines are cut. One to two hours after dusk is regarded as the most favourable time for the attack.

The scene of the attack is left the same night. Retreating units endeavour to cover up their tracks.

When a unit stays in the same area for some time, actions are carried out only in neighbouring areas. Conspicuous movements are forbidden in the locality where the unit is situated except for essential tasks, e.g. procurement of supplies.

Movements of larger formations take place mostly by night. Marching in the day time is only possible in large stretches of forest. A company proceeds by platoons. Guides escort the units from place to place, or from forest to forest. The destination is reconnoitred a day or two before hand. While on the march roads and inhabited places are avoided. Occasionally a platoon will be billeted in one place. Camps are pitched in the forest. Camps are guarded day and night by double sentries up to a radius of half a mile. Persons with local knowledge are sent out to spy out the land and procure food. When a unit intends to stay some time armed patrols are sent out into the neighbouring countryside. It is difficult to take a UPA unit by surprise, since the population to the extent of 99% work for the UPA willingly and with enthusiasm. The population is extraordinarily suspicious and wary of any stranger.

IV. *Armament.* Units are armed for the most part with Russian weapons. Pistols and hand-grenades are 80% of German or Hungarian origin. German sub-machine guns and machine guns occasionally. Members of the ss division *Galicia,* however, are armed and equipped 90% with German material (RG 34 and 42; MP 40 and 43). Automatic weapons of Slovakian or Hungarian origin are rare.

Armament of a group:
  1 light machine gun (Russian)
  2-3 carbines (Russian)
  1-2 carbines (German or Hungarian)
  2-3 sub-machine guns (Russian).

Platoons mainly armed with heavy machine-gun; occasionally mortars and special weapons.

The local and political combat-groups are less heavily armed. Occasionally machine pistols, mainly pistols or carbines, small arms being better for their tasks.

Ammunition:

Apparently plentiful. Dump about seven miles away from actual quarters. Shortage of pistol ammunition 7.65 mm and 9 mm. German weapons are preferred, but German ammunition in short supply.

Care and maintenance of weapons: great shortage of material for this purpose. Weapons, nevertheless, in good condition.

V. *Equipment.* A great shortage of equipment of all kinds. Bivouac tents, haversacks, slings are uncommon; rucksacks are improvized from sacks; spades and axes are even more scarce; ammunition pouches are likewise improvized by individual; mess tins and water bottles are also in short supply; shortage of washing and shaving utensils, tooth powder and tooth brushes (one rasor blade to ten to twenty men).

VI. *Dress.* Footgear is mainly of German and Hungarian

origin. Shoes and boots are made locally. However, material available does not suffice to cover requirements. German Army and locally produced underwear is worn. As a result of the shortage of underwear there is widespread infestation.

For uniform, items of German, Russian and Slovak uniforms are worn. Greatcoats are in short supply.

VII. *Supplies.* The inhabitants of individual villages are made collectively responsible for supplies to UPA units 90% of which process takes place without friction. In some places "Ukrainian State Stores" are formed for this purpose. Elsewhere a village headman *(Starichi)* is made responsible for supplies to the troops.

Inside the units distribution of food takes place through a QMS equally for officers and men. The usual cooked dish is a nourishing tasty stew. Captured field kitchens are available. Distribution of provisions for morning and evening, e.g. butter, etc., takes place according to availability (similarly tobacco). Salted and smoked ham, and sausage, are put by as an "iron ration." A great shortage of salt and spices.

Signed in draft

KIRN

Captain & Kdo. führer

* * *

APPENDIX II

DEFENSIVE AND COUNTER-ESPIONAGE MEASURES
AGAINST THE BANDERA MOVEMENT

*Translation
of Regimental Order of the 258th* Khabarov *Rifle Regt
of 14 Jan. 1944*

With the entry into the Western regions of the Ukraine the regiment may come into contact with anti-Soviet elements, the bands of Bandera, and must be prepared in the near future for acts of terrorism.

It is ordered that:

1. No one may go out alone.

2. No one may go out unarmed.

3. Baggage wagons may not go out singly, but only in groups of not less than five. For every group of wagons a baggage commander is to be detailed. Drivers must be armed. Ammunition supplies are to be guarded.

4. The rear services will deal with the security of the operational zone.

5. Headquarters guards are to be strengthened. Their quarters must be close together.

6. If necessary the civil population is to be moved out of houses occupied by HQ personnel.

7. No arms are to be left unguarded in quarters.

8. Care is to be taken in guarding W/T stations, telephone cable-offices and telephone lines.

9. The vigilance of personnel is to be intensified. All necessary measures for the preservation of secrecy are to be strictly carried out.

10. Acceptance of alcoholic drinks from the civil population is to be strictly forbidden.

11. Individual partisans and partisan groups in the battalion area are to be carefully scrutinized.

12. Guard duty in the battalion is to be strictly maintained.

The battalion commander is personally responsible for the execution of the above orders.

A report that the order has been carried out is to be submitted by 0800 hours 15.1.1944.

[sgd.] *Chief of Staff*
Maj. KHARLAMOV

* * *

Minutes

This is a most interesting report. The odd thing about it is that the local population seems to have been willing to support both Ukrainian Nationalist Partisans and Soviet Partisans. This seems to indicate that they were not greatly interested in the Ukrainian Nationalist issue as such, but were willing to help anybody who claimed to be fighting in their interests.

[sgd.] J. B[RIMELOW]

*

This report is most useful, but in places so much telescoped as to be somewhat misleading. For example, no mention is made of any Ukrainian political organization save OUN. This was admittedly the most important but there were several others. In particular the most pro-German of all the movements, the SHD, followers of Hetman Skoropadsky, had by no means died out. Skoropadsky himself died in April 1945, but before his death he appointed one Boris Honoinev his successor. His followers have recently made application to the British authorities in Germany to contact the old Hetman's son Danylo who is living in England.

It seems most unlikely that Andreas Melnik should have joined the Soviet partisans, as he was the leader of the OUN movement, even though Bandera and Lebed, being younger and more fanatical, have usurped some of his authority.

According to a Stockholm source, Bandera died in a German concentration camp about November 1943. In connection with Mr. Brimelow's point concerning the volatility of Ukrainians some distinctions must be made. First, the main nationalist centre was Galicia — the Volhynians were more inclined to compromise. Second, the communist partisans were strongest in the towns, and the local population there tended to go in with them, while in the countryside the Ukrainian partisans were better able to continue with their war against every man.

Anywhere the Soviet partisans were far better armed, the Ukrainians joined them simply in order to secure arms.

[sgd.] B. MILLER

SOURCE: FO 371/47957
Public Record Office

37

Despatch from the High Commissioner for Canada to the Canadian Department of External Affairs, 9 August 1946, Regarding Treatment of Ukrainians in Germany and Representations from Canada.

OFFICE OF THE
HIGH COMMISSIONER FOR CANADA

LONDON
9TH AUGUST, 1946

Sir,

I have the honour to refer to my despatch No. A. 101 of 19th February, concering the position of Ukrainians in Germany and Poland.

2. In view of the natural interest taken in this subject by Ukrainian organizations in Canada, we have kept in close touch with the Foreign Office on developments. The Foreign Office are themselves the recipients of numerous protests and requests from the Ukrainian Canadian Committee and other Ukrainian organizations in Canada. In fact, the pressure exerted by the Ukrainian Canadian Committee has not been without influence on recent developments in United Kingdom policy towards Ukrainians in the British Zone.

3. I am enclosing a copy of an undated telegram addressed some months ago to Mr. Attlee by the Ukrainian Canadian Committee in Winnipeg, drawing attention to an order said to have been issued by the British Military authority in Germany to the effect that the Ukrainians were not recognized as a nationality, that no recognition could be given to any Ukrainian organizations or representatives as such, and that Ukrainian welfare organizations were not to be allowed. This attitude towards Ukrainians was contrasted with the attitude towards Jews, who were said to be accorded special protection. Although this telegram somewhat overstated the case, it did refer to an order which had in fact been issued on 29th December by the Headquarters of 30 Corps

District. When the complaint of the Ukrainian Canadian Committee was brought to the attention of the Foreign Office the latter
made representations to the Control Office for Germany and
Austria which has the responsibility for deciding upon any change
in the policy represented in this order.

4. This order had provided for the dissolution of all Ukrainian
organizations in Germany. The Foreign Office pointed out that the
Russians, so far as they could ascertain, had never asked for more
than the breaking up of the organizations set up by the German
Ministry for the Occupied Eastern Territories, with particular
reference to the Ukrainian National Committee and the Ukrainian
Red Cross. These two latter organizations had quite rightly been
broken up by the Military Government and certain of the members
arrested. The Foreign Office thought, however, that they might
have overshot the mark in insisting on the breaking up of all Ukrainian organizations and the prevention of all Ukrainian activities.
Non-political welfare work by the Ukrainians for the benefit of
their own countrymen, they thought, would not appear to fall
within the scope of the ban which had been imposed at the request
of the Russians.

5. This order also raised the question whether Ukrainians in
Germany should be allowed to organize welfare work amongst
themselves on the basis of self help. The Foreign Office pointed out
that if the Ukrainians were not to be permitted to conduct welfare
work amongst themselves they would be dependent on the minimum welfare facilities afforded to displaced persons in camps.
Although the Foreign Office understood that these minimum
facilities were not inconsiderable and included schooling for
children, they referred to the statement by the Ukrainian Canadian
Committee in their telegram that educational work amongst
Ukrainians had to be carried out in Russian or Polish. This did not
seem to the Foreign Office to be a necessary conclusion from the
principle that they did not recognize the claim of the Ukrainians to
be treated as a separate nation. Multi-lingual nations were common enough for them to admit the desirability for educational
work in Ukrainian without prejudice to their policy of recognizing
only the USSR and Poland as the homelands of these people.

6. The Foreign Office referred to recommendations which they
had earlier made concerning the treatment of the Balts and which
have now been accepted as policy. These recommendations had
been made because the Foreign Office Representatives in Germany had warned them that there was a risk of demoralization
among the Balts if the basic welfare work in camps where they

were kept was not supplemented by self help. I am enclosing a copy of a letter of 31st October, 1945, from Brimelow, of the Foreign Office, to King, of the Control Commission, which will give you a detailed picture of the proposals which were subsequently adopted for treatment of the Balts in Germany. Care was taken at this time to prevent this welfare work among the Balts from being used as a cover for political activities. The Foreign Office considered that there was a reasonable case for extending similar facilities to such Ukrainians as were unlikely to be able to return to their homes. They admitted that at first sight the Ukrainians appeared to be in a different position from the Balts in that they could ask to be sent to Poland if they did not wish to go to the USSR. However, the British Ambassador at Warsaw had reported that the Polish and Soviet Governments had an understanding whereby Ukrainians living in South Eastern Poland might be deported to the USSR and he had been unable to obtain an assurance that the same treatment would not be meted out to any Ukrainians returning to Poland from abroad. The Ukrainians in Germany were therefore faced with the same alternative as that which confronted the Balts – the USSR or exile. If, as seemed most likely, large numbers persisted in their refusal to return to their homes there would presumably be advantage in promoting welfare work amongst them in order that they should not go to pieces as a result of enforced inactivity.

7. The Ukrainian Canadian Committee in their telegram had raised the question of the forcible repatriation of Ukrainians in Germany. British policy in this regard was at the time under consideration and the decision to bring this policy into line with that of the United States is reported in my despatch No. A.671 of 8th August.

8. The Control Office has now agreed to the suggestions of the Foreign Office with regard to the treatment of Ukrainians in Germany, and instructions have been sent to the British authorities in Germany to carry out a policy in accordance with the views described above. I learn, however, that the results of this policy in the field are not very successful as yet. It is the British view that the Ukrainians are by no means as reliable and co-operative in carrying out this policy as are the Balts. It was explained to both the Balts and the Ukrainians that if they would behave sensibly, in other words not indulge in activities which would provoke protests from the USSR, then the British authorities would find it much easier to help them. The Balts seemed to understand, but the Ukrainians to a much lesser extent.

9. One of the difficulties has been that the Ukrainians have got hold of publications and propaganda from the Ukrainians in Canada, and the circulation of this material has drawn sharp protests from the Russians. The Foreign Office discussed this matter informally with representatives in London of the Ukrainian Canadian Committee. They pointed out to them that the British authorities would be forced to forbid the entry of this provocative material, but they thought it would be much better if the Ukrainian Canadians could stop it at its source. The Foreign Office state that they have found the Ukrainian Canadian Committee representatives in London understanding and sensible. They doubt if the Committee itself has been responsible for sending this material, but attribute it rather to other organizations associated in some way with the Ukrainian Canadian Committee. Since representations were made to the Ukrainian Canadians in London the flow of this material stopped.

10. The Foreign Office were asked if they would wish to make any representations to the Canadian Government for assistance in restraining the Ukrainian Canadian Committee. They stated, however, that they had no desire to do so. They welcomed, however, my describing the situation to you so that if opportunities should arise the Canadian authorities might be able to advise the influential Ukrainians in Canada that the best way in which to help those Ukrainians who were left in Germany was to behave reasonably and not force the British authorities into a position which would make it difficult for them to help.

11. I am sending copies of this despatch, together with the enclosures, to the Chargé d'Affaires in Moscow and to the Head of the Canadian Military Mission in Berlin.

I have the honour to be,
Sir,
Your obedient Servant,

[sgd.] [—————]
Acting High Commissioner

Source: File 8296 - 40c
Department of External Affairs
(Canada), Historical Division

38

Proposal of British Foreign Secretary to British Cabinet, Presenting Arguments in Favor of Diplomatic Relations with the Government of the Ukrainian SSR.

[NOVEMBER, 1946]

ESTABLISHMENT OF DIPLOMATIC RELATIONS WITH
THE GOVERNMENT OF THE UKRAINIAN
SOVIET SOCIALIST REPUBLIC

TOP SECRET

I should welcome the approval of the Cabinet for an approach to the Government of the Ukrainian Soviet Socialist Republic through the Ministry for Foreign Affairs of the USSR suggesting that diplomatic relations be established between the Ukraine and the United Kingdom. I have discussed this proposal with H. M. Ambassador in Moscow and have reached the conclusion that we have little to lose and a good deal to gain by such a move.

RECOMMENDATION

I recommend that the Governments of the Dominions be first consulted on this proposal and, if they agree, the United States Government.

CONSIDERATIONS

Present Position. Neither the United Kingdom nor the Dominions have at present any representative in the USSR outside Moscow. The Soviet Government on the other hand has diplomatic representatives in London, Ottawa, Canberra and Wellington, and in addition has Consular representatives in Halifax (Nova Scotia) and Pretoria, with an acting Consular agent at Capetown. Taking the Commonwealth as a whole, the balance is thus heavily in favour of the Soviet Union.

For purposes of comparison it may be mentioned that the

United States Government have a diplomatic representative in Moscow, a consular representative in Vladivostok and a Naval Control Officer at Odessa. The Soviet Government have a diplomatic representative in Washington and consular representatives in New York, San Francisco and Los Angeles. Again the balance is in favour of the USSR. There are also some Chinese and a Persian consul in the Soviet Union; but in spite of this the Soviet Government steadfastly refused during the war to agree to the opening of British consulates on a basis of reciprocity and there is thought to be no likelihood of their changing their attitude. If, therefore, our representation in the Soviet Union is to be extended outside Moscow, it will be necessary to enter into direct relations with one or more of the constituent Republics.

Diplomatic representation in the Constituent Republics of the USSR. Under a law of the 1st February, 1944, an article (18a) was added to the Soviet Constitution under which each Constituent Republic has the right to enter into direct relations with foreign States, to conclude agreements with them and exchange diplomatic and consular representatives with them. So far as is known, no Union Republic has yet availed itself of the right thus conferred upon it to exchange representatives with other States.

The War Cabinet decided on the 5th June 1944, that the question of the recognition of the constituent Republics of the USSR for purposes of international representation should be postponed until the peace settlement and that the Governments of the Dominions and the United States should be informed of this decision. It was agreed at the time that HMG would keep in touch with the Governments of the Dominions in the event of the Russians making any move bearing on this matter. In August 1944 the State Department agreed informally with His Majesty's Embassy at Washington that there should be a full exchange of views and information on this subject. We are thus committed to consulting the Dominions and the US Government before we alter our attitude. Subsequently the Soviet Government pressed for the admission to the United Nations of all sixteen constituent Soviet Republics. HMG, the Dominions and the United States Governments all declined to agree to this, but after prolonged discussion the Ukraine and Byelorussia were admitted to membership of the United Nations Organization (the War Cabinet's concurrence was given on the 8th February, 1945). It may be added that on two recent occasions officials of the State Department have said that the United States Government were reluctant to take official action of the Ukrainian Government for purposes other than membership of the United Nations.

The admission of the Ukraine and Byelorussia to UNO constituted recognition of these two constituent republics as separate
entities for international purposes and a proposal to exchange
diplomatic representatives with the Ukraine would not, therefore,
be a departure from principle. It is with the Ukraine that it would
be most worthwhile to have direct diplomatic relations. The advantages would be:

(i) we should have a regular source of reports on an area of the
USSR which is of great economic and military, if not political, importance. (The Ukraine is the second largest Republic in the USSR);

(ii) we should have another centre in the Soviet Union for contacts and the spread of cultural, if not political, influence;

(iii) we should learn about the working in practice of the Soviet
machinery of Government outside Moscow.

In return we should merely have to accept the addition of a few
Ukrainians to the Diplomatic Corps in London. They would really
be little more than additions to the staff of the Soviet Embassy. If
we are refused permission, as is probable in view of the difficult
conditions at present prevailing in the Ukraine, we shall have done
something to expose the unreality of the Ukraine's pretensions to
independence and we shall have an additional argument for refusing to recognize or to admit the separate representation of other
constituent republics, especially the three Baltic republics, on international bodies. Incidentally the fact that we are asking for
diplomatic relations to be established with the Ukraine might, in
itself, deter the Soviet Government from asking for recognition of
other parts of the Soviet Union.

The possible disadvantage of the proposal is that whereas it is
generally known that we agreed to the admission of the Ukraine
and Byelorussia to the United Nations Organization because there
was no other way in which Soviet concurrence and participation
could be obtained, and whereas it is generally recognized at present that both republics are, in foreign affairs at any rate, mere
puppets of the Soviet Government, we might by ourselves propos-
ing an exchange of diplomatic representatives with the Ukraine
confer a certain air of respectability on it. It may, however, be
argued that the principle of separate representation was really
given away when we admitted these states to UNO and that having
given the principle away we might as well derive what advantage
we can from it.

SOURCE: FO 371/66354
Public Record Office

39

British Embassy, Warsaw, to the British Foreign
Secretary E. Bevin, 27 May 1947,
Reporting on Polish-Soviet Population Exchanges
and Effects on Ukrainian Insurgency.

BRITISH EMBASSY

WARSAW
27TH MAY, 1947

Sir,

I have the honour to report that a joint communique issued by the Polish Government and the Government of the Ukrainian Soviet Socialist Republic announcing the formal termination of repatriation of Polish and Ukrainian citizens from the respective territories, was published here on the 7th May.

2. The repatriation movement referred to resulted from the Agreement of the 9th September, 1944, which provided for the transfer to present-day Poland of Poles domiciled in Ukrainian territory to the east of the new frontier, and of such Ukrainians as were still domiciled in Poland to the territories which are now incorporated in the Ukrainian Republic. Its termination has several times been postponed, owing to transport difficulties and to the unwillingness of numbers of both Poles and Ukrainians to opt for transfer. No official figure has been given for the number of persons finally involved. M. Wolski, Vice-Minister of Public Administration, however, informed press correspondents some two months ago that 484,000 Ukrainians had been transferred from Poland and that these were "believed" to be the whole community.

3. Even now according to reports from persons recently arrived from Lwow, many Poles have remained in the Ukrainian Republic. In a recent conversation with Mr. Russell, First Secretary at this Embassy, M. Mikolajczyk assessed the number of Poles in all the former Polish territory now in the Soviet Union at a figure as high as 600,000. At the same time, a member of the staff has been informed privately from an official source that there

are still 74,000 Ukrainians on Polish territory. They are mainly Ukrainians who are partners in a mixed Ukrainian-Polish marriage, or *Lemki* (a mountain race belonging to the Uniate Church and akin to the Ukrainians) who, as far as the repatriation agreement is concerned and against their will, have been counted in with the Ukrainians. They also include a number of pure Ukrainian families which have escaped transfer.

4. Both the Polish Government and the itinerant Soviet Commissions which "registered" the Ukrainians desirous of transfer, showed a keen desire to remove all Ukrainians from Poland. To dispose of those who, in spite of all, still remain and thus it would seem, extinguish the Ukrainian Question as far as Poland is concerned, the Polish Government have instituted strong measures. They have started to deport the 74,000 persons referred to above to the Western Territories, where they are being settled in scattered groups, and inaugurated (in early April) a military manoeuvre of some magnitude to wind up, once and for all, the armed Ukrainian bands, which have been attempting to hinder expatriation and taking vengeance on the Poles settled in former Ukrainian farms, many thousands of whom they have rendered homeless. I have no exact figures bearing on the deportation to the Western Territories, but I am reliably informed that on one day last week, 7,000 persons were awaiting transport in premises attached to the State Repatriation Office at Przemysl. They are said, incidentally, to have included a number of Polish families known for their political hostility to the Government.

5. Action against the Ukrainian bands has been in progress in somewhat desultory and ineffective fashion for the past two years. Since the murder of General Swierczewski, however, officially attributed to a Ukrainian band and reported in my *Weekly Summary* No. 12 of the 1st April 1947, the Military Attaché at this Embassy estimates that units, at any rate, of two divisions of the Regular army have been used, as well as the Security Police and the Internal Security Corps. Stories of the fighting have been featured in the press. An interesting development in this connection is that the Polish authorities are said to be receiving some measure of help from both the Soviet and the Czechoslovak Governments. On the 11th May, M. Modzelewski, Minister of Foreign Affairs, told the Finance Committee of the *Sejm* that the three Governments had decided on a "common policy of action." There is no evidence, however, that troops of any of the Governments concerned have crossed a frontier.

6. Henceforth apart from the small number of Ukrainian com-

munities in North Eastern Slovakia, there will be no Ukrainians in Europe outside the Soviet Union. Thus the vexed Ukrainian Question should at last cease to trouble international relations in Eastern Europe and become an internal affair of the Soviet Union.

7. I am sending copies of this despatch to His Majesty's Ambassadors at Moscow and Prague.

I have the honour to be, Sir,
Your most obedient, humble, Servant,

The Right Honourable   [sgd.] PHILIP OSWALD
Ernest Bevin, M.P.

SOURCE: FO 371/66355
Public Record Office

40

Memorandum by H. F. Matthews, Director of the Office of European Affairs, to D. Acheson, US Under Secretary of State, Describing Advantages and Disadvantages in Establishing Diplomatic Relations with the Ukrainian SSR, 23 June 1947.

OFFICE OF EUROPEAN AFFAIRS

SECRET   [WASHINGTON]
                                                        JUNE 23, 1947

The British have informed us of their intention to raise the question in Moscow of the establishment of direct diplomatic relations with the Ukrainian SSR and have requested the observations of this Government thereon. There follows a list of the principal advantages and disadvantages to this Government in following a similar course:

ADVANTAGES

1. The establishment of direct diplomatic relations with the Ukraine would give this Government a valuable listening post in one of the most important Republics of the Soviet Union. Internal security regulations in the USSR have recently been tightened and increased barriers placed between contacts of Soviet citizens with foreigners. Our Mission in Moscow is finding it increasingly difficult to arrange for travel within the Soviet Union. A mission in Kiev would enable at least some additional contacts to be made and would provide an excuse for travel between Moscow and the Ukraine. Apart from contacts much information could be obtained merely from observation. For example, weather reports would be useful to the Department of Agriculture and it would be possible to obtain information concerning the work of reconstruction industrial development, etc. even though our mission were subjected to close surveillance.

2. We have had indications that the establishment of dip-

lomatic relations with the Ukrainian Government would have to take place before an application to open a consulate in Odessa could be considered. We have long desired to open a consulate in that port and it is likely that the Soviet Government will shortly insist upon the withdrawal of our Naval representative who is now there.

3. We have a pressing need throughout the world for officers who have had experience in the Soviet Union. We are now beginning to give special language training to junior officers to be followed by assignments to the USSR. Due to the critical housing shortage in Moscow it will not be possible to send a sufficient number of officers for service there or in Leningrad and the establishment of a mission in Kiev would be of great assistance in the carrying out of this training program.

4. The Ukrainian Government already enjoys the full privileges of membership in the United Nations and its subsidiary organizations as well as in conferences organized under its auspices. Ukrainian officials are assigned to the Soviet Embassy in Washington and the Ukrainian Government, therefore, enjoys a number of advantages without according any similar advantages to the United States.

5. There has long been a strong autonomous feeling in the Ukraine and in times of stress dissatisfaction with the Central Government would probably be more evident in Kiev than in any other capital. The Polish Government has already received permission to open a consulate at Kiev and it is probable that if the British are allowed to establish diplomatic relations, similar permission will be given to other states, particularly those bordering on the Ukraine. It may be possible to obtain valuable information from other diplomatic missions there.

DISADVANTAGES

1. The Ukrainian SSR is not an independent sovereign state and does not even have a very large degree of autonomy. The agreement to admit the Ukraine into the United Nations was made under the pressure of wartime necessity. To establish diplomatic relations with the Ukraine would assist the Soviet Government in its maneuver to have the fiction of the autonomy of the Soviet Republics accepted by foreign governments. While we are now well committed to separate Ukrainian participation in any conference organized under the auspices of the United Nations, the establishment of diplomatic relations would preclude us from objecting to Ukrainian participation in any non-United Nations conference on

the ground that it was not a sovereign state.

2. Separate recognition of the Ukraine would increase the complexity of our relations with the Soviet Union and would give the Soviet Government increased maneuverability in advancing its own special interests in international affairs. For example, the Soviet Government could arrange for the Ukrainian Mission in Washington to take a strong position on a given question without involving the Soviet Government in direct responsibility therefor.

3. Establishment of direct relations would provide the Soviet Government with an additional propaganda channel and the mere fact of recognition would lead many Americans to accept the fiction of the autonomy of the Soviet Republics.

RECOMMENDATION

It is recommended that we reserve our decision on this matter until we have had an opportunity to see whether or not the British are successful in establishing direct relations and what benefits they receive therefrom. It is recommended that the attached *aide-mémoire* be sent to the British Embassy and that the attached telegram be sent to Moscow informing the Ambassador of the Department's decision.

[sgd.] H. F[REEMAN] M[ATTHEWS]

SOURCE: M 1286, Reel 5
State Department Records
US National Archives

41

H. H. Wrong, Canadian Embassy, Washington, to L. B. Pearson, Under Secretary of State for External Affairs, 14 July 1947, Relating to Establishment of a British Diplomatic Mission in Kiev, Ukrainian SSR.

SECRET

WASHINGTON
JULY 14TH, 1947

Dear Mr. Pearson:

With reference to my message WA-2111 of July 7th about the British proposal to open direct diplomatic relations with the Ukraine, I mentioned this matter to Mr. Bohlen of the State Department a couple of days ago and asked him what he thought of it. He said he thought that there was little harm in the British trying an experiment in order to see whether they could, in fact, open a mission in Kiev which would be a useful source of information. He was doubtful, however, that the Russians would permit the members of such a mission to see more than a very few officials or to have any liberty of movement.

There was some danger in the recognition in this way of the claim to alleged sovereignty of one of the Soviet republics. He went on to tell me the story of the proceedings at the Yalta Conference at which Mr. Roosevelt and Mr. Churchill had agreed to the admission of the Ukraine and Byelo-Russia as separate members of the United Nations. He said that he had been strongly opposed himself to this decision and called it the worst decision taken at Yalta. It had been pushed by Mr. Churchill because of the difficulties which he had encountered over the admission of India, and Mr. Roosevelt had at first opposed it.

The matter had come up at a meeting of the Foreign Ministers one morning, and was accepted by the three Heads of Government the same afternoon. Mr. Bohlen had come into the conference room almost simultaneously with Marshal Stalin, and had found Mr. Stettinius verbally reporting to Mr. Roosevelt the discussions of the Foreign Ministers. Mr. Bohlen was surprised when Mr.

Roosevelt opened his talk with Mr. Stalin simply by saying that he agreed that the two republics should be admitted so that that problem was off their list. He added that it was one of Mr. Roosevelt's "bad days" at Yalta.

He thinks that an exchange of diplomatic missions between the UK and the Ukraine ought not to do much harm, although it might possibly have some rather difficult repercussions in the unlikely event that the Russians decided that they had to turn Poland into a Soviet republic. He commented on the vote in the Universal Postal Union excluding the Baltic republics from membership as evidence that there was little likelihood of Russian pressure for international recognition of other republics succeeding in its object.

Yours sincerely,

[sgd.] H.H. WRONG

SOURCE: FO 371/66357
Public Record Office

42

New York Times *Article, 29 January 1948, Describing Ukrainian National Liberation Movement, with Minutes by British Foreign Office Officials.*

NEW YORK TIMES

JANUARY 29, 1948

SOVIET DIVISIONS SAID TO FIGHT UKRAINE AND CAUCASUS DISSIDENTS

Two divisions of Soviet troops in the Ukraine and two in the Caucasus area are aiding local police forces in intermittent but bloody warfare against anti-Communist guerrillas in those regions, according to information seeping out of Russia.

The guerrillas, who are no present threat to the Moscow regime, are nevertheless sizable in numbers. Their determined resistance, which has persisted since the war, has not yet been broken, and the periodic raids they make from their mountain and forest hideouts are of sufficient scope to require military as well as police counter-measures.

The Ukraine always has been a hot-bed of dissidence in Soviet Russia, and the nationalist and separatist tendency of this region never has been completely crushed by the Moscow regime.

During and after the German wartime invasion, the region was torn by civil strife, and the Ukrainian insurgent army, or the so-called UPA, became a very sizable force. In 1947, the Kremlin sent Lazar Kaganovitch, dubbed the "Iron Commissar," to the Ukraine to repress the rebellion, and his purges and executions, together with strong combined military measures by Russia, Czechoslovakia and Poland cut down severely the strength of the UPA.

The pitched battles that sometimes occurred two years ago between the UPA and MVD (secret police) troops no longer occur, it is understood, but the UPA, though weakened, still carries out periodic raids, and serves as the nucleus of a fairly extensive Ukrainian underground.

The Ukrainian resistance is centered in the Carpathian Mountains, but some resistance also has been reported from Bukovina and elsewhere. Reports from Ukrainian sources indicate the names of some of the leaders of the insurgent forces are Bandera, Melnyk, and Stohul, which are quite possibly fictious names intended to protect the relatives of these guerrilla leaders.

Somewhat less is known about the guerrilla fighting in the Caucasus, but the insurgents there seem to be composed of Cossacks, deserters from the Soviet Army, and dissidents of various types. The movement, however, is heavily tinctured with some of the same nationalist, separatist fervor that marks the Ukrainian insurgency.

Neither of these small-scale "civil wars" within Russia is any threat to the regime in the Kremlin, according to the best analysis available in this country, and the strength of the guerrillas has decreased steadily since the war. But it is considered significant in Washington, and an index of the internal political weaknesses of the Soviet regime, that guerrilla resistance, sufficient to require military counter-measures, still exists in the so-called "monolithic state."

* * *

Minutes

26. 5.

I suspect that this article is largely speculative, based on reports received from the various Ukrainian organizations in the USA.

Nevertheless, on the very slender evidence available, this is probably a more or less correct picture. [........]

[sgd.] C. RAE

*

8. 6.

The names of Bandera and Melnyk are so familiar in Ukrainian nationalistic and insurgent 'lore' that they have acquired solidity and reality irrespective of whether they are, by origine, fictitious.

Melnyk, who took over the pre-war OUN (Union of Ukrainian Nationalists) after the killing of its leader Col[onel] Konovalets in 1938, is, in any case, unlikely to be a pseudonym. About Bandera, who just seems to first seems to come into history about 1941, one is not so sure; 'Stohul' is a name new to me.

I agree that this article gives quite a balanced and accurate picture in the light of our knowledge of the subject, in particular it emphasizes that times and situations have changed — that UPA is now probably only a shadow of its former self from the point of view of military power, owing to the anti-insurgent drive of 1946-1947. Much Ukrainian nationalist propaganda tends to ignore thus circumstance unpalatable but probably true.

[sgd.] N.W. JONES

SOURCE: FO 371/77584
Public Record Office

43

Restricted Despatch to the US Secretary of State from the American Ambassador to the Soviet Union, 29 January 1948, Commenting on Remarks Made by V. Molotov on Ukrainian Nationalism in a Speech to the Ukrainian Supreme Soviet.

RESTRICTED

Moscow
JANUARY 29, 1948

The Ambassador has the honor to report that the Soviet Government devoted considerable effort and attention to the celebration of the 30th anniversary of the Ukrainian SSR on January 25. The event was preceded and accompanied by one of those propaganda campaigns at which the Soviet system is so efficient. The importance of the affair in the eyes of the local rulers was indicated by the fact that Vyacheslav Mikhailovich Molotov himself went down to Kiev to give the speech which formed the high point of the celebration. A translation of Mr. Molotov's remarks on this occasion is enclosed.

The most important point of this speech appeared to the Embassy to be a reiterated emphasis on the Ukraine's loyalty to and solidarity with the Soviet regime. In the light of the long history, extending right up to the present moment, of official criticism directed against the Ukraine for an alleged tendency to submit to "bourgeois influences," it is interesting and probably significant that Molotov stated: "Ukrainian science and arts are successfully overcoming anti-popular bourgeois influences and are gaining ever wider recognition among the peoples of the Soviet Union and beyond its borders."

Moreover, Molotov emphasized that the Ukrainian people had proved their loyalty to the Soviet regime during the recent war, a statement obviously more distinguished by propaganda value than by objective truth. His actual words were as follows:

> *The great difficulties and trials of our patriotic war served as a test of the firmness of the moral and political unity of the Ukrainian people, of their loyalty to the Soviet state and*

of the Bolshevik devotion of the Ukrainian Communists to
principle. At present we know that the Ukrainian people and
their vanguard — the Bolsheviks of the Ukraine — passed
through all these trials with flying colors.

Nevertheless, the Soviet Government well knows that hostile manifestations in Ukrainian culture and political life are by no means completely suppressed and it will undoubtedly continue to struggle against them. Nikita Sergeyevich Khrushchev, present political boss of the Ukraine, who replied to Molotov's speech, reemphasized that point:

In strengthening the friendship of the Soviet peoples, we
are obliged to wage a merciless struggle against all the
enemies of Communism, and, first of all, against the
Ukrainian-German nationalists who, after the smashing of
their German fascist masters, passed into the service of the
Anglo-American imperialists — the most evil enemies of
democracy and all progressive mankind. The Ukrainian peo-
ple have destroyed the insignificant group of Ukrainian na-
tionalists and will root out their remnants to the last one.

In addition to the Jubilee Session of the Ukrainian Supreme Soviet at which the above speeches were delivered, the celebration was marked by a host of other meetings, events, exhibits, congratulatory messages, and the usual devotional letter to Stalin. All the written material, including the editorials which followed, were highly congratulatory in tone and often similar to Molotov's speech in content.

Source: M 1286, Reel 6
State Department Records
US National Archives

44

*Report of the Office of Intelligence Research,
Department of State, 17 March 1948, Describing
Ukrainian Resistance Movement and Citing
the Impossibility of Success.*

DIVISION OF RESEARCH FOR EUROPE
OFFICE OF INTELLIGENCE RESEARCH

SECRET

MARCH 17, 1948

NATURE AND EXTENT OF DISAFFECTION
IN THE UKRAINE

[........]

THE UKRAINIAN UNDERGROUND

Reports of underground partisan activities in the Ukraine, which have recurred intermittently since the end of the war, received indirect substantiation in the Soviet press in August 1947. From other sources it would appear that Ukrainian guerrillas have operated in Poland and Czechoslovakia as well as in the western *oblasts* of the Ukraine. They have tried to oppose the power of the Polish authorities in southeastern Poland and have helped to resist the extension of collective farming into the western areas of the Ukraine. There have been indications that in both southeastern Poland and the Western Ukraine some of the local people have assisted the partisans.

The first postwar admission by the Kremlin that Ukrainian nationalist guerrillas opposed to the Soviet system were still active appeared in the two letters sent to Stalin in the name of the peasants in the Lvov and Rovno *oblasts* in August 1947 [........]. The letters referred to activities of "Ukrainian-German nationalist bands" in these areas. Moreover, an editorial in the Ukrainian Party newspaper implied that the partisans were active in other Western Ukrainian *oblasts*.

According to the letters, the bands were trying "with the support of the *kulaks*" to hinder the extension of collectivized agriculture. A report transmitted by the American Military Attaché in Moscow actually describes one such attempt. Apparently two or three peasants living near the city of Lutsk in the Western Ukrainian *oblast* of Volyn succumbed to the pressure applied by a Party organizer during a mass meeting to organize a collective farm. The same night a group of guerrillas reportedly appeared in the homes of these individuals and chopped off the arms which the peasants had raised at the meeting to signify assent.

There have been no Soviet reports on measures taken to liquidate the partisan bands operating in the Ukraine; the information available originates with sources outside of the Soviet Union. The Polish and Czechoslovak Governments, on the other hand, have released public statements on their actions against the partisans within their areas.

On various occasions the Poles have revealed that their military forces had been engaged with the "Ukrainian White Partisans" or the "Fascist-Ukrainian bands of the UPA" *(Ukrainska Povstanska Armiya* — Ukrainian Insurrectionary Army). Apparently the most recent major operation occurred in May 1947, when "400 bandits" were allegedly killed and several hundred captured. This took place shortly after the partisans had succeeded in killing the Polish Vice Minister of National Defense, Colonel General Karl Swierczewski, near Sanok, a border town in southeastern Poland. It appears, however, that even after this date the Ukrainian guerrillas were still operating in Poland, since at the end of June 1947 the Warsaw radio reported that the UPA bands "would be finally liquidated" in the "near future."

At least some of the population in southeastern Poland aided the Ukrainian partisans active in that region. When the Poles carried out their operation in May 1947, they "arrested a number of persons" for having "cooperated" with the guerrillas. A London *Times* correspondent who entered Poland shortly before the middle of August 1947 was shown a village near the Slovak border that had been completely burned by Polish military forces, allegedly as a reprisal measure against the villagers for having aided the Ukrainian bands. The officers of a Ukrainian partisan group that reached the American Zone of Germany in September 1947, after leaving Poland and crossing Czechoslovakia, also reported that they had been aided by the civilian population in southeastern Poland. According to them, their position in the area became untenable in the spring of 1947, when the Polish Army began to

evacuate the local population into East Prussia and Silesia, thus
cutting off "the partisans' main source of supply."

The activities of Ukrainian partisans in Slovakia and Moravia
received much attention in the Czechoslovak press during the summer of 1947. In those areas, too, the guerrillas were reported to
have received assistance from some elements in the local population. The partisans apparently singled out Communists and prosperous Jews for attack. General Ludwig Svoboda, Czech Minister
of Defense, reported in October 1947 to a committee of the National Assembly on the measures that had been taken against the
bands. He claimed that Czechoslovak troops had successfully kept
the partisans from breaking into Slovakia from Poland in April
1946. In the spring of 1947, however, Svoboda said, "several large,
organized bands" totalling 400 to 600 men crossed into Slovakia
from Poland, where they had been under combined pressure from
Polish and Soviet troops. They were immediately attacked, according to Svoboda, and either liquidated or dispersed, so that by the
time he spoke there were only 100 to 200 Ukrainian partisans remaining at large in Czechoslovakia.

In his description of the bands, the Czechoslovak Minister of
Defense asserted that they were "militarily organized," had been
"well trained, ... had had several years of experience in guerrilla
warfare," and were "strongly armed with machine guns and other
automatic weapons." From this it would appear that the Ukrainian
partisan units comprised a more formidable force than mere bandit
bands whose sole motivation was plunder.

The claim made in the summer of 1946 that there was a
political organization in Europe to which Ukrainian guerrillas in
Western Europe owed allegiance seems also to have been substan-
tiated during 1947. Both the Civil Censorship Division of the
United States Forces in Europe and the Ukrainian partisans who
surrendered to American units in Germany in September 1947
have reported that an organization exists in Europe which sup-
posedly is coordinating the activities of all Ukrainians struggling
for the independence of their homeland. This organization, whose
name is translated variously as Ukrainian Supreme Council of
Liberation and Ukrainian Supreme Free Peoples' Council *(Ukrainska Golovna Vyzvilna Rada)*, apparently hopes to become the official Ukrainian government if the partisans should gain control of
the Ukraine. Almost nothing is known about the individuals composing this council or about the subordinate governmental agencies it allegedly has organized in preparation for assuming control
in the Ukraine. The Ukrainian guerrillas interned in Germany in

September 1947 said that Stepan Bandera, well-known Ukrainian nationalist leader, is rumored to be the head of the Council as well as the commander in-chief of the Ukrainian Insurrectionary Army (UPA). This statement would complement the 1946 report on the Ukrainian Supreme Council, which claimed that Bandera recognized the Council's authority.

The military organization of the UPA, as described by the Ukrainian partisans who surrendered to American troops in Germany, resembles the description given in the 1946 report on the Ukrainian Supreme Council of Liberation. According to that report, the UPA was operating in the western part of the Soviet Ukraine in bands of 60 men and had a total strength of 100,000 men. The Ukrainian partisans in Germany asserted that the UPA was organized operationally into squads, plutoons, companies, and in some cases even battalions. For administrative purposes, it was alleged, the smaller units were grouped into regiments. The usual unit of operation, however, was the company, which generally numbered about 160 men but varied in size according to the desires of the company commander. In all, it was claimed, there were between 50,000 and 200,000 active partisans in Poland and the Soviet Union. The numerical distribution of these men between the two countries, however, was not revealed.

The equipment of each Ukrainian partisan company, it was claimed, generally included from six to eight machine guns and a similar number of mortars, as well as the usual side arms for the individual guerrillas. This statement would imply that, given sufficient ammunition, the Ukrainian company would have firepower comparable to that of a wartime American infantry company. This condition has probably been rare, however, since the military supplies of the UPA were reported to depend upon what it could seize from its Polish and Soviet opponents and upon contributions from sympathetic civilians who had stolen supplies from Polish or Soviet forces.

Conclusions

Resistance to Soviet policies obviously continues to find support in the postwar Ukraine. The nationalist and separatist tendencies among the Ukrainians which Moscow viewed with so much concern during the 1930s still persist and are being attacked with vehemence. That the Kremlin has had only limited success in suppressing Ukrainian separatism was indicated as late as January 1948, when Khrushchev clearly implied that this sentiment still existed and urged continued efforts "to extirpate the remnants" of the local nationalists. [........]

The Ukrainian guerrilla bands will probably be exterminated in the near future. If the relatively weak Soviet military forces were able by 1921 to subdue the Ukrainian nationalist forces of Simon Petlura and the partisan bands of the Ukrainian anarchist Nestor Makhno, which developed during the Russian Civil War, it can be expected that present Soviet military and police forces, which are infinitely stronger, will eventually overpower all armed groups resisting the integration of the entire Ukraine into the Soviet Union. The real significance of the Ukrainian nationalist bands lies rather in the fact that they have already been able to operate for more than two years against the established governments of both Poland and the USSR. This could have happened only with the support of at least a part of the local population. These bands have had no normal sources of supply and have depended upon what they could seize from their adversaries and what was obtained from civilian sympathizers. Their continued survival suggests that the local population furnished them at least with food despite near-famine conditions in 1945 and it is evident that only people who strongly hate the Soviet way of life would have supported what many of them undoubtedly realize is a lost cause.

[........]

Source: OSS Research Analysis
Reports, No. 4228-R, M1221
UN National Archives

45

Note to National Security Council, Washington, by S. W. Souers, Executive Secretary, 18 August 1948, on US Objectives with Respect to Russia and the Issue of Ukrainian National Liberation.

UNITED STATES OBJECTIVES WITH RESPECT TO RUSSIA

AUGUST 18, 1948

TOP SECRET

The enclosed paper on the above subject, prepared by the Policy Planning Staff of the Department of State, is circulated herewith for the information of the National Security Council in connection with NSC 20, Appraisal of the Degree and Character of Military Preparedness Required by the World Situation.

At the request of the Under Secretary of State, the enclosure is being referred to the National Security Council Staff for consideration and the preparation of a report to the National Security Council.

[sgd.] SIDNEY W. SOUERS

Executive Secretary

[........]

PARTITION VS. NATIONAL UNITY

First of all, would it be our desire, [........] that the present territories of the Soviet Union remain united under a single regime or that they be partitioned? And if they are to remain united, at least to a large extent, then what degree of federalism should be observed in a future Russian government? What about the major minority groups, in particular the Ukraine?

We have already taken note of the problem of the Baltic states. The Baltic states should not be compelled to remain under any communist authority in the aftermath of another war. Should the territory adjacent to the Baltic states be controlled by a Russian authority other than a communist authority, we should be guided by the wishes of the Baltic peoples and by the degree of moderation which that Russian authority is inclined to exhibit with respect to them.

In the case of the Ukraine, we have a different problem. The Ukrainians are the most advanced of the peoples who have been under Russian rule in modern times. They have generally resented Russian domination; and their nationalistic organizations have been active and vocal abroad. It would be easy to jump to the conclusion that they should be freed, at least, from Russian rule and permitted to set themselves up as an independent state.

We would do well to beware of this conclusion. Its very simplicity condemns it in terms of eastern European realities.

It is true that the Ukrainians have been unhappy under Russian rule and that something should be done to protect their position in future. But there are certain basic facts which must not be lost sight of. While the Ukrainians have been an important and specific element in the Russian Empire, they have shown no signs of being a "nation" capable of bearing successfully the responsibilities of independence in the face of great Russian opposition. The Ukraine is not a clearly defined ethnical or geographic concept. In general, the Ukrainian population made up of originally in large measure out of refugees from Russian or Polish despotism shades off imperceptibly into the Russian or Polish nationalities. There is no clear dividing line between Russia and the Ukraine, and it would be impossible to establish one. The cities in Ukrainian territory have been predominantly Russian and Jewish. The real basis of "Ukrainianism" is the feeling of "difference" produced by a specific peasant dialect and by minor differences of custom and folklore throughout the country districts. The political agitation on the surface is largely the work of a few romantic intellectuals, who have little concept of the responsibilities of government.

The economy of the Ukraine is inextricably intertwined with that of Russia as a whole. There has never been any economic separation since the territory was conquered from the nomadic Tatars and developed for purposes of a sedentary population. To attempt to carve it out of the Russian economy and to set it up as something separate would be as artificial and as destructive as an attempt to separate the Corn Belt, including the Great Lakes industrial area, from the economy of the United States.

Furthermore, the people who speak the Ukrainian dialect have been split, like those who speak the White Russian [Byelorussian] dialect, by a division which in eastern Europe has always been the real mark of nationality: namely, religion. If any real border can be drawn in the Ukraine, it should logically be the border between the areas which traditionally give religious allegiance to the Eastern Church and those which give it to the Church of Rome.

Finally, we cannot be indifferent to the feelings of the Great Russians themselves. They were the strongest national element in the Russian Empire, as they now are in the Soviet Union. They will continue to be the strongest national element in that general area, under any status. Any long-term US policy must be based on their acceptance and their cooperation. The Ukrainian territory is as much a part of their national heritage as the Middle West is of ours, and they are conscious of that fact. A solution which attempts to separate the Ukraine entirely from the rest of Russia is bound to incur their resentment and opposition, and can be maintained, in the last analysis, only by force. There is a reasonable chance that the Great Russians could be induced to tolerate the renewed independence of the Baltic states. They tolerated the freedom of those territories from Russian rule for long periods in the past; and they recognize, subconsciously if not otherwise, that the respective peoples are capable of independence. With respect to the Ukrainians, things are different. They are too close to the Russians to be able to set themselves up successfully as something wholly different. For better of for worse, they will have to work out their destiny in some sort of special relationship to the Great Russian people.

It seems clear that this relationship can be at best a federal one, under which the Ukraine would enjoy a considerable measure of political and cultural autonomy but would not be economically or militarily independent. Such a relationship would be entirely just to the requirements of the Great Russians themselves. It would seem, therefore, to be along these lines that US objectives with respect to the Ukraine should be framed.

It should be noted that this question has far more than just a distant future significance. Ukrainian and Great Russian elements among the Russian emigré-opposition groups are already competing vigorously for US support. The manner in which we receive their competing claims may have an important influence on the development and success of the movement for political freedom among the Russians. It is essential, therefore, that we make our decision now and adhere to it consistently. And that decision should be neither a pro-Russian one nor a pro-Ukrainian one, but one which recognizes the historical, geographic and economic realities involved and seeks for the Ukrainians a decent and acceptable place in the family of the traditional Russian Empire, of which they form an inextricable part.

It should be added that while, as stated above, we would not deliberately encourage Ukrainian separatism, nevertheless, if an independent regime were to come into being on the territory of the Ukraine through no doing of ours, we should not oppose it outright. To do so would be to undertake an undesirable responsibility for internal Russian developments. Such a regime would be bound to be challenged eventually from the Russian side. If it were to maintain itself successfully, that would be proof that the above analysis was wrong and that the Ukraine does have the capacity for, and the moral right to, independent status. Our policy in the first instance should be to maintain an outward neutrality, as long as our own interests − military or otherwise − were not immediately affected. And only if it became clear that an undesirable deadlock was developing, we would encourage a composing of the differences along the lines of a reasonable federalism. The same would apply to any other efforts at the achievement of an independent status on the part of other Russian minorities. It is not likely that any of the other minorities could successfully maintain real independence for any length of time. However, should they attempt it (and it is quite possible that the Caucasian minorities would do this), our attitude should be the same as in the case of the Ukraine. We should be careful not to place ourselves in a position of open opposition to such attempts, which would cause us to lose permanently the sympathy of the minority in question. On the other hand, we should not commit ourselves in their support to a line of action which in the long run could probably be maintained only with our military assistance.

[........]

Distribution:
The Secretary of State
The Secretary of Defense
The Secretary of the Army
The Secretary of the Navy
The Secretary of the Air Force
The Chairman, National Security
Resources Board

Source: NSC 20/1, RG273
National Security Council Records
US National Archives

46

Minutes by British Foreign Office Officials on Central Ukrainian Relief Bureau Memorandum, 18 August-September 1948, Commenting on Official Status of Ukrainian DPs and Ukrainian Nationality.

AUGUST 18, 1948

I cannot help thinking that the main purpose of this memo is to request that Mr. Panchuk himself be appointed Ukrainian Ambassador [........] In fact Mr. Panchuk fulfils (not to everybody's satisfaction) the functions already quite unofficially, and the Home Office would, I think, throw a fit if it ever came to be more than that. I am sure this proposal need not go any further.

I expect copies of this memo have gone to other Departments, and I do not know how seriously we have to take the question of Ukrainian nationality. Treaty Department will have to advise. But even if, as a historical-sociological argument, Mr. Panchuk's definition is correct, nationality does mean "political citizenship" for our purposes, and coming from such an one as Mr. Panchuk, his reliance on the "statehood" of the Ukrainian SSR is an appalling sophistry. If, on these grounds (in themselves, I believe, fallacious), he wants to use the term Ukrainian citizen, he would have to accept such to be Soviet citizens as well; we may be sure he does not mean that.

We shall have to keep Ukrainians in this country happy, and one can sympathize with their desire not to be classed as Poles and Rumanians. It is, though, clearly impossible to call them Ukrainians pure and simple. Are there any objections against "stateless Ukrainian" [........]

[sgd.] C.R.A. RAE

*

AUGUST 23, 1948

Mr. Panchuk (who still, I imagine, calls himself a "Canadian" and not a "Ukrainian" for official purposes!), forgets that the national anonymity of many Ukrainians is often a matter of distinct advantage to them, especially where alleged "war criminals" and quislings are concerned. If they are to be given a special designation, I think that "Undetermined nationality" is preferable to "Ukrainian" or "Stateless."

[sgd.] A.W. WILLIAMSON

*

SEPTEMBER 1, 1948

It is unlikely that the Home Office will ask for our advice as to how "Ukrainians" should be described in documents issued to them in the UK, but if they do, we can give appropriate advice. Whatever local police authorities or Ministry of Labour Exchanges may do, the Home Office are not likely to regard or use "Ukrainian" as a term defining nationality.

[————]

SOURCE: FO 371/71636, 31437
Public Record Office

47

Secret Memorandum to the US State Department from R. F. Corrigan, Assistant to the US Political Adviser for Germany, 27 October 1948, Referring to Intelligence Division Report, European Command, US Army, Setting out Details on the Organization of a Ukrainian State on Ukrainian Territory.

UNITED STATES POLITICAL ADVISER
FOR GERMANY

SECRET

HEILDERBERG
OCTOBER 27, 1948

TRANSMITTING FURTHER INFORMATION REGARDING
UKRAINIAN DISSIDENT ELEMENTS

Sir:

    With reference to my despatch number 515 of September 29, 1948 and to previous correspondence on the subject of Ukrainian dissident elements, I have the honor to enclose (with original only) a single photostatic copy of a document given to this Office by the Office of the Deputy Director of Intelligence, European Command, United States Army that, I am informed, sets out details as to the organization of a Ukrainian State on Ukrainian territory if ever that should become possible. I understand that this document has been quite restricted in circulation.

The Honorable
The Secretary of State
Washington

Respectfully yours,
For the Political Adviser:

[sgd.] ROBERT F. CORRIGAN
Foreign Service Officer

48

Secret Letter from British Chancery, Prague, 9 February 1949, to the Foreign Office Research Department, Describing Ukrainian Insurgent Activities in Czechoslovakia.

BRITISH EMBASSY

PRAGUE
FEBRUARY 9TH, 1949

Dear Department,

Reference your letter without number of 21st January, 1949. The allegations are founded on fact, as will be seen from the following answers to the four questions arising out of your letter.

(1) Did TVORBA refer to large scale activities by the Ukrainian underground movement in Slovakia?

Answer: Yes, in a series of three articles entitled "Operation B" by Vaclav Slavik in TVORBA, Nos. 22, 23 and 24 of 2nd June, 9th June and 16th June, 1948, respectively, in which he described military operations, in which he participated and which took place against the Bandera forces between June, 1947, and the end of 1947, when the latter were liquidated.

(2) Was there any admission in TVORBA of "heavy fighting" in Slovakia?

Answer: Yes, in No. 22 there was a reference to "heavy fighting" and it was stated "the initial battles were very heavy." In No. 24 the author wrote "this struggle has no parallel in the history of our security."

(3) Was it stated that the number of Czech and Slovak recruits to UPA was "alarmingly large"?

Answer: Not in so many words but in No. 23 it was stated "the enemy ... had accomplices very frequently in the most influential local circles of Slovak public life ... these traitorous reactionary circles were to be found in widely different places."

(4) Was there any reproach of the Soviet-Polish-Czech command for failing to liquidate UPA which had turned the armed forces of these powers into a laughing-stock?

Answer: Not in so many words but in No. 22 it was stated "there were deficiencies in the ranks and organization of our warriors. The inconsistently effected purge of our army then became evident. A number of officers had to be relieved of their posts on account of conducting themselves badly in the face of the enemy. There were even cases of men preparing to betray their own units and desert to the enemy."

Yours ever,

CHANCERY

* * *

Minutes

Disappointing, as these particular admissions seem to refer only to matters of somewhat ancient history, and not to more recent operations, as, frankly, I had hoped! Since our letter to Prague was written, however, much more recent admissions on the Czech radio & in the Czech press during December 1948 have come to light, and have been incorporated, incidentally, in a more cautious redraft of my 'magnum opus' on the underground movements.

[sgd.] JCD

SOURCE: FO 371/77584
Public Record Office

49

Memorandum by N. W. A. Jones, British Foreign Office Research Department, March 1949, Regarding the Ukraine, Ukrainian Insurgency, and Emigré Organizations. Minutes by C. R. A. Rae and R. Faber.

TOP SECRET   MARCH, 1949

Mr. Hankey
Northern Department

I mentioned to you some time ago that we contemplated a paper on the alternatives to the present Soviet set-up in the Ukraine. Mr. Jones has now completed his analysis of the alternatives and their feasibility. We feel that it may be useful to have surveyed the ground in case the Ukraine should eventually become a 'hot' political question.

As you expressed an interest in this question I am sending you a copy of the draft.

[sgd.] V. CONOLLY
Research Department
Foreign Office

ALTERNATIVE FORMS OF GOVERNMENT TO "SOVIET FEDERALISM" FOR THE UKRAINE

The true nature of "Soviet Federalism", i.e. rigid centralization and the control of the entire Union in almost all matters from Moscow is fully exemplified in the present relationship between the Ukrainian SSR and the USSR. In addition to the patent fact that all vestiges of real political autonomy have long since vanished, Soviet economic plans for the Ukraine have always been subordinated to a general policy aimed at the complete absorption of the Soviet Ukraine by the USSR — this being, of course, in accordance with the Communist tenet that absolute unity, including political unity, can only be based upon economic fusion.

Several solutions present themselves as possible alternatives to the present system:

THE INSTITUTION OF AN INDEPENDENT NATIONAL UKRAINIAN STATE

An assessment of the feasibility of this proposition requires the preliminary examination of a number of vital factors.

Historical Tradition and Justification

The Ukrainians claim that their country is the direct successor to the tradition and authority of Kievan Russia, a period of history which all Russians, including the Soviets, rightly regard as one of outstanding glory in many fields. In support of their claim the Ukrainian nationalists maintain that the Ukrainian language is the direct descendant of the ancient Slavonic spoken in the Kiev of the 11th-13th centuries, and further, under the influence of their nationalist historians notably Michael Hrushevsky they claim that a state of almost complete ethnic homogeneity unites modern Ukrainians with those of the middle ages. The differing and often "unpleasant" characteristics of the Great Russians are ascribed to the strong Tatar and Finnish admixture which the peoples of the north and east acquired after the 13th century Mongol invasions.

The most extreme Ukrainian claim to unsullied continuity of either language or race cannot, however, be seriously maintained in the forms in which they present it. The Ukrainian language has certainly deviated very considerably from ancient Slavonic, but on the other hand it does retain more of its features than does modern Great Russian: and in spite of Ukrainian nationalist claims to the contrary, the Mongol invasion, after breaking the social and political order in South Russia, almost certainly led to the wholesale extermination or dispersal of the population. When South Russia including the Ukraine was re-colonized, largely in the 16th century, it is thus improbable that there were strong elements of the original Slavonic population remaining, and this re-colonization was carried out by Poland and Muscovy. This may furnish an explanation of why Ukrainian nationalists often experience difficulty in accepting even the dashing and picturesque Bohdan Khmelnitsky as a national hero, owing to his more or less enforced adoption of the Pereyaslav agreement (1654) which recognized Russian sovereignty over the Ukraine; and prefer the poet Taras Shevchenko (1814-1861) whose social and political tendencies were largely confined to literature. Similarly the Ukrainian School's sug-

gestion that the sack of Kiev by Andrew Bogolyubsky (1169) was
an early example of Great Russian and Ukrainian antagonism does
not bear serious examination, there being many contemporary indications that no consciousness of such a broad division existed at
the time; the Russian abbot Daniel (early 12th century) during his
pilgrimage to Palestine lighted a candle for "all the Russian land";
the theme of unity is likewise the keynote in the *Tale of Igor's Army* written, if genuine, soon after 1185.

Nevertheless, it can be safely maintained firstly, that
whatever its relationship to ancient Slavonic, Ukrainian does exist
as an independent Slavonic language, greatly strengthened and
developed, like several of the others, during the 19th century and
secondly, that whatever the Ukrainian line of descent from Kiev,
the present-day Ukraine exists in territory which was formerly the
centre of a powerful and prosperous Russian community, and the
institution of an independent State centred on Kiev can claim
sound historical justification.

Such were the historical origins of the birth, if not of the rebirth of Ukrainian nationalism in the 19th century. Receiving a
great impetus, like many other similar phenomena, from the Romantic movement, nationalism was at first confined to a heightened interest in native customs and folklore. This found its expression in the society of St. Cyril and St. Methodius, founded in Kiev
about 1846, of which the members, among them Shevchenko
himself, were revolutionary in temperament, rather than in
thought or intention. The succeeding phase, rather more serious
and scientific in its methods, but still not concerned with any idea
of separatism or indeed with any alteration in the existing political
and social order, was headed by the Kiev Society known as the
Hromada, the members of which from 1860 onwards carried out a
vast amount of historical research and provided Ukrainian nationalism with its historical *raison d'être.* Increasing Tsarist opposition, hitherto having paid slight attention to the matter, led to
a transfer of the centre of activity to the Austrian dominions where
the Habsburg Government was not unwilling to countenance
Ukrainian activity, provided that it was anti-Russian and also
because it was usually anti-Polish. As a result, Lvov became the
foyer of Ukrainian nationalism and was the ground which first
received the seeds of overt political propaganda.

Michael Dragomanov (1841-1895), a Professor from Kiev who
carried on his activity later from the greater safety of Switzerland
was probably the first Ukrainian to suggest a radical political re-
alignment; as a solution for the Ukrainian problem he proposed the

foundation of a Slav federation aimed at ending the tyranny of Moscow but avoiding a complete breach between Moscow and Kiev. Dragomanov's ideas may have survived to the present since it is very probable that the Ukrainians who played an important part in the anti-Soviet Promethée organization, consciously modelled their programme on the same lines. The final stage in the development of nationalist thought was reached when another and more radical solution was suggested by Michael Hrushevsky (born 1866) who, like Dragomanov, left Kiev for Lvov and the West but, unlike the latter formulated a policy of complete separation from Russia. The influence and indeed the personal activity of Hrushevsky, heightened by his reputation as a historian, led directly to the Ukrainian Rada of 1918, of which he was for a time the nominal head, and to the Ukrainian National Republic which still continues in exile.

The Numbers of the Ukrainian Population

The actual number of those speaking Ukrainian and considering themselves Ukrainians has long been a subject of great doubt and speculation. The task of arriving at even an approximate estimate has been rendered more difficult by the fact that the numbers of specifically Ukrainian casualties in the last war are unknown and can only be guessed at.

All serious estimates of the Ukrainian population are based on the official Soviet census figures of 1926 and 1939. Of these the former was probably fairer in its estimate than the latter which was carried out at a time when nationalism was scarcely encouraged. At the time of the 1926 census there were stated to be 29,018,000 persons inhabiting the Ukrainian SSR, while the 1939 census gave the figure as 30,960,000. In 1926 the total number of persons in the entire USSR who called themselves Ukrainians was given as 31,194,976, 87% of whom spoke the Ukrainian language. The 1926 census also reported that approximately 8,000,000 Ukrainians lived outside the borders of the Ukrainian SSR in the rest of the Union, leaving the number within the national republic as approximately 23,200,000.

In 1939 the number of those inhabitants of the USSR who considered themselves Ukrainians was stated as 28,070,404, representing a considerable decrease on the 1926 figures. As was indicated above, this is undoubtedly due in part to the fact that in 1939 the policy was to treat nationality as a "psychological phenomenon" (Lorimer) indicating the major group to which each individual felt that he belonged, thus inducing many who had previously called themselves Ukrainians to register as Russians (who increased in number according to the 1939 census from 77.7 millions to 99 millions). In 1939 approximately 19,600,000 of the 28,000,000 "ethnic" Ukrainians lived in the Ukrainian SSR, the remainder of the 1939 population of 30,960,000 being largely Russians.

With the causes and extent of the inter-census decrease in the Ukrainian population — undoubtedly the deaths and deportations at the period of collectivization and subsequent or rather consequent famine were greatly responsible — we are not immediately concerned, except to note that the subject forms one of the principal grounds for the Ukrainian nationalists' hatred of the Soviets: some of their estimates place the losses suffered by the Ukrainian nation at as high as 4½ to 5 millions. Whatever the facts concerning the tragedy of 1932-4 in the Ukraine, it appears probable that in 1939 the number of nationally conscious Ukrainians in the USSR was composed of the 19½ millions in the Ukraine proper to which must be added a proportion of those living outside the national republic. It is reasonably certain that those living in regions bordering the Ukrainian SSR, numbering about 3½ millions (distributed in the Kursk-Voronezh, Don and North Caucasus), escaped the russification of the inter-census period. It is probably also that the Ukrainians in the Far East numbering 315,000 in 1926 (census figures) also retained their identity. This yields a total of approximately 23½ millions for the USSR in 1939.

Of the 9,240,000 persons (according to Sulkevich, *Territoriya i Naseleniye SSR*, Moscow, 1940), who were added to the Ukrainian SSR between the census date (17th January, 1939) and the 1st May, 1940, a large proportion were of Ukrainian origin. According to the Polish census of 1931 there were in Poland 4,441,600 Ukrainians, nearly all of whom were later incorporated into the USSR. (The principal exceptions were those in the Kholm area, numbering, according to the same source, 73,000). However, according to many authorities a large proportion of the Polish Ukrainians could not be considered as nationally conscious: it has been suggested that the number of "conscious" Ukrainians would be more safely estimate at 2 millions. Accepting this figure and omitting the 700,000 inhabitants of the Sub-Carpatho-Ukraine who, until their incorporation into the USSR at least, showed very little enthusiasm for Ukrainian nationalism, we arrive at a very tentative figure of 25½ millions for those who may safely be regarded as Ukrainians. This makes no allowance for war losses which in the case of the Ukraine must run into millions, particularly in view of the fact that the

Ukraine was the most devastated area in the USSR. Neither is any account here taken of the Ukrainians who inhabited the Bukovina, estimates of whose numbers vary enormously (from about 200,000 to 400,000), and whose interest in the nationalist idea is as in the case of Sub-Carpatho-Ukraine, problematical.

However, these figures, tentative though they be, provide a corrective to the impression gained from a casual survey of Soviet population figures or from émigré literature, which often promises that a Ukrainian state could number as many as 50 million ardent nationalists. In fact, a Ukrainian state could scarcely count on more than half that number of natives. In addition it would, at the outset, be faced by very serious minority problems. In the immediate pre-war period, of the 8 million urban dwellers only 30% were Ukrainians: of the rural population the Ukrainians constituted a majority, ranging from about 80% in some areas to 50-60% in others (e.g. Odessa province). In the Western Ukraine a similar phenomenon was to be observed: an urban population predominately non-Ukrainian (in this case Polish) accompanied by a predominately Ukrainian peasant population. According to the 1931 Polish census the population of Lvov (312,231) was 63.5% Polish and 24.1% Ukrainian; of Stanislavov (59,960), 43.7% Polish and 38.3% Ukrainian; of Tarnopol (35,644), 77.8% Polish and 14.0% Ukrainian. (In all these cities there were large Jewish populations.) In addition, in the region of Lvov and in that of Tarnopol, along the pre-1939 Polish-Soviet frontier there were large enclaves of Polish-speaking peasantry. Some of these were Catholics, others, who were more pro-Ukrainian in outlook, Uniates.

Assuming the Western Ukraine were to be included, a Ukrainian national state would be faced with a minority of perhaps 15 million persons. Transfer of population, even if feasible from the Ukrainian point of view would be an enormous undertaking and would have effects largely unforeseeable, but probably unfavourable if not fatal from the economic standpoint. Indeed, the minority question constitutes the most serious objection to the purely nationalist conception.

The Territory of the Ukraine

Except for a compact area of Ukrainian settlement in the Kursk-Voronezh district, containing (in 1926) almost 1½ million Ukrainians, the northern boundary of the pre-1939 Ukrainian SSR coincided approximately with the limits of Ukrainian speech. It is, of course, on the Western and Eastern flanks of the country that the principal disputed areas lie. In the East, the substantial numbers of Ukrainians in the North Caucasus area, where (excluding the mountain republics themselves) Ukrainians constituted 41% of the population (1926 census), and a fairly dense settlement numbering about 600,000 on the lower Don, led the nationalists to claim large areas in the Kuban and Don regions.

The question of Western Ukraine, however, would constitute the most serious problem in delimiting the frontiers of any new Ukrainian State. The main facts of this complicated historical and political situation, insofar as they are ascertainable, have been repeatedly expounded. The attainment of a just decision in the matter is still attended by extreme difficulties; however, in view of the fact that some of the most important émigré organizations are linked with Galicia and particularly because Western Ukraine has been the scene of well-attested insurgent activity, it would perhaps be difficult to envisage a Ukrainian State without accepting, in principle at least, the inclusion of certain Western territories. This would mean that the frontier of the new State would approximate far more to the Curzon line and, incidentally, to its present limits, than to the pre-1939 Polish-Soviet border. Polish opposition to the establishment of a frontier approximating to the Curzon line would doubtless be violent: Ukrainians on their part would in many cases be dissatisfied with boundaries which would still exclude the Kholm area (north-west of where the projected Curzon line was to join the Bug) and the disputed Sanok, Dobromil, Lesko area, both of which regions are outside the present frontier of the Ukrainian SSR. Much partisan activity has been reported in the latter region; efforts made by the Poles to transfer the Ukrainians to the USSR are alleged to have been largely unsuccessful and many apparently returned to Poland with the connivance or ignorance of the Soviet authorities.

As an indication of Ukrainian nationalist claims at their widest extent, reference may be made to the map forming part of the title page of each issue of the Ukrainian Congress Committee of America's *Ukrainian Quarterly*. The area shown on this map as Ukrainian includes not only extensive North Caucasian and Kuban territory and all the customary claims in the West (with Sub-Carpatho-Ukraine, the Kholm area, the "Sanok triangle" and the Northern Bukovina) but also the Crimea, which can scarcely be considered Ukrainian ethnic territory; in addition, as has already been indicated, the loyalty of the Sub-Carpatho-Ukrainians to the idea of Ukrainian rather than of Russian nationalism has so far not been strong. Another map, published in *L'illustration* in June, 1941, accompanying an article by Shumitsky, a leading Ukrainian émigré in Paris at the time, claimed similar areas with the exception of the Rumanian territories; the fact that the map had presumably to be submitted to German censorship no doubt explains this.

Economic Viability of the Ukraine

A brief mention of a few outstanding facts will suffice as a reminder of the Ukraine's mineral wealth and of its importance as an agricultural centre. In 1940, the Ukraine produced 61.6% of the total union pig-iron, 43.3% of the steel, 47.8% of the rolled metal, 63% of the iron ore, 34.9% of the manganese, 72.1% of the aluminium, 20% of the machine-building, 33% of the organic dyes, 40% of the superphosphates and 80% of the soda. The Donbas coalfield is important not only for its large output (60% of the Union total in 1938) but also for its essential supplies of coking coal in which the Urals are comparatively poor. An enormous distance separates the Western part of the USSR from the Kuzbas, the only other large coking coal area in large-scale operation. The Ukrainian grain harvest in 1940 amounted to about 19 million tons out of an all Union total of 115 million. Figures recently published claim that the 1948 Ukrainian grain harvest represented an increase of about 1,200,000 tons on 1940.

As was indicated earlier the Soviets have in the past made great efforts to render the Ukraine dependent on the rest of the Union by means of the manipulation and control of industrial organization and management, and have so rendered even more abnormal the already abnormal phenomenon of a modern capitalist heavy industry superimposed upon the structure of a rather backward rural economy in the latter half of the 19th century. However, these are circumstances which are not by definition immutable and the wide-spread impression that the Ukraine could be a viable economic unit is in general borne out by an examination of the available data. "The most remarkable feature of Ukrainian economic potentialities is the fortunate balance between agricultural and industrial riches", according to W. E. D. Allen, a recent historian of the Ukraine. It is pertinent to ask, as this author proceeds to do, to what extent the Ukrainians are or would be capable of producing from their own ranks alone the necessary personnel to exploit these potentialities efficiently. An indication that this problem might be solved is provided by the partial analogy of the Czechoslovak republic, doubts as to the viability of which were

expressed in 1918. Moreover, on one of the rare occasions on which
Ukrainians have had an opportunity of showing their organizational and administrative abilities, these capacities have been
shown to be considerable – the case in point being the inter-war
Galician Ukrainians' social, educational and co-operative organizations (the *Maslosoyuz* or "Butter League", etc.)

In conclusion it may be said that the institution of an independent Ukrainian national state would be feasible though attended
by considerable difficulties. A sufficient historical tradition exists,
economic problems would probably be those most easily solved
and questions of population, minorities and precise frontier
delimitation would present the most serious obstacles.

The fact that precisely these would be the greatest difficulties
leads to the consideration of any alternatives which might obviate
them. One such alternative which has been suggested on a number
of occasions is outlined below.

Federation of the Ukraine with Neighbouring States or Ethnic Groups

The most recent excursion into this field is a plan attributed to
'General' Taras Chuprynka, reported to be the chief of the Ukrainian Liberation Army (upa) whose activities constitute the only
reasonably well attested indications of armed revolt in the Soviet
sphere of influence. The General's plan envisages the division of
the ussr into four distinct regions: 1) Siberia; 2) the Caucasus;
3) Turkestan; 4) the "Scandinavian-Black Sea Unit." It is this last-
named division which contains the Ukraine proper, the other com-
ponents being "a free Karelia," the Baltic States, White Ruthenia
(Belorussia), "Kozakia" and "Is-ed-Ural" (sic). This combination,
according to a commentary on the plan published together with it
in the 1st January 1949 issue of the Pan-American Ukrainian Conference's publication *The Ukrainian Bulletin*, would result in a
block of 70 million people, well able to defend itself against Great
Russian aggression. The idea is interesting in that it indicates that
settlement of East European problems on a non-nationalist basis is
being considered by some anti-Soviet and anti-Communist groups.
Similar aims are professed by the so-called "Federal Club of Central Europe" which envisages, as far as knowledge of it goes, a diplomatic and military union of the Countries of Central and Eastern
Europe. The participants are stated to be representatives of "free
opinion in Belorussia, Bulgaria, Croatia, Estonia, Hungary, Latvia, Lithuania, Poland, Rumania, Serbia, Slovakia and the
Ukraine."

As is well-known, Ukrainians play a leading part in some of the better known international émigré organizations, notably the ABN (anti-Bolshevik Block of Nations) and the Freedom International which, together with the *Promethée*, re-constituted by the Poles, forms the ALON (Anti-Bolshevik League for the Liberation of Nations). With the exception of ABN (of which the leaders are connected with UPA and the UHVR) these organizations have as little likelihood of being influential and active behind the iron curtain as has the "Federal Club of Central Europe." But of greater importance for the present purpose is the apparent fact that in spite of their names, they have little interest in federation but aim at national independence for their component member groups.

The principal danger inherent in the federal idea as represented by the "Chuprynka plan" is the risk that the resulting federal union in effect admits the superiority of one nation, the most powerful, over the rest, as in the present Soviet system. It is possible to see in the "Chuprynka plan" a resurrection of the idea of *Rzecz Pospolita*, except that the former rôle of Poland is to be assumed by the Ukraine. This form of federation would be as little welcome to the Baltic nations as is the existing Soviet variety.

As another alternative to the present régime, it might be appropriate to suggest a method whereby certain of the advantages accruing from an independent Ukraine or from a Ukraine acting in federation with other Slavonic or non-Slavonic nations might be obtained without actually dividing the Ukraine from Great Russia. This effect might be realized by well-planned decentralization and by attempting to lessen the importance and influence of Moscow in favour of that of Kiev. This would call for judicious administrative changes and the engendering of a new mental and psychological attitude to the Ukraine and to Moscow on the part of the inhabitants of the USSR concerned both delicate and difficult matters calling for a high degree of statemanship and good will.

Although this is not a complete novelty and was regarded as a possible policy by the Germans (cf. *Polish Fortnightly Review*, No. 20, 15th May 1941), it has, as far as is known, no active supporters at the present time, either in émigré or other circles; nevertheless, it is a possibility that ought not to be overlooked and would, if successful, attain many of the aims of the other alternatives without encountering the difficulties with which they are beset.

POSSIBILITIES OF LEADERSHIP AMONG UNDERGROUND AND
EMIGRE ORGANIZATIONS AND PERSONALITIES

An analysis of the available information shows that there are
in effect two major émigré groupings active, both of which are supported by others of less importance and one of which is believed to
carry out underground activity directed against the present
régime. These groupings are as follows:

a) the Ukrainian National Republic *(Ukrainska Narodna
Republika)*.

This group originated in the exile government which was
driven from the Ukraine in 1919-20. The last Ukrainian body able
to claim free elections (albeit the elections in question were carried
out under conditions of considerable confusion), it can claim to
represent the entire Ukraine. Its president and also its only well-
known member is Andrew Livitsky, a collaborator of one of the
original founders, Simon Petliura. Domiciled in Poland until 1944
and afterwards in Paris, the UNR is handicapped by the lack of
direct contact with the Ukraine since the beginning of its exile. Its
politics as far as they are ascertainable would still appear to bear
marks of the mild socialism inherited from the *Rada* and *Directoria*
days of 1918. It is unique in that originally at least it laid no claim
to Western Ukraine – a circumstance which explains its exile
home in Poland and its failure to collaborate with the regular
Polish Ukrainian Party of the inter-war years, the UNDO (Ukrainian
National Democratic Union).

b) Since 1945, the UNR has had a competitor for the leadership
of the émigré movement in the form of the UHVR (Ukrainian
Supreme Liberation Council – *Ukrainska Holovna Vyzvolna
Rada*).

In considering the respective merits of the two organizations it
should be noted that the UNR (as opposed to the short-lived
Western Ukrainian Government which amalgamated with it on the
23rd January, 1919 and which was soon liquidated by the Poles)
was and remains (so far as is known) pro-Polish in its orientation.
This is a direct legacy of Simon Petliura's final position of agreement with the Poles and his secret recognition (2.12.19) in the
name of *Directoria* of Polish claims to Galicia, the Kholm area,
Polesia and Western Podolia.

The UHVR-OUN-UPA grouping, however, is scarcely likely to
share any such view with relation to the Western Ukraine. The
head of OUN until his assassination in 1938, (probably by Soviet
agents) was Colonel Konovalets, who had driven Hetman

Skoropadsky from the Ukraine after the German withdrawal in 1918 but who had later broken with Petliura over the latter's 'Polish' orientation. Konovalets and the entire OUN movement became more and more pro-German, a tradition carried on under his successor Melnyk (or Yary, whom some reports state to have become the real leader of OUN after Konovalets' death). When Bandera and Stetsko broke away from the main policy of OUN during the war and attempted to found an entirely independent Ukrainian State in 1941, adopting an anti-German as well as an anti-Soviet policy, their pan-Ukrainian sentiments gained in strength and they were accordingly violently anti-Polish as well. Hence the UHVR-UPA are strongly opposed to any foreign influence in the Ukraine. It may, perhaps, be placed upon record at this juncture that the UHVR-UPA is the only one of those organizations which can claim well-attested military or partisan activity within the Ukraine; the recent Prague and Bratislava trials leave little room for doubt on this point and provide more convincing proof than the lavish and expensive publicity which the UPA receives from American and Canadian émigrés. Of the personalities, figuring in UHVR and UPA, the best known are Stetsko, a former leader of OUN and who now heads the UHVR inspired Anti-Bolshevik Block of Nations, Lebed, who styles himself Secretary General for Foreign Affairs of the UHVR, and General Taras Chuprynka who is persistently reported as Commander in Chief of UPA. About him nothing is known and it is highly probable that this name, almost suspiciously Ukrainian, is a pseudonym.

The recent reports of a union, urged by UHVR but not willingly accepted by UNR and Livitsky between the two organizations is an interesting development and would have the effect of combining the superior *Salonfähgkeit* of the UNR with the greater "actuality" of UHVR. There is to date too little precise information about this new "Ukrainian Council" (in which Livitsky continues as president, the elderly social democrat Mazepa as Prime Minister and Stetsko Vice Premier) on which to base a reliable judgement, but within the limits of 'formal' émigré circles it may prove to be the most important combination of forces.

It would appear to be unfortunate that the UNDO, the most serious Ukrainian opposition party in pre-war Poland, which had the aim of eventually establishing a free Ukraine by legal and constitutional means shows few if any signs of activity as a movement in exile; but for the disadvantage that its activity was, of course, never able to extend to the Soviet Ukraine (although the party was considerably feared by the Soviets), the UNDO could, were it not quiescent, take a powerful lead in providing a stable rallying point for other groups.

In view of the difficulty of determining the degree of popular support at home and in exile enjoyed by any given group, and indeed of distinguishing on occasions between the vociferous minority of émigrés and the largely inarticulate majority, any support lent to these organizations at present might be best directed towards using them for information and intelligence purposes, financial or other encouragement of their internecine quarrels being carefully avoided.

[sgd.] N.W.A. JONES

* * *

Minutes

17 MAY, 1949

This is an extremely interesting memorandum, which should be read in full. As the various alternative governments are hardly actual political questions at the present time, detailed minutes are not called for. We should, however, certainly not lose sight of this study, and unless this draft is going to be revised, we should bring this paper up at regular intervals. SLD and Mr. Halford may also like to know of its existence. (It is regrettable that for security reasons, we cannot send a copy to Moscow).

[sgd.] C.R.A. RAE

*

8 MAY, 1950

Still scarcely relevant.

[sgd.] RICHARD FABER

SOURCE: FO 371/77586
Public Record Office

50

British Chancery, Washington, to the British Foreign Office, 16 December 1949, Concerning American Policy towards the Ukrainian National Liberation Movement.

BRITISH EMBASSY

CONFIDENTIAL

WASHINGTON
16TH DECEMBER, 1949

Dear Department,

Please refer to your letter of the 2nd December last about the Annual Congress of the "Ukrainian Congress Committee of America."

2. We have understood from previous correspondence with Research Department [........] that they received the publication entitled *The Ukrainian Bulletin*. You may, therefore, have seen the special issue of this publication (Vol. II, Nos. 22-23) reporting in some detail the Fourth Congress of Americans of Ukrainian Descent. In that event you may have noticed that Mr. Truman sent a special messages to the Congress. We asked the State Department whether this message had any special significance and they replied in the negative, pointing out that it was normal practice for the President to address messages of this sort to this type of organization.

3. The State Department informed us in this connection that no special significance should be attached to the fact that the *Voice of America* had recently inaugurated a broadcast to the Soviet Union in the Ukrainian language. The Department had felt for some time that it would be useful if some of the *Voice's* broadcasting to the Soviet Union could be in other than the Russian language. They had chosen Ukrainian as the second largest Soviet language. They were hoping to follow this up with broadcasts to the Soviet Union in some of the Caucasian and Baltic languages.

4. The State Department also assured us that their policy towards the Ukrainian émigré organizations and the Ukrainian separatist movement in general remained as before — namely one of neutrality. They did not propose at this stage either to play up, or to discourage, Ukrainian separatist feeling.

Yours ever,
CHANCERY

Northern Department,
Foreign Office
London, S.W.1

Source: FO 371/77585
Public Record Office

51

L. Scopes, British Foreign Office, to Canada House, 4 September 1950, Replying to Canadian Enquiry with Respect to the 14th Galician Grenadier Division.

FOREIGN OFFICE
S.W.I.
4TH SEPTEMBER, 1950

CONFIDENTIAL

Sir,

With reference to your letter No. AR 408/7 of the 21st August regarding Ukrainian refugees now in the United Kingdom who formerly served in the German armed forces, I am directed by Mr. Secretary Bevin to inform you that while in Italy these men were screened by Soviet and British missions and that neither then nor subsequently has any evidence been brought to light which would suggest that any of them fought against the Western Allies or engaged in crimes against humanity. Their behaviour since they came to this country has been good and they have never indicated in any way that they are infected with any trace of Nazi ideology.

When they surrendered to the Allied forces at the end of the war, they were members of the 1st Ukrainian Division of the Wehrmacht which was formed about September, 1944 and which was only in action once (against the Red Army in Austria during April 1945) being employed in training and guard duties in Austria and Yugoslavia during the rest of its existence. Some of its members, however, appear to be survivors of an earlier formation known as the 14th Galician Grenadier Division. This was also a Wehrmacht unit, an attempt made by the Germans to make it into an s.s. Division having apparently been resisted by the Ukrainians themselves. This unit seems to have been formed about July, 1943 and to have been destroyed at the Battle of Brody in June, 1944.

From the reports of the special mission set up by the War Office to screen these men, it seems clear that they volunteered to fight against the Red Army from nationalistic motives which were given greater impetus by the behaviour of the Soviet authorities during their earlier occupation of the Western Ukraine after the Nazi-Soviet Pact. Although Communist propaganda has constantly attempted to depict these, like so many other refugees, as "quislings" and "war criminals" it is interesting to note that no specific charges of war crimes have been made by the Soviet or any other Government against any member of this group.

I am, Sir,
Your obedient Servant,

[sgd.] L. SCOPES

The Official Secretary,
Canada House, S.W.1.

* * *

Minutes

29 AUGUST, [1950]

As will be seen from WR 2384 02685 (1947), these charges have been made against these Ukrainians before, but there is nothing to show that there is any truth in them. Let us inform Canada House of the facts at our disposal.

[sgd.] A.W.H. WILKINSON

SOURCE: FO 371/87433
Public Record Office

52

British Foreign Office Minutes, January 1951,
Commenting on Political Views of Mr. Stewart,
Scottish League for European Freedom, with
Specific Reference to National Liberation
Movements in the Soviet Union.

Minutes

JANUARY 6, 1951

Copies of this letter have been sent to the Prime Minister, and presumably to other public men as well.

[........]

There is no doubt that Mr. Stewart has a case; but there is also no doubt that he considerably over-emphasizes it. He is blind to the possibilities, still present, if somewhat diminished, of achieving a balance of power that will lead to peace. He is also blind to the essential importance of obtaining full support from public opinion, by making every effort, however, hopeless such efforts may be, to find a modus vivendi *with the USSR. He also exaggerates the strength of the resistance movements behind the Iron Curtain, which, according to our information, are, though often still active, losing rather than gaining strength. Where Mr. Stewart is, of course, right is in his awareness of the aggressive character of the Soviet régime; and of the great value which, in the event of war, the resistance and separationist movements could have for us. Whether or not disintegration of the Soviet Union on ethnic lines would, in the event of war, be a proper objective for the Western Powers, is another and very controversial question; but there is at least a good deal to be said for Mr. Stewart's views on this score.*

Mr. Stewart's letter has been acknowledged; and a fuller reply is not, I think, required.

[sgd.] RICHARD S. FABER

*

Mr. Stewart has swallowed the Ukrainian nationalist line whole. His violent anti-Russian, as distinct from anti-Soviet, feelings are a poor guide to the formulation of a rational foreign policy and his obstinate insistence on the value of the near-apocryphal resistance movements behind the Iron Curtain makes his practical recommendations not merely foolish but dangerous.

2. Mr. Stewart's conviction that all Russians sub-divide into masochistic mystics and aggressive imperialists may be emotionally satisfying to him, and not without profit to the ABN. As a contribution to the solution of our problem, it is about as useful as "Mein Kampf."

3. With regard to the ABN's plan to convert the USSR into numerous ethnical state entities, a project with which Mr. Stewart is in full agreement, I can only reiterate FORD's statement (on N 1073/1) that this is an attempt to put the clock back some 400 years. As regards the potential strength of national anti-Moscow sympathies in the Soviet Union itself, it is probably true that its strength is diminishing rapidly under Soviet Communist influences, especially those brought to bear on the young. Nor can we wash our hands of all national movements in case they may be of future use to us.

4. Of Mr. Stewart it can only be said that though his heart is in the right place it is perhaps excessively large.

[sgd.] J.H. PECK

SOURCE: FO 371/94964
Public Record Office

53

Memorandum from Defence Liaison to Canadian Department of External Affairs, 21 February 1951, Commenting on Utility of Audience with Ukrainian Emigré Leader Y. Stetsko in View of Possible Exploitation of Ukrainian Nationalism.

SECRET

OTTAWA
FEBRUARY 21, 1951

ADMISSION TO CANADA OF YAROSLAV STETSKO

[........]

We have not yet enough information on Stetsko and on the ABN (Anti-Bolshevik Bloc of Nations) for me to give a firm opinion on them or on the desirability of admitting Stetsko to Canada. From the available evidence I see no reason to hope for particularly useful or desirable results from Stetsko's visit and some reason to be mildly apprehensive about it. My doubts are due to my impression that Stetsko and the ABN are preaching the inevitability of war with the Soviet Union (it may be believed but should not be preached) and advocating the complete dissolution of the Soviet Union and the setting up a galaxy of successor states. Western thinking is proceeding very cautiously on the subject of war aims and the future of a defeated Soviet Union and it would probably be premature, embarrassing and of adverse effect in psychological warfare if too much attention were drawn to the ABN at the present time — assuming that its policy is the one suggested above.

On the other hand, it is useful and valuable to us to be well informed about all émigré movements and accordingly it might be worthwhile to let Mr. Stetsko come here and acquaint us with the details of his thinking and planning. Perhaps a condition of granting his visa could be the restricting of his political activities in Canada. It should be easier to make a decision in this case when we have received further information from London.

[........] Despatch D. 385 [........] asked for a variety of information on Ukrainian nationalism and Ukrainian organizations in exile which it was felt was needed to help clarify our thinking on the possible exploitation of Ukrainian nationalism for the purposes of psychological warfare at the present time and in war-time. One reason for this is that we are under constant pressure from Ukrainian groups in Canada to broadcast in Ukrainian and to give support to movements advocating an independent Ukraine.

[sgd.] M. WEISHOF
Defence Liaison

SOURCE: 10919 - 40 Historical
Division, Department of
External Affairs (Canada)

54

J. A. McCordick, Defence Liaison, to J. Legér, Under Secretary of State for External Affairs, 4 May 1951, Regarding Use of Foreign-born Canadians for Psychological Warfare Operations Overseas and Anti-communist Work within Canada.

MEMORANDUM
FOR MR. LEGER

OTTAWA
MAY 4, 1951

EUROPEAN EMIGRE ORGANIZATIONS

On May 2nd I sent you a memorandum on this subject which listed a number of recent proposals which have come to our attention. I think we should have an early discussion of this problem and I submit below a proposed policy which could serve as point of departure for the discussion:

1. It would be very difficult to prevent émigré organizations, of the kind we already know about, from establishing themselves in Canada.

2. Anyway we would not want to deter the establishment of reputable organizations which might perform a useful function.

3. As mentioned in my previous memorandum, we need to find out more about the organizations and the possibility of conflicting or rival ambitions. Perhaps the best we can do is to ask those concerned; for example, we might ask Mr. Nemec if he knows about Mr. Mott and whether there is any rivalry or lack of co-ordination as regards the setting up of a Canadian branch of "The National Committee for a Free Europe."

4. At present the approaches are not being uniformly handled: some go to the Prime Minister, some to the Under Secretary; some are referred to your Division, some to me. We should set up a standard procedure. I would recommend that the correspondence go first to the European Division and be handled jointly by the European Division and myself, with Defence Liaison kept in the general picture and consulted when necessary.

5. We should adopt a general policy towards the organizations and I would suggest:

(a) That we give similar answers to approaches from reputable individuals or organizations, and send no more than acknowledgements to others whose *bona fides* are still in doubt.

(b) That the answers go over the signature of the Under Secretary even if the original approach was to the Minister or the Prime Minister.

(c) That the answers avoid giving tacit official approval or encouragement while stating that we do not object to the establishment of the organization in question as long as it does not contravene the laws of Canada. We might wish to add that we expect the organization to refrain from activities which might embarrass the Canadian Government.

(d) That we keep the RCMP informed about the various organizations.

(e) That we keep in touch with the Citizenship Branch, who will probably have continuous contact with the organizations, and that we request the Citizenship Branch to refer to us any original approach made to them by individuals or organizations.

(f) That we bear in mind the possibility that we may eventually be able to cooperate profitably with one or more of the organizations for the purposes of: (1) counteracting communist influence amongst foreign-born Canadians and recent immigrants; and (2) conducting Psychological Warfare abroad.

[sgd.] J. A. Mc Cordick

Source: File: 11387 - 40
Department of External Affairs
(Canada), Historical Division

Selected Bibliography

J. A. Armstrong, *Ukrainian Nationalism*, 2nd rev. ed. (New York: Columbia University Press, 1963; Reprint, Littleton, Colo.: Ukrainian Academic Press, 1980).

Y. Bilinsky, *The Second Soviet Republic: The Ukraine After World War II*. (New Brunswick, N.J.: Rutgers University Press, 1964).

Y. Boshyk (ed.), *Ukraine During World War II: History and Its Aftermath*. (Edmonton: Canadian Institute of Ukrainian Studies, 1986).

R. Conquest, *The Harvest of Sorrow: Soviet Collectivization and the Terror-Famine*. (New York: Oxford University Press, 1986).

M. R. Elliott, *Pawns of Yalta: Soviet Refugees and America's Role in Their Repatriation*. (Urbana, Ill.: University of Illinois Press, 1982).

G. Fisher, *Soviet Opposition to Stalin: A Case Study in World War II*. (Cambridge, Mass.: Harvard University Press, 1952).

I. Kamenetsky, *Hitler's Occupation of Ukraine, 1941-1944: A Case Study of Totalitarian Imperialism*. (Milwaukee: Marquette University Press, 1956).

B. S. Kordan and L. Y. Luciuk, *A Delicate and Difficult Question: Documents in the History of Ukrainians in Canada 1899 - 1962*. (Kingston: The Limestone Press, 1986).

B. Krawchenko, *Social Change and National Consciousness in Twentieth Century Ukraine*. (London: Macmillan, 1985).

J. E. Mace, *Communism and the Dilemmas of National Liberation: National Communism in Soviet Ukraine 1918-1933*. (Cambridge, Mass.: Harvard University Press, 1983).

A. J. Motyl, *The Turn to the Right: The Ideological Origins and Development of Ukrainian Nationalism, 1919-1929.* (Boulder, Colo.: East European Monographs, 1980).

P. R. Magocsi, *Galicia: A Historical Survey and Bibliographical Guide.* (Toronto: University of Toronto Press in association with the Canadian Institute of Ukrainian Studies and the Harvard Ukrainian Research Institute, 1983).

P. J. Potichnyj and Y. Shtendera (eds.), *The Political Thought of the Ukrainian Underground.* (Edmonton: Canadian Institute of Ukrainian Studies, 1986).

M. Proudfoot, *European Refugees, 1932-1952: A Study in Forced Population Movement.* (London: Faber and Faber, 1957).

J.S. Reshetar, *The Ukrainian Revolution, 1917-1920: A Study in Nationalism* (Princeton, NJ: Princeton University Press, 1952).

G. Reitlinger, *The House Built on Sand: The Conflicts of German Policy in Russia, 1939-1945.* (New York: Viking Press, 1960; Reprint, Westport, Conn.: Greenwood Press, 1975).

N. Tolstoy, *Victims of Yalta.* (Toronto: Hodder and Stoughton, 1977).

Y. Tys-Krokhmaliuk, *UPA Warfare in Ukraine: Strategical, Tactical and Organizational Problems of the Ukrainian Resistance in World War II.* (New York: Vantage Press, 1972).